THE NEW CREATIONISM

*If you thought you knew what creationism was,
this book will probably surprise you.*
(Dr Arthur Jones,
Science and Education Consultant)

*If you want a clear, concise, balanced and well-referenced overview of current young-universe
creation science, The New Creationism is a great place to start.*
(Dr Gordon Wilson,
Senior Fellow of Natural History,
New Saint Andrews College, Idaho, USA)

THE NEW CREATIONISM

Building scientific theories on a biblical foundation

Paul A. Garner

Foreword by Dr Andrew Snelling

EP BOOKS

1st Floor Venture House, 6 Silver Court, Watchmead,
Welwyn Garden City, UK, AL7 1TS

www.epbooks.org

admin@epbooks.org

EP Books are distributed in the USA by:
JPL Distribution
3741 Linden Avenue Southeast
Grand Rapids, MI 49548
E-mail: orders@jplbooks.com
www.jplbooks.com

First published 2009
Second impression 2009
Third impression 2011
Fourth impression 2015
Fifth Impression 2017

British Library Cataloguing in Publication Data available

Print: ISBN 978–0–85234–692–1
Kindle: ISBN 978-1-78397-203-6
ePub: ISBN 978-1-78397-204-3

Scripture quotations in this publication are from the Authorized/King James Version

Dedicated to the memory of my Dad,
Ian Collen Garner (1946–2003),
who always encouraged me
in everything I did.

Acknowledgements

'Without counsel purposes are disappointed: but in the multitude of counsellors they are established' (Proverbs 15:22).

I would like to acknowledge the many friends and colleagues who provided feedback on earlier drafts of this book. Their advice and suggestions have made this a much better volume than it would otherwise have been. In particular I would like to thank Professor Edgar Andrews and Dr J. H. John Peet for their thorough comments on the entire first draft. Other reviewers, including Dr Geoff Barnard, Dr Nancy Darrall, Dr Arthur Jones, Dr Andrew Snelling, Dr David Tyler, Dr Todd Wood and Dr Bill Worraker, made helpful suggestions for the revision of individual chapters. They do not necessarily agree with everything I have written and, of course, any remaining errors are solely mine. My brother, Stuart Garner, and two church friends— Kathryn Faulkner and Linda Jones—provided useful feedback from the non-specialist viewpoint and their comments have greatly improved the book's clarity. I am deeply indebted to Jack Lewis for his many hours of conscientious work in preparing the illustrations. Finally, I wish to express my love and gratitude to my wife, Debra, and our children, Chris and Cara, for their patience and understanding while I have been engaged in writing this book.

Contents

Part IV: The Flood and its aftermath

Foreword

As I recall, when I first met Paul Garner some years ago he was just finishing his undergraduate studies, and he was already committed to, and heavily involved in, creation ministry. For this he was very well equipped, with his degree training in both geology and biology.

Over the years since, I have always appreciated and enjoyed Paul's friendship. I have stayed in his home, we have travelled together and we have done field work together. I have also had the joy of taking Paul on a trip down the Colorado River through the Grand Canyon.

Paul's warm and winsome personality readily commends him to all he meets. He has always had an insatiable appetite for more knowledge, and the demonstrated mental skills to grapple with it and integrate it. And his burden and passion have led him in recent days to wholly follow the Lord into full-time service in creation ministry. This has now enabled him to forge strategic partnerships in cutting-edge creation biology and geology research efforts.

So why am I extolling the author of this book? It's because his personality and broad up-to-date knowledge are very evident through and in its pages. Indeed, this is quite an astounding book. In so few pages, in an easy-to-read style, Paul manages to present a comprehensive, understandable overview of the origins issue, yet he touches on all the latest, robust technical details. And he does so in a warm, inoffensive manner that commends this book to lay Christians for whom it was written, yet scientifically informed non-Christians would also be challenged by it.

Everyone has a fascination about their origins, where they came from, their roots. Our history gives us significance and meaning. That's why so many people today are disillusioned with, and cynical about, life and its seeming lack of purpose. After all, this is to be expected, because public education systems around the globe for more than a generation have been teaching impressionable children that they are just another animal which evolved by accident from a random collection of chemicals in some primordial 'soup' many millions of years ago. Indeed, to them, unborn children seem to have less value than whales needing to be saved.

On the other hand, it's only God's Word that brings a message of value and purpose to human life. The book of Genesis tells us that man was created by the infinite, all-powerful Creator God revealed in the Bible, and in his image. However, the first man and woman chose to disbelieve God's Word and rebel, which brought God's judgement on all of the creation, resulting in the pain, sorrow, sickness and death we all now experience. Yet God still loved mankind whom he had created. He therefore demonstrated that love by eventually sending his only beloved Son as the perfect God-man, Jesus Christ, both to reveal himself directly to us, and to die on our behalf to pay the penalty for our ongoing rebellion. And that same Jesus was resurrected from death, so he can offer us eternal life with him if we renounce our rebellion and accept his forgiveness.

Now that's good news! We are that incredibly valuable to our Creator. And there is so much purpose to life now. However, this teaching that we evolved from a cosmic accident totally undermines this good news. Ask any Christian who has tried to tell a modern teenager that God created him. Hasn't science proved the Bible to be all wrong? Scientists can explain how the universe and then life started, so there is no god and Christianity is irrelevant! Faced with this apparent onslaught against the plain reading of the opening chapters of the Bible, many Christians either retreat powerless to respond, shift their message to just 'Jesus loves you', or, worse still, question their understanding of God's Word and compromise their faith to accommodate the world's message.

This is exactly why this book is an absolute must for all Christians to read! Paul Garner systematically and masterfully works through, and succinctly yet thoroughly deals with, the claimed major scientific evidences that are today arrayed against those Christians who desire to be faithful to God's Word. Paul starts with an unwavering commitment to the plain reading of the opening chapters of Genesis, and presents his detailed case in support of his Bible-believing position against the backdrop of what those chapters clearly teach. And he does this not simply by criticizing scientists and their claimed evidences, but by presenting the latest and best scientific models totally consistent with and supportive of God's Word proposed by other equally well-qualified scientists, who, like Paul, are absolutely committed to God and his Word.

Read the contents page, and you will immediately recognize that the chapter titles cover the key issues in this origins debate, and many of the questions most asked by Christians and non-Christians alike. In the opening chapters Paul launches into dealing with the supposed Big Bang for the origin of the universe, and the creation of the Sun, Moon and stars, before reminding us just how well designed is our earthly home. The pivotal questions of time are next treated—the biblical case for literal creation days and 6,000 or so years for earth history are resoundingly established; the present-is-the-key-to-the-past philosophy is shown to be contrary to the evidence for catastrophic formation of sedimentary rock layers; the radioactive clocks in rocks have run fast and therefore cannot yield absolute ages of millions of years; and yet there is robust evidence that the solar system, the earth and mankind are young. However, biological issues are not neglected, as Paul then skilfully discusses the origin of life, diversity by design, similarities and relationships, defects and degeneration, and embryonic recapitulation and vestigial organs. Then the global Flood catastrophe is defended biblically and a plausible mechanism for it is described, as well as how the fossil record is explained by the Flood. Furthermore, only the Flood can explain the single ice age that occurred as an immediate consequence of it, while the dispersion of mankind from the Tower of Babel is the only viable explanation for the origin of languages and the subsequent cultures. Finally, a glossary at the back provides a very helpful aid for non-technically trained readers to refer to for explanations of technical terms.

I therefore enthusiastically commend this book. It is a gem— short enough and easy to read, so as not to be daunting to lay people, but deep and comprehensive for the more technically inclined, supported by copious references in the endnotes for those who want to chase more in-depth details. It would be my prayer that this book will enjoy wide circulation, and that the Lord would use it to strengthen many in their Christian faith and equip them to boldly defend the truth of God's Word.

Andrew A. Snelling
Ph.D. (geology)
Director of Research
Answers in Genesis
Kentucky, USA

Introduction

In the increasingly secular age in which we live, it is all too easy to forget that the major disciplines of science were founded by men of broadly Christian convictions.[1] Their names are perhaps familiar to us—Boyle, Ray, Hooke, Newton, Faraday—but there is often an embarrassed silence concerning the spiritual beliefs that motivated these scientific giants. Like the astronomer Kepler, they perceived that in their scientific insights they were 'thinking God's thoughts after him'. Today, however, there is a sense of collective amnesia about the religious motivations of these men. Over the last two or three centuries, science has become almost completely disconnected from its biblical roots, with the result that the academic culture in which science is practised today is one of tacit—if not explicit—atheism. Nowhere is this more evident than in the scientific study of how the universe began and developed—the field of origins.

This book has been written in the conviction that the first eleven chapters of the book of Genesis—the Bible's book of beginnings—provide a trustworthy and accurate account of the early history of the universe. Plainly understood, these foundational chapters of the Bible give us the following outline of 'primeval history':

1. They speak of *creation*. All things were created by God in six
   days as laid out in Genesis 1:1–2:3 and affirmed in Exodus
   20:8–11. Adam, the first man, was made from the dust of
   the ground on the sixth day and the genealogies of Genesis
   chapters 5 and 11 allow us to place his creation within the last
   few thousand years. All human beings are descendants of
   Adam and his wife Eve.
2. They tell us of *the fall of man*. Adam was instructed by
   God to rule over the Earth as a righteous steward, but
   the entrance of sin brought God's curse upon mankind
   and all his dominion. One of the consequences of Adam's
   rebellion, as Genesis 3:14–19 makes clear, was that death
   and bloodshed became a part of the creation.
3. We learn about *the Flood* of Noah's day, Following Adam's
   fall into sin, the wickedness of mankind grew until the
   whole world was full of violence and corruption. This
   culminated in the intervention of God in a global flood
   which destroyed the world that then existed. Genesis
   7:21–23 records that every human being and air-breathing
   land animal perished except for those preserved with
   Noah in the ark.
4. We read about *the confusion of the languages at Babel*.
   After the Flood, Noah's descendants rebelled against God
   by disobeying his command to repopulate the world.
   Genesis 11:1–9 tells us that they set about building a
   city and a tower, to make a name for themselves, but
   God confounded them by confusing their languages and
   causing them to disperse.

Of course, many people today regard these events as little
more than pre-scientific myths. In their view, the theory of
evolution has replaced the concept of biblical creation and the
idea of long geological ages has replaced the Bible's account of
the Flood. However, the book of Genesis presents these events
to us as a record of real history—things that actually happened.

This means that we are faced with an apparent conflict between what science says concerning origins, on the one hand, and what the Bible says, on the other.

How are Bible-believing Christians to handle this conflict? One approach is to focus upon the scientific problems faced by conventional evolutionary theories. There are many books that do this, although the approach has often proved unsatisfying to people who, quite understandably, want to know what we are going to put in the place of the theories we have rejected. Other creationists have taken a more positive approach, which is to show that rigorous scientific ideas about the past can be built upon the historical foundation provided in the Bible. This is a much more challenging task—but ultimately more fruitful. In this book, I will, where necessary, offer criticisms of conventional theories; however, my main aim is to summarize the work of modern-day scholars who are seeking to restore the biblical foundations of the scientific enterprise and build positive creationist theories in the field of origins. It is my conviction that many of the scientific puzzles concerning the origin and development of our world can be solved when we take these early chapters of the Bible seriously and use what they say to build our theories. I hope that even those readers who disagree with me will persevere long enough to discover why I hold this view.

Of course, the very idea that scientific theories can be built upon a biblical foundation may be surprising to some readers. The first book of the Bible is not, in the words of the cliché, 'a scientific textbook'. If it were, how could it possibly have been understood by generations of people before modern science was developed? Nevertheless, I am convinced that Genesis is a book of history—and that it provides a satisfying framework for scientific study relating to origins.

As you read, however, I want you to keep in mind that scientific theories—even those developed upon biblical foundations—are not of the same level of certainty as Scripture itself. Scientific explanations are always incomplete and often our understanding is limited or unsatisfactory. We must remember that science is a dynamic process, and theories change as a result of new evidence and new ways of thinking. The inevitable consequence is that some material in this book will become out of date—perhaps even by the time it is published! Although I have tried to summarize what I regard as the best research available at the time of writing, not all the ideas in this book will stand the test of time. Some of these theories will have to be revised or abandoned, while Scripture remains true for all time. This should not be disturbing to us because our faith in God's Word is not dependent upon scientific argument; nevertheless, it is exciting for the Christian believer to know that biblical truths can help us to frame our scientific theories and promote genuine enquiry.

Inevitably this book will deal with some concepts that may be unfamiliar to those without a scientific background. However, the intention is to help the non-specialist reader think through the topic—so when it has been necessary to introduce unfamiliar concepts, I have tried to explain them in everyday language. There is also a glossary of technical terms at the end of the book.

It is my prayer that this book will help to build up your confidence in God's Word and excite you about the scientific study of God's world. It will not necessarily answer all your questions, but I trust that it will help you to think seriously about some important issues. If you want to dig deeper, each chapter has many references to follow up and there are recommendations for further reading at the end of the book. I have also included details of some websites where you can find more information.

Part I:

The heavens and the Earth

1

In the beginning

The Bible begins with a profound statement: 'In the beginning God created the heaven and the earth' (Genesis 1:1). In this opening verse of Scripture we learn at least two important things.

First, we learn that *before anything else was in existence, God was there*. The Bible nowhere argues for God's existence—it simply presupposes it. As we read elsewhere, 'Before the mountains were brought forth, or ever thou hadst formed the earth and the world, even from everlasting to everlasting, thou art God' (Psalm 90:2).

The second thing we learn is that *the whole universe*—time, space and matter—*is the creation of this eternal, self-existent God*. He had only to speak and a universe came into being. Psalm 33:9 says, 'For he spake, and it was done; he commanded, and it stood fast.' This was an act of creation *ex nihilo* (from nothing), as the writer to the Hebrews makes plain: 'Through faith we understand that the worlds were framed by the word of God, so that things which are seen were not made of things which do appear' (Hebrews 11:3). Here is a basic teaching of Christianity. Unlike God, the universe had a beginning and is not eternal; rather the universe is here because the eternal God willed it to be so.

In presupposing the existence of a Creator God, Christianity is not, however, an irrational faith; for the Bible tells us that God has made the universe in such a way that it clearly reveals his existence and nature. The psalmist writes, 'The heavens declare the glory of God; and the firmament showeth his handiwork. Day unto day uttereth speech, and night unto night showeth knowledge. There is no speech nor language, where their voice is not heard. Their line is gone out through all the earth, and their words to the end of the world' (Psalm 19:1–4). In other words, the universe has been so designed that it points all people in all places and at all times to the one who made it. The New Testament letter to the Romans develops this thought in the context of man's accountability to God: 'For the invisible things of him from the creation of the world are clearly seen, being understood by the things that are made, even his eternal power and Godhead; so that they are without excuse' (Romans 1:20).

The heavens declare the glory of God

Assuming that what we have said so far is true, we ought to expect to see something of God's glorious nature displayed in the things he has made and, indeed, this seems to be the case. Let us consider some of the ways in which the universe reflects the nature of its Creator.

1. The immensity of the universe

Perhaps the best way to think about this is in terms of the light year, defined as the distance that light can travel in one year through a vacuum, going at 300,000 kilometres (186,000 miles) per second. One light year is equivalent to about twelve million round trips to the Moon! The closest star to the Earth, besides the Sun, is Proxima Centauri, 4.2 light years away. The Andromeda Galaxy is two million light years away. The most distant objects detected in space are estimated to be almost fourteen billion light years away.[1] Surely the size of the universe reflects something of the greatness of the God who spoke it into being.

2. *The complexity of the universe*

The more that scientists study the universe, the more levels of structure they discover. It is rather like opening up a series of 'Russian dolls'. On the largest scales, looking through powerful telescopes, we find that stars are grouped into systems called galaxies, galaxies into clusters, and clusters into superclusters. On the smallest scales, we find that molecules are made up of atoms, atoms are made up of protons, neutrons and electrons, and still more fundamental and exotic particles probably await discovery. The multi-layered complexity of the universe reminds us of the infinite knowledge of the one who made it.

3. *The beauty of the universe*

Is there any sight in creation more awe-inspiring and magnificent than the night sky? Psalm 8, which considers the glory of the heavens, the Moon and the stars which God has set in place, was written nearly three thousand years ago by King David who, as a young shepherd boy, would have pondered the universe and his own position in it. With the aid of modern telescopes we can see wonders that David could not have imagined. There are stars of every size and colour, beautiful spiral galaxies, radiant nebulae and pillars, clouds and filaments of glowing gas. The beauty of the universe surely points us to the splendour and majesty of the God who adorned it.

The regularity of the universe

Another feature of the universe that we ought to note is its regularity. The universe behaves in a consistent manner. It is governed by natural laws and physical constants which apparently apply everywhere throughout space and time. Where did these laws and constants come from? Science presupposes their existence, but can offer no ultimate explanation for them. Even more remarkable is the fact that human beings are able to discover and mathematically describe these natural laws. Why should this be so? The great physicist Albert Einstein once commented: 'The most incomprehensible fact of nature is the fact that nature is comprehensible.'[2] However this 'most incomprehensible fact' can be understood by those who acknowledge that God made the universe in such a way that we might come to know him through it.

Of related significance are the many 'cosmic coincidences' that maintain the fabric of the universe and make it possible for life to exist.[3] Specifically, the universe looks as though it has been designed for mankind. This has been referred to as the anthropic principle—from the Greek word for man (*anthropos*).[4] Some scientists have tried to avoid the obvious theological implications of this principle by arguing that the universe *must* look as though it were designed for man, even if it were not, for otherwise we would not be here to observe it. That might explain those features that are *necessary* for life to exist on the Earth—such as the properties of carbon and oxygen atoms—but it would not explain those features that are 'nice to have' but not strictly essential—such as the ability of man to comprehend the universe mathematically.[5] Some scientists, including Sir Martin Rees, Britain's current Astronomer Royal, have suggested that there are an infinite number of parallel universes and we are here simply because 'our' universe happened to have the right conditions for life to emerge.[6] Others have suggested that 'our' universe is simply the latest in a never-ending cycle of universes. Of course, both ideas are completely untestable and therefore not really scientific at all.

What about the Big Bang theory?

Despite the beauty, harmony and regularity of the universe, many people today are of the opinion that there is no Creator and that the universe is ultimately purposeless. We are confidently told that science can explain the universe without recourse to God. According to physicist James Trefil, it is now possible to reconstruct the history of the universe to within less than a millisecond of its beginning.[7] Statements like this have persuaded many people that increased knowledge of our universe has pushed God out of the picture.

Various secular theories for the origin of the universe have been proposed, but the one that has gained the widest currency today is the Big Bang theory. According to this theory, the universe began about 13.7 billion years ago with all the matter and energy of the universe compressed into an almost infinitely hot, dense state. From there, it has expanded to generate the universe we observe today. The Big Bang is commonly, but erroneously, referred to as an 'explosion'. The word 'explosion' suggests expansion *into* space; by contrast, space and time are themselves considered to have been generated during the Big Bang. As the universe expanded outwards, temperatures dropped sufficiently for hydrogen and helium atoms to form. About 100 million years after the Big Bang, the first stars began to form from clouds of gas in the young universe. This star-forming process eventually gave rise to the Milky Way and other galaxies. When these first-generation stars had grown old, some of them exploded as supernovae. The resulting fragments later recombined to form new stars, which repeated the process. Our Sun is said to be a third-generation star, a relatively recent addition, and to have formed around five billion years ago. Around some of the stars debris coalesced to form planets and on at least one planet—the Earth—living things evolved.

There are three main pieces of evidence supporting the Big Bang theory.

1. The universe is bathed in weak radiation

In 1965, the American physicists Arno Penzias and Robert Wilson detected faint radio noise coming from all directions in space. The reason for this radiation is that space is not entirely cold, but has a temperature of 2.73 degrees above absolute zero (the coldest temperature possible). Most cosmologists think that this radiation is the 'dying ember' from the Big Bang—light waves from the initial fireball, 'stretched' by the expansion of space and now detectable as microwaves.

2. Distant galaxies seem to be rushing away from us

The light from almost every galaxy, except for a few nearby ones, is shifted towards the red end of the electromagnetic spectrum

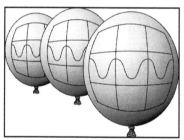

(in other words, the wavelength of the light has been increased). This phenomenon is known as the red-shift. What is more, the red-shift is greater the further away a galaxy is from us. This suggests that the galaxies are speeding away from one another, thus 'stretching' the wavelength of the light they are emitting.[8] The conventional understanding of this is that the universe is expanding as a result of the Big Bang.

According to the Big Bang theory, light waves from distant galaxies are being stretched in wavelength as the universe expands. The stretching of the waves on this expanding balloon offers a helpful analogy.

3. The light elements are found in the right amounts

If a hot Big Bang took place, it is possible to predict the proportions of the light elements—hydrogen, deuterium, helium, beryllium and lithium—that ought to exist in the universe. This prediction seems to be consistent with what we observe.

Doubts about the Big Bang theory

It is clear that the Big Bang theory has some impressive support. However, it also has some deficiencies that are often overlooked.

1. *The cosmic radiation is too smooth*

The Big Bang theory says that density irregularities in the primordial fireball grew into stars, galaxies and clusters of galaxies. These irregularities should be evident today as hot and cold spots in the radiation—as we point our detectors into space we should find slight differences in the temperature of the microwaves across the sky. Slight variations have been detected by the satellites COBE (COsmic Background Explorer) and WMAP (Wilkinson Microwave Anisotropy Probe), but they appear to be far too small to account for the large-scale structure of the universe.[9] Big Bang proponents have adjusted their model in an attempt to 'fix' this.

2. *The most distant galaxies are too mature*

According to conventional cosmology, as we look more deeply into the universe we are looking back in time. Assuming that the Big Bang theory is correct, as we look further into space we should see galaxies at an earlier stage of development ('proto-galaxies'). We should also see the number of galaxies drop off with increasing distance. However, astronomers are finding mature galaxies at great distances, and more of them than expected.[10] The discovery of an enormous string of galaxies 10.8 billion light years from Earth poses a similar problem. Computer models of the early universe are unable to explain how such a colossal structure could have formed so soon after the Big Bang.[11]

3. The light-element abundances were not really predicted by the Big Bang theory

They were generally known before the theory was developed.[12] Indeed, the assumed conditions in the early stages of the Big Bang can be adjusted by cosmologists to give the correct proportions of light elements in the universe. Even so, some objects have light-element abundances that are different from what the Big Bang theory predicts.[13]

Developing a creationist theory of cosmology

Although the Big Bang theory is dominant today, a host of alternatives have been proposed.[14] In 2004 a letter by thirty-three scientists, openly critical of the Big Bang, was published in the British popular science magazine *New Scientist*[15] and on the Internet.[16] It pointed out that there are many observations that the Big Bang theory cannot explain and that most of the evidence in favour of the theory can be explained in other ways. There is clearly great scope to develop a cosmological theory that is superior to the Big Bang in its explanatory power.

In the last ten years, some creationists have applied themselves to the development of biblically based theories of cosmology. Theories of this kind are needed because the Big Bang does not seem to be compatible with Scripture. The Big Bang theory requires billions of years, while the Bible says that creation was accomplished in six days (see chapter 4), and even the order of events is significantly different.[17] This latter point is one of the reasons why interpreting the 'creation days' as long eras of time is not helpful in harmonizing the Bible with secular theories.

The most promising creationist cosmologies are, like the Big Bang, based upon Einstein's equations of general relativity. According to Einstein's equations, gravity has a distorting effect upon time. We tend to think of time as a constant, but Einstein

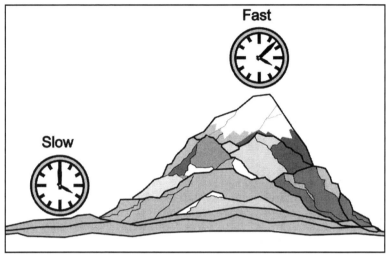

An atomic clock at a high altitude will tick slightly faster than an atomic clock at a low altitude. This is because gravity distorts time.[18]

proposed that time can be stretched and compressed—only the speed of light remains constant. This phenomenon—referred to as 'time dilation'—has been known for about a century and is supported by numerous experiments. It has been demonstrated, for instance, that an atomic clock—an extremely accurate clock based on the vibrations of an atom or molecule—ticks slightly faster at a high altitude than an identical clock at a lower altitude, because the clocks are at different locations within the Earth's gravitational field. The observed difference is precisely what general relativity predicts for the different altitudes.

In 1994, physicist D. Russell Humphreys applied this principle of time dilation to propose a creationist cosmology to replace the Big Bang. Humphreys derived his new cosmology from the equations of general relativity by replacing what he regarded as the unbiblical assumptions of the Big Bang theory with more biblically based ones.[19] For example, the Big Bang theory assumes that the universe, when viewed on a sufficiently large scale, is basically the same in all directions and that the location of the Earth is not

A finite universe without boundaries can be represented in two dimensions by the surface of a balloon. An insect crawling on its surface would never encounter a 'centre' or an 'edge' even though the surface is not infinitely large.

special in any way. A related, and equally arbitrary, assumption of the Big Bang theory is that the universe has no edge or centre and is therefore 'unbounded'. This is difficult to visualize, but perhaps an analogy will help. Consider an insect confined to the surface of an inflated balloon. The insect can crawl around the balloon surface for ever but it will never encounter a 'centre' or an 'edge', for there is none! Although this analogy cannot be pressed too far—after all, the surface of the balloon, unlike the universe, is only two-dimensional—it may help us to grasp something of what is meant by the 'unboundedness' of the universe according to the Big Bang theory.

Humphreys considered the intriguing alternative that the Earth might have been created at or near the centre of a 'bounded' universe (i.e. one *with* an edge and a centre).[20] Big Bang cosmologists reject the concept that the Earth is in a special place because it is philosophically unacceptable to them. However, the idea has recently received some surprising observational support. Surveys have shown that galaxy red-shifts—and therefore the distances of these galaxies from the Earth—tend to fall into discrete groups (astronomers say that they are 'quantized'). It looks as though the galaxies are arranged in concentric 'shells' around our own home![21] The odds for the Earth having such a striking position in the universe by accident are less than one in a trillion. Moreover, the best three-dimensional map of the universe yet published—from the Sloan Digital Sky Survey—clearly shows shells of galaxies centred on the Earth.[22] The idea that the Earth is in a special place is not only compatible with Humphreys' biblical cosmology but also, it seems, with the latest scientific observations.

Humphreys also incorporated into his model the apparent expansion of the universe based on the red-shifts of distant galaxies—an observation usually regarded as confirming the Big Bang theory. In that theory, the recession of the galaxies from one another is extrapolated backwards in time until all the matter and energy of the universe are contained within an infinitesimally small point (called a singularity).

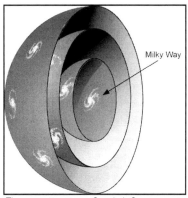

The quantization of red-shifts suggests that the distant galaxies are arranged in concentric 'shells' around the Milky Way. In reality the situation is more complex than depicted here because several different distance intervals exist between the galaxies.

The limits of this extrapolation can obviously be questioned, but the conclusion that the universe has undergone some degree of expansion from a smaller size seems robust. The evidence for expansion has added significance when we consider the large number of Bible verses that refer to God 'stretching out' or 'spreading out' the heavens (e.g. Job 9:8; 37:18; Psalm 104:2; Isaiah 40:22; 42:5; 44:24; 45:12; 48:13; 51:13; Jeremiah 10:12; Zechariah 12:1). On the basis of the frequency, diversity and widespread distribution of these verses throughout Scripture, Humphreys argued that they should be understood as more than mere metaphor. The Bible, he suggested, seems to teach that at some time in the past God stretched out space itself.

Humphreys' ground-breaking contribution in 1994 was to bring these three basic ideas together—the time-dilating effects of gravity, the quantized red-shifts suggesting that the Earth is at or near the centre of a bounded universe, and the apparent expansion

of the universe based upon the red-shifts of distant galaxies—as the
foundation for a new creationist cosmology.

A full discussion of Humphreys' theory is beyond the scope
of this book, and for a more detailed account readers should
consult Humphreys' volume on the subject, entitled *Starlight
and Time*.[23] However, the basic proposal is that, at creation, God
caused the expansion of the universe from an initially very dense
state called a white hole. A white hole is similar to a black hole
(see chapter 2), except that matter and energy stream *out* of a
white hole and *into* a black hole. Humphreys was able to show
mathematically that with these initial conditions there would
have been a net gravitational effect towards the centre of the
early universe. Since gravity has a distorting effect upon time,
time would inevitably have passed at different 'rates' in different
parts of the universe. Time dilation would have led to clocks at
the edge of the universe running faster than clocks at the centre.
The extraordinary implication is that only a few days might have
passed on the Earth (which observations suggest is at or near the
centre), while the equivalent of 'billions of years' were passing
further out in the universe.

Humphreys' theory not only provides the first-ever outline of a
creationist cosmology, but also, in principle at least, a solution to
the long-standing puzzle of how light from distant stars and galaxies
managed to reach the Earth within the short biblical time frame.
Humphreys' 'white-hole cosmology' shows that gravitational
effects in the early universe could have allowed starlight to travel
the required distances while only a short time passed as measured
by Earth-based 'clocks'.

As with any new theory, Humphreys' cosmology has come in
for criticism and modification, and it is unclear at present whether
his version of the theory will survive the challenge of scientific and
biblical analysis. Other creationists have been developing their
own time-dilation theories in an attempt to deal with perceived
weaknesses in Humphreys' initial work. A prime example is
the model proposed by Australian physicist John Hartnett and

described in his book *Starlight, Time and the New Physics*, which seems to explain how starlight reached the Earth within a short time frame as well as providing an elegant solution to several other outstanding cosmological problems.[24] This is an area of origins research where creationist contributions are only now being formulated and debated. Nevertheless, such 'cutting-edge' research shows that it is possible to develop new theories of the universe that incorporate information from both Scripture and our scientific observations. They demonstrate that the Bible can guide our scientific thinking about cosmological questions and suggest innovative avenues of enquiry. Readers who would like to know more about this active area of research are directed to one of the books that deal with it in more depth.[25]

In the next chapter we will look at some of the objects with which the Creator has populated the heavens—the Sun, Moon and stars—and consider how they point us to the goodness and faithfulness of God.

2

The Sun, Moon and stars

On the fourth day of creation, God made the Sun, the Moon and the stars as lights to populate the heavens. Genesis 1:14–15 says:

And God said, Let there be lights in the firmament of the heaven to divide the day from the night; and let them be for signs, and for seasons, and for days, and years: and let them be for lights in the firmament of the heaven to give light upon the earth: and it was so.

In the last chapter we noted that one purpose of the heavens is to reveal the glory of God, but this passage tells us that they were also made for the benefit of man. Each created light—Sun, Moon and stars—was endowed with the particular characteristics and properties needed to fulfil its God-ordained function. The stated purpose of the lights is threefold.

1. To separate day from night

'And God made two great lights; the greater light to rule the day, and the lesser light to rule the night' (Genesis 1:16). The Sun, 'the greater light', is a nuclear furnace that provides the Earth with light and heat. The Moon, 'the lesser light', does not shine with its own light; it reflects light from the Sun. The Hebrew word for 'light' (*'ôr*) in this passage is broad enough to include a light-reflector such as the Moon.[1]

2. To serve as signs to mark seasons, days and years

There are many ways in which the heavenly lights fulfil this purpose. The daily circuit of the Sun across the sky, the phases of the Moon, the changing star patterns in the sky, lunar and solar eclipses—all act as timekeepers for man.

3. To give light on the Earth

The Sun is the right brightness and distance from us to provide illumination during the day. At night the Moon and the stars provide light, but the light they give is subdued so that the difference between day and night is maintained.[2]

Let us consider the origins and design of each of these heavenly lights. As we think about them, let us direct our praise and adoration to the one who set them in space and appointed them for our good and to his glory. We will begin with the stars.

The number and diversity of the stars

First of all, what is a star? A star is basically a ball of gas (mostly hydrogen) that gives out its own light and heat. Stars are powered by nuclear reactions which turn the hydrogen into helium, releasing energy in the process. The temperature at the core of a star, where these reactions take place, is estimated to be sixteen million degrees Kelvin[3] (300 degrees Kelvin is approximately room temperature). Stars like our Sun 'burn' their nuclear fuel at a staggering rate, transforming five million tons of mass into energy every second.[4] This is a huge amount, but negligible when compared with their total mass. At this rate, it would take around ten billion years for a star like our Sun to exhaust its fuel supply.

Stars occur in immense systems called galaxies, bound together by gravity and orbiting around a common centre. Our Sun is one of about 100 billion stars that make up our galaxy, the Milky Way. Our galaxy is one of about thirty galaxies in a cluster called the Local Group. This cluster is about ten million light years across— astronomers use the word 'local' in a very different way from its colloquial use! A large and famous cluster, containing many thousands of galaxies of different types, is the Virgo Cluster, about forty million light years away. One recent estimate suggests that, in total, there are ten times more stars in the observable universe than all the grains of sand on the world's deserts and beaches.[5] With this in mind, we can only marvel at the fact that God 'telleth the number of the stars; he calleth them all by their names' (Psalm 147:4). Even more remarkably, their creation is summed up by the writer of Genesis in just a few extraordinary words: 'He made the stars also'!

Stars are not only numerous; they are also diverse. To a casual observer of the night sky it might seem that stars differ only in their apparent brightness. In fact, stars vary widely in a whole range of properties, such as colour, temperature, luminosity, mass and density. There are yellow stars like our Sun, red supergiants that are hundreds of times larger and white dwarfs that are only the size of the Earth. Despite their great number, no two stars are absolutely identical. They are like snowflakes, all made to an understandable pattern yet amazingly diverse. Truly, as 1 Corinthians 15:41 reminds us, one star differs from another in glory.

Star 'lifecycles'

Astronomers typically organize these different types of stars into a sequence which they interpret as a lifecycle. According to this idea, young stars settle into a stable phase of existence, called the 'main sequence', with steady light output. Our Sun is one of these

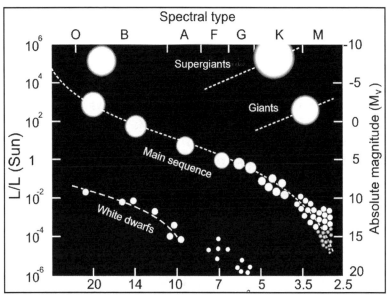

When stars are plotted according to their luminosities and temperatures, they fall into three main distributions: the main sequence, white dwarfs, and giants plus supergiants. Spectral types and stellar magnitudes are also shown in this diagram. Star diameters are not to scale.

main-sequence stars. However, when the fuel supply in the core is depleted, hydrogen-burning moves outwards and the star swells in size. As it swells, its surface temperature drops so that it becomes red. The star has become a red giant. Next, the star's helium core may become sufficiently hot to participate in nuclear reactions and the outer layers of the star shrink. At this stage, it resembles a main-sequence star once again. After the helium fuel in the core runs out, the star begins to burn both hydrogen and helium in concentric shells around the core. This causes the star to swell, so much so that the outer layers drift off into space to form a 'planetary nebula'. At the centre of this expanding shell of gas is the exposed core of the former red giant. This type of star is small, hot, extremely dense and known as a white dwarf. All stars of less than four times the mass of our Sun are thought to go through this lifecycle, although at different rates depending on their mass. In most cases these stars will die quietly as white dwarfs, but occasionally they may 'cannibalize' a companion star, leading to a violent explosion which destroys them (a Type I supernova).

Stars of more than four solar masses are thought to end their life in a similarly spectacular manner. Such a star evolves into a red supergiant, even larger and brighter than a red giant. Eventually a series of runaway nuclear reactions occurs in the core with the result that the star explodes (a Type II supernova). In most, if not all, cases the dense core of the dead star is left behind. This is called a neutron star. Gravity is so strong in a neutron star that the whole mass becomes extremely dense and, incredibly, a thimbleful of neutron-star material would weigh a billion tons. In theory, if the remnant core is dense enough it may continue to collapse under its own gravity to become a black hole. In a black hole, the collapsing star reaches a point of zero size and infinitely large density. Although black holes are invisible because even light cannot escape from them, it is theoretically possible to detect them. In binary systems where one star has died and become a black hole, it may continue to orbit a normal companion star. The intense gravitational field may cause gas to stream from the companion star into the black hole, heating up to millions of degrees before it disappears out of sight. At such temperatures the gas emits X-rays, which can be detected by observation satellites. There are currently about 300 objects within our galaxy which are candidates for being black holes. One of the best known is an X-ray source called Cygnus X–1 which orbits a faint star in the constellation of Cygnus.

The lifecycle theory we have described makes sense of our observations of different star types in the universe and also seems to be soundly based in physics.[6] If stars derive their energy from thermonuclear reactions—and recent studies of particles emitted by the Sun seem to confirm that this is the case[7]—then it is inevitable that all stars will change given sufficient time. Some creationists have instinctively reacted against this idea because the process of change is usually referred to as 'stellar evolution'. However, it is perhaps better to think of it as 'stellar ageing' because the changes are nothing more than a natural outworking of the law of entropy, the tendency of all natural systems to move towards a disordered state. The Bible itself leads us to expect these kinds of 'downward' changes. From the perspective of a human lifetime it may seem that the heavens are static and unchanging, but in fact they are 'wearing out'. In Psalm 102:25–27 we read:

Of old hast thou laid the foundation of the earth: and the heavens are the work of thy hands. They shall perish, but thou shalt endure: yea, all of them shall wax old like a garment; as a vesture shalt thou change them, and they shall be changed: but thou art the same, and thy years shall have no end (see also Isaiah 51:6 and Hebrews 1:10–12).

You may, however, have noticed my comment that the process of stellar change is inevitable *given sufficient time*. A potential problem for biblical creationists is that our current understanding of physics suggests that star lifecycles take billions of years. According to a straightforward understanding of the biblical timescale there has not been enough time for stars to pass through this cycle. How then are we able to observe a variety of stars at different stages in their lifecycles? One suggestion is that the universe was created as a fully functioning and diverse system from the very beginning. In this view, God originally created a variety of stars, and each star follows its lifecycle from the stage at which God created it. This 'mature creation' view is favoured by many creationists. Another possible solution to the problem is the phenomenon of gravitational time dilation which we discussed in chapter 1. Creationist cosmologies based upon time dilation suggest that, during the early history of the universe, 'billions of years' of processes were able to take place in outer space while only a few days passed as measured by 'Earth standard time'. If these theories are on the right lines there would have been adequate time for stars and galaxies to age and develop, and Adam and Eve would have been able to look into the heavens on the sixth day of creation and observe much the same kind of universe that we see today.[8]

The origin of stars

The most controversial aspect of the theory of star lifecycles concerns how stars form in the first place. The Bible tells us that the first stars were called into being by God during the Creation Week. However, according to conventional astronomy, the life of a star begins with the collapse of a gas cloud in space. As the cloud contracts under the influence of its own gravity, it becomes smaller and more dense. Eventually its centre becomes sufficiently hot for nuclear reactions to begin. This is how stars are said to be born. Astronomers even point to areas of the universe where they believe stars may be forming. One of these is the Eagle Nebula, 7,000 light years from the Earth. In 1995, the National Aeronautics and Space Administration (NASA) released spectacular Hubble Space Telescope images of gigantic pillar-like clouds of glowing gas and dust in this region of space. The infrared radiation emitted from these clouds is said to be associated with the start-up energy from new stars.

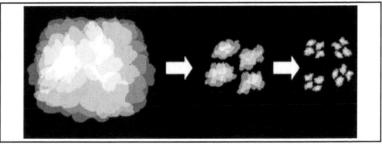

The theory of stellar evolution proposes that stars form by the fragmentation and gravitational collapse of gas clouds.

However, the assumptions regarding star formation remain very speculative. Calculations show that if a gas cloud can be collapsed to a critical size then it is possible for nuclear reactions to begin and a star to form.[9] The difficulty is in getting the cloud to collapse to this critical size so that gravity can take over. The gas clouds in 'star-forming' regions are very hot—that is why they are glowing—and hot gas clouds are more likely to disperse than collapse. It has been suggested that a nearby supernova explosion might compress the cloud enough to start the process of gravity collapse, but this begs the question of where the star that exploded came from. In fact, all the suggested ways to get a gas cloud to collapse require stars to exist already.

The Sun—a special star

Let us now consider the nearest star to the Earth—the Sun. Like other stars, our Sun is made mostly of hydrogen and helium. It is extremely hot; the surface temperature of the Sun is about 6,000 degrees Kelvin. The Bible describes the Sun as 'the greater light' that governs the day. The Sun truly is a great light; it is over 100 times the diameter of the Earth. An express train moving at 160 kilometres per hour would take nearly one year to travel from one side of the Sun to the other.[10] The Sun is also a very long way from the Earth—about 150 million kilometres (ninety-three million miles). A journey to the Sun at the speed of sound would take fourteen years. Even light travelling at 300,000 kilometres (186,000 miles) per second takes eight minutes to cover the distance.

All life on Earth depends on the Sun. If the Sun suddenly stopped shining, we would be doomed. Darkness would rapidly descend. In the course of a few hours, summer would turn to winter and the lakes and oceans would begin to freeze. Food and fuel would soon disappear and civilization would come to an end. Finally, the atmosphere would condense, liquefy and freeze, encasing the whole Earth in ten metres of solid air at the chill temperature of deep space.[11]

Although the Sun is often described as an ordinary or average star, it is actually a very special star.[12] Consider the following facts:

- Most stars are smaller, cooler, dimmer and have less mass than the Sun.[13]
- One-half to two-thirds of stars have a companion star; our Sun does not.
- The light and heat from most stars is very variable, but the Sun is relatively constant.
- Most Sun-like stars produce enormous superflares about once a century; our Sun does not.[14]

These features make it possible for life to exist on the Earth. The Bible's account of creation explains why: it was designed with man in mind.

The Moon—our nearest neighbour

We also find evidence of plan and purpose when we study our satellite, the Moon. This 'faithful witness in heaven' (Psalm 89:37) has many features that are useful to life on the Earth. Here are a few of them.

1. The Moon is an efficient reflector

The amount of light reflected depends on its surface area. Since the Moon is relatively large—over a quarter of the Earth's diameter—it reflects sunlight well.[15] This enables the Moon to fulfil its role as 'the lesser light' that governs the night.

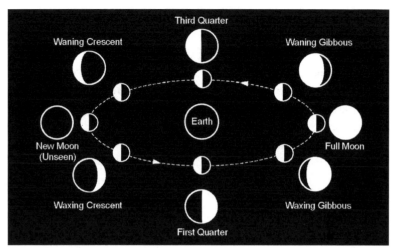

In this diagram, the inner loop shows the Moon's orbit around the Earth and the outer loop shows how the Moon appears from the Earth. The sunlight is coming from the left. The Moon exhibits different phases as the relative positions of the Sun, Earth and Moon change. It appears as a Full Moon when the Sun and Moon are on opposite sides of the Earth, and as a New Moon when they are on the same side.

2. The Moon helps us keep time

It orbits the Earth about once a month, giving us a regular cycle of phases (new moon, first quarter, full moon, third quarter).[16] Also, the Moon is just the right distance from the Earth to eclipse the Sun. Although the Sun is 400 times larger, it is also 400 times farther away.[17]

3. The Moon helps keep the oceans clean

Its gravitational pull raises tides which circulate oxygen and nutrients in shallow seas. The tides can also be harnessed to provide energy for man.[18]

The origin of the Moon has been something of a mystery to those who reject the Bible's account of its creation. Before the

Apollo Moon landings, a variety of different theories had been proposed, but the rock and soil samples brought back from the Moon seemed to rule out all of them.[19] Today, the most widely accepted idea is that the Moon was formed from material that was blasted off the Earth by the impact of another huge object. Calculations show that to produce enough material to form the Moon, the impacting object would have had to be at least as massive as the planet Mars. This is called 'the giant impact theory'. However, there are doubts about whether this theory can account for the chemistry of the Moon,[20] and there is also the unsolved problem of how to get rid of the excess spin this event would cause.[21] Explaining the origin of the Moon by natural processes is so difficult that one astronomer reportedly joked that perhaps the Moon is really an illusion![22] Of course, even if a plausible scenario is eventually produced which shows how the Moon could have formed by a giant impact, this would not necessarily indicate that it *actually* happened that way. We know from Genesis 1:14–17 that the Moon was spoken into being directly by the word of God.

Remembering the Creator

We have seen that the Sun, Moon and stars were created by God to separate day from night, to serve as signs to mark seasons, days and years, and to give light on the Earth. The Bible's witness is clear— these objects were specially designed with man in mind. As we contemplate the heavens, our response should be to remember our Creator and give thanks to him for his goodness. This would surely have been the testimony of these two lunar astronauts, whose experiences drew them close to God:

> While I was on the moon my belief was in the theory of evolution. However, since that time I have put my heart to Jesus and the reality of the Holy Bible. I believe now with all my heart

in God as the Creator and this book has been a tremendous inspiration to me to understand more fully the reality of God's creation (*Charles M. Duke, Lunar Module Pilot of Apollo 16*).[23]

I was born into a family in which both my mother and my father knew God. I learned about Jesus Christ from my mother, and I am grateful to her for this. I will never forget the day when I first visited an Evangelical Baptist church. God Himself seemed to say: 'Now it's your turn. I want to enter your life and fill it with Myself.' So I turned to the Lord, and He began controlling my life in His all-wise and loving way. I didn't know where the Lord would lead me, but my only desire was that it would be *upwards*! (*James B. Irwin, Lunar Module Pilot of Apollo 15*).[24]

In our next chapter we turn our attention to the Earth itself—the place that the Creator prepared to be our home.

3

There's no place like home

Our home, the Earth, is the centre-stage of God's universe. It is of prime importance in the fulfilment of God's purposes. It was made on the first day of creation—but was originally formless, empty and dark (Genesis 1:1–2).[1] The rest of Genesis 1 describes the way in which God gave the Earth its shape and form and filled it with living creatures. On the second day, God made an expanse, which he called 'the firmament', or 'the sky', to separate water from water (Genesis 1:6–8). Then, on the third day, he commanded the water under the sky to be gathered to one place, so that dry land would appear. God called the dry land 'earth' and the gathered waters 'seas' (Genesis 1:9–10). In this way, he fashioned our world in order that it might be inhabited:

> For thus saith the LORD that created the heavens; God himself that formed the earth and made it; he hath established it, he created it not in vain, he formed it to be inhabited: I am the LORD; and there is none else (Isaiah 45:18).

A recurring theme of the Bible is that God's wisdom is manifested in the world that he has made. This is expressed in Jeremiah 51:15, which says, 'He hath made the earth by his power, he hath established the world by his wisdom, and hath stretched out the heaven by his understanding.' Similarly, Proverbs 3:19–20 tells us, 'The LORD by wisdom hath founded the earth; by understanding hath he established the heavens. By his knowledge the depths are broken up, and the clouds drop down the dew.'

In this chapter we will explore the many ways in which the Earth, in its suitability to sustain and nurture life, demonstrates God's wisdom. We will begin by taking a look at our close neighbours in space—the planets of our solar system—because they will help us realize how the Earth has been uniquely prepared as man's home.

Our astronomical backyard

The Earth was made on the first day of Creation Week, but when did God make the planets beyond the Earth? The Bible does not directly mention their creation. However, Genesis 1:16 tells us that, along with the Sun and Moon, God made 'the stars' on the fourth day of creation. The Hebrew word for stars (*kôkāb*) refers to any bright object in the sky and probably includes comets, asteroids, meteoroids and the planets.

Mercury is the nearest planet to the Sun and it is an inhospitable and barren world. In 1975, the Mariner 10 spacecraft flew within 330 kilometres (205 miles) of Mercury and revealed a surface of craters, lava plains and sinuous cliffs up to 3,000 metres (9,840 feet) high. The thin atmosphere is composed mainly of sodium and potassium and the surface temperature varies between –173°C and 427°C.

Venus is often called the 'morning star' or 'evening star' because it is the brightest object in the sky after the Sun and Moon. It has a dense atmosphere of carbon dioxide and nitrogen, and clouds of sulphuric acid obscure its surface. However, maps of Venus have been made by radar. It is a hostile world with surface pressures ninety times greater than those on Earth and temperatures reaching 472°C—sufficient to melt lead.

Mars is known as the 'Red Planet' because of its iron-rich rocky surface. Thanks to the many orbiters and landers that have visited the planet, we have a number of images of barren Martian landscapes. The southern hemisphere of Mars is dominated by volcanoes, including Olympus Mons, 600 kilometres (375 miles) across and towering 26,000 metres high (over 85,000 feet). There are also vast canyon systems such as Valles Marineris, 4,500 kilometres (2,800 miles) long from east to west and as much as 700 kilometres (435 miles) wide from north to south. Huge dust storms occasionally engulf the whole planet and may last several months. The thin atmosphere is mainly composed of carbon dioxide.

Jupiter is the largest planet in our system and the first of the 'gas giants'. Eleven Earths could be placed side by side across its equator! Jupiter is thought to have a small rocky core surrounded by liquid hydrogen. The thick atmosphere is made up of hydrogen and helium. Despite its great size, Jupiter spins on its axis in under ten hours. This means that the clouds in its atmosphere are spun into belts and zones, with wind speeds of more than 700 kilometres (435 miles) per hour. The famous Great Red Spot is an immense storm that has been raging on Jupiter for centuries.

Saturn is also a gas world with a thick atmosphere of hydrogen, helium and traces of methane and ammonia. Remarkably, the density of Saturn is less than that of water—it would float if you could find a bathtub big enough! The winds on Saturn are even faster than those on Jupiter, reaching nearly 3,000 kilometres (1,865 miles) per hour at the equator. Saturn, of course, is famous for its spectacular system of rings. Although Jupiter, Uranus and Neptune also have ring systems, it is Saturn that boasts the best display. Amazing photographs of the fine structure of the rings were returned by the Cassini spacecraft in 2004.

Uranus is perhaps the most mysterious of the outer planets. Once thought to be a bland and unchanging world, it has been shown to be surprisingly active by the latest images from the Keck Observatory in Hawaii.[2] At the centre of Uranus is thought to be a small rocky core which grades into a deep liquid ocean which, in turn, thins out into a deep atmosphere of hydrogen and helium. The blue-green colour of this world is caused by traces of methane in its atmosphere.

Neptune is smaller than Uranus but has a similar atmosphere of hydrogen, helium and methane. The images taken by Voyager 2 in August 1989 revealed a beautiful blue world. The most prominent feature in Neptune's atmosphere is the Great Dark Spot, a huge storm about half the size of the Earth. Voyager 2 also discovered a fast-moving white cloud, which became known as the 'Scooter'.

Pluto, formerly considered to be the smallest of the planets, was demoted to the new category of 'dwarf planets' in 2006. Two other solar-system objects—the asteroid Ceres and a distant icy body called Eris—are also included in this newly defined group of objects and it is likely that others will eventually be reclassified to join them. Pluto has a very elliptical orbit, so that it is sometimes nearer to the Sun than Neptune. Very little is known about Pluto because it is so far away. However, it is thought to have a thin atmosphere and a frozen surface of methane, nitrogen and carbon monoxide.

When we consider the planets in our solar system, we are reminded that God loves variety. One scientist has said, 'The most striking outcome of planetary exploration is the diversity of the planets.'[3] Another said, 'The more that we look at the different planets, the more each one seems to be unique.'[4] It is a tribute to God's creativity and versatility that no two planets in our solar system are the same.

What about the solar nebula theory?

How did such a complex and diverse system of planets come into being? Just as the Big Bang theory was devised to provide an explanation for the origin of the universe without reference to the Creator, so a theory has been devised to explain the origin of our

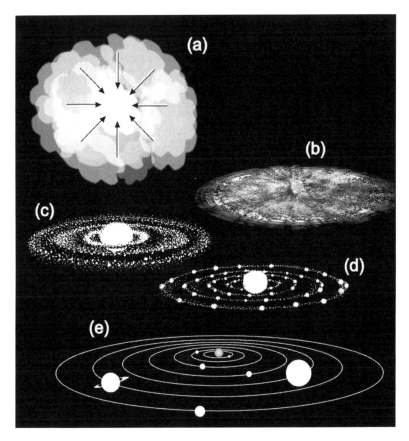

According to the solar nebula theory, our planetary system formed from a cloud of gas about 4.6 billion years ago. The cloud is said to have collapsed into a flattened disc (a, b), with material in the centre becoming our Sun (c) and the orbiting debris coalescing to form the planets and moons (d, e).

solar system by solely natural processes. It is called the solar nebula theory.

According to this theory, our planetary system formed from a rotating cloud of gas surrounding the young Sun about 4.6 billion years ago. The cloud is thought to have collapsed into a flattened disc and gradually cooled down. This led to dust grains condensing out of the gas. Within the disc, these grains are said to have collided with one another, sticking together to form larger and larger pieces. This process, known as accretion, eventually led to the formation of the rocky inner planets. In the outer parts of the nebula, where temperatures were much lower, water, methane and ammonia grains formed and accreted into icy bodies. Some of these objects became so large that they were able to collect and retain helium and hydrogen atoms and become giant gas planets. Eventually, as the Sun grew hotter and more luminous, it blew away the remaining gas and dust to leave the orbiting planets and moons.

This theory is popular with most astronomers because it seems to make sense of the major features of our solar system. It explains why the planets revolve around the Sun in nearly the same plane, in nearly circular orbits, and in the same direction that the Sun rotates. It explains the different compositions and distances from the Sun of the inner and outer planets. It also accounts for the existence of small solar-system objects, such as asteroids and comets, as 'left-over' pieces from the accretion process. Furthermore, the theory is said to have been indirectly confirmed by observations of 'young' stars elsewhere in our galaxy surrounded by discs of gas and dust. One example is the star Beta Pictoris, which is surrounded by a dust disc about 100 times the diameter of our solar system. The disc even has an inner 'hole' which, astronomers suggest, may be a place where planets have already formed.

Doubts about the solar nebula theory

However, not all the evidence unambiguously supports the solar nebula theory. It faces several unresolved scientific problems.

1. The accretion of particles in the dust cloud

The theory says that the planets and moons grew when dust particles in the cloud began to stick to one another. But experiments show that particles of this type tend to break up when they collide, not stick together.[5] A recent review of the scientific data concluded that the growth from dust grains to kilometre-size bodies remains unexplained.[6]

2. The distribution of angular momentum (i.e. rotational movement) in the solar system

It is well known that the spin rate of an object will increase as it contracts in size. We observe this principle in action when an ice-skater spins faster as he pulls his arms inward towards his body. Now consider the nebula theory, which says that the Sun formed from a contracting cloud of gas and dust. As the cloud collapsed, the spin rate of the young Sun would have dramatically increased. Today the Sun—which has most of the mass of the solar system—should be spinning rapidly and the planets should be revolving around the Sun relatively slowly. In fact, the opposite is true. The planets possess 98% of the angular momentum of the solar system and the Sun only 2%. Scientists who accept the nebula theory have tried to devise ways to transfer the angular momentum from

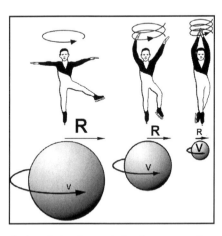

An ice skater demonstrates the conservation of angular momentum when he spins faster by drawing his arms and legs closer to his axis of rotation. As the radius (R) decreases, the velocity (V) increases.

the Sun to the planets, but these explanations have been only partially successful.[7]

3. The unexpected motions of some planets and moons

Venus spins in the opposite direction to the other planets—this is called retrograde rotation—and Uranus is spinning on its side. According to the nebula theory, they must have started off spinning the same way as the other planets.[8] Explaining how the spin direction of some objects was changed remains a major puzzle. In the case of Uranus, it has been suggested that the planet was knocked onto its side when another large body struck the planet near one of its poles. However, five moons of Uranus are in highly circular orbits around the planet's equator. The impact theory does not explain how they escaped being scattered into random orbits or lost from the system altogether.[9] Others have suggested that the Uranus system gradually evolved to its present state, but no detailed explanation has been forthcoming.

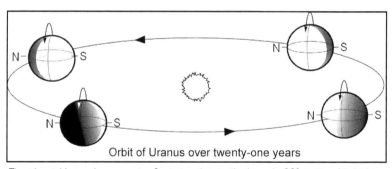

Orbit of Uranus over twenty-one years

The planet Uranus has an axis of rotation that is tilted nearly 98° to its orbital plane. This means that the north and south poles point alternately towards the Sun. (Drawing not to scale).

As is often the case in science, these problems are not sufficient to completely disprove the nebula theory. It is always possible that naturalistic solutions to these difficulties will be discovered in the future. At present, however, they do cause us to question the theory and prompt us to come up with alternative scientific scenarios concerning the history of the solar system that are consistent with the Bible. These scenarios will have to explain, among other things, the numerous craters that are found on the Earth and the other planets and moons. These craters indicate that our solar system has been bombarded by meteorites or asteroids at least once—and perhaps more than once.[10] It has been suggested that catastrophic events of this kind may have been associated with the Flood of Noah's day (see chapter 13), although these ideas have not been well thought out so far. What is certainly true is that there is a trend, even in the mainstream scientific literature, to explain the peculiarities of our solar system by invoking catastrophic events in the past.

The 'Goldilocks planet'

When we consider the diversity of the planets revealed by modern solar-system exploration, and the difficulties faced by the solar nebula theory, we begin to realize how special the Earth is. Venus is very similar to the Earth in size and distance from the Sun, yet it is extremely different in almost every other respect.[11] Only the Earth is equipped to support life. Let us review some of the characteristics that make life on the Earth possible.

1. Earth's surface temperature

This depends largely upon the Earth's distance from the Sun. If the Earth were only a few million kilometres closer to the Sun, the temperature would dramatically rise. If the Earth were a few million kilometres further from the Sun, there would be profound cooling. Some scientists call the Earth 'the Goldilocks planet' because it is not too hot or too cold—it is just right.[12] The atmosphere also helps to regulate the temperature of the Earth, acting as a thermal blanket and preventing the radiation of heat into space at night. In addition, the oceans function as a giant thermostat, regulating seasonal temperatures. As a consequence, the average annual temperature of the Earth is about 14°C and is remarkably stable.

2. Earth's tilt

The 23½° tilt of the Earth's vertical axis causes the four seasons. During May–July the northern hemisphere is pointing towards the Sun (summer in the north, winter in the south). During November-January the southern hemisphere is pointing towards the Sun (summer in the south, winter in the north). If the Earth had no tilt, there would be no seasons and the surface temperature at any particular spot would always be about the same. It is estimated that only one half of the lands which are currently suitable for agricultural production would be able to grow crops. On the other hand, if the tilt were double the current value, temperature extremes between the seasons would be even greater. Even the mid-latitudes would be unbearably hot in the summer and intolerably cold in the winter. Most of Europe and North America would become uninhabitable.[13]

3. Earth's day

On the Earth we have a day that is about twenty-four hours long. If it were much longer than this, the temperature differences between day and night would be exaggerated. Living creatures on the daylight side would be scorched, while those on the dark side would be frozen.[14] If the length of our day was similar to that of Mercury or Venus, for example, animals and plants would face serious difficulties.

4. Earth's atmosphere

Our atmosphere contains an optimal mixture of oxygen and nitrogen. In this way the oxygen is diluted to the proper strength for use by living organisms. Interestingly, no appreciable amounts of oxygen have been found in any of the other atmospheres in the solar system. Those planets which do have atmospheres contain poisonous gases. Our atmosphere also protects us from meteors. Several billion small meteors enter the atmosphere each day, but almost all of them burn up before they reach the ground. Very few, perhaps half a dozen, actually land on the Earth's surface as meteorites. Another benefit of our atmosphere is that it protects us from the harmful ultraviolet rays of the Sun. This form of light can cause problems such as cataracts and melanomas.[15] However, the ozone layer in the stratosphere (ten to fifty kilometres, or six to thirty miles, high) helps to absorb this radiation.

5. Earth's oceans

Probably the most obvious difference between the Earth and the planets when viewed from space is water. Liquid water is scarce elsewhere in the solar system, yet over 70% of the Earth's surface is covered with water, to depths of up to 11,000 metres (over 36,000 feet). There are seventy billion gallons (265 billion litres) of water for every single person on Earth.[16] Water has some extraordinary properties.[17] It is a universal solvent which can carry the essential nutrients needed by living organisms. It is transparent, allowing ocean animals to see through it and light to reach marine plants and algae. It has a high heat-holding capacity, which means that the oceans can retain and circulate heat efficiently. Water is also one of only a few substances which expand and become less dense when they freeze. This means that ice floats on water, thus preventing oceans and lakes from freezing from the bottom up—something that would be disastrous for life. Furthermore, our optimum distance from the Sun allows this water to exist in three forms—vapour, liquid and ice—to supply the hydrological cycle.

6. Earth's continents

The continents cover almost 30% of the Earth's surface and have a mean height of about 840 metres (2,756 feet) above sea level. There is enough water on Earth to flood the land to a depth of about 2,500 metres (8,200 feet)—so how is it that any land is exposed? The answer is that the continents are made of rocks which are, on average, less dense than the rocks that make up the ocean floor. Also, the continental crust is usually double the thickness of the ocean crust. These factors are balanced in such a way that the continents maintain their elevation above the ocean waves.[18]

We undoubtedly live on a 'user-friendly' planet with countless features that benefit mankind. By comparison with the Earth, the other worlds of our solar system are bleak and desolate. Our solar system has vast barren expanses of craters, mountains, rocks, gas and dust. There are unbearable extremes of heat and cold, and oxygen and water are lacking. Yet here on Earth the requirements for life are all present in abundance. There really is no place like home! The uniqueness of the Earth confirms what the Bible tells us about its origin—that it was designed by the wisdom and understanding of God to be inhabited.

Part II:

Questions of time

4

A matter of days

Our lives are governed and regulated by the passage of time and the natural cycles of our world. We operate on a twenty-four-hour schedule—the day. We get up in the morning when the Sun rises and we go to bed at night after the Sun sets. We group our days into months of about thirty days each, based on the cycle of phases of the Moon. In our calendar, there are twelve months in each year—a period of 365 days defined by the Sun's yearly path around the sky against the backdrop of the distant stars.

All these time periods—day, month and year—are astronomical cycles of one kind or another. By contrast, however, the seven-day week has no basis in astronomy and its origin is a mystery until we consider the record of creation in Genesis 1 and God's own commentary on it in Exodus 20:8–11:

Remember the sabbath day, to keep it holy. Six days shalt thou labour, and do all thy work: but the seventh day is the sabbath of the LORD thy God ... For in six days the LORD made heaven and earth, the sea, and all that in them is, and rested the seventh day: wherefore the LORD blessed the sabbath day, and hallowed it.

Genesis 1 tells us that the Lord God completed his work of

creation in six days and rested on the seventh day. Exodus 20:8–11 reveals that God did this as a pattern for us: we are to work for six days and set aside the seventh for rest because that is what the Lord did.

This biblical information has enormous implications for how we are to understand the history of our world. We are immediately faced with a conflict between what the Bible seems to say and the conclusions of conventional science, because according to the most widely accepted scientific theories the development of the universe and the Earth took billions of years—not six days. Indeed, the conclusion that the universe and the Earth are extremely old seems so secure that many Christians are reluctant to stand against the scientific consensus.

How long is a day?

This conflict has led many to try to harmonize the biblical account with the conventional timescale by taking a non-literal view of the 'days' in Genesis 1. The suggested interpretations are many and varied, but here we will briefly describe three of them.

1. The framework theory

This theory says that the Creation Week can be divided into two sets of three days each—days one to three are seen as 'days of forming' and days four to six as 'days of filling'. There are said to be parallels between days one and four, days two and five, and days three and six. Proponents of this view regard the 'days' as nothing more than a literary device and say that they should not be understood in a chronological or historical sense. However, others have pointed out that the parallels between days one to three and days four to six are somewhat artificial and, even if granted, they do not preclude a literal understanding of the days.[1]

2. The day-age theory

This theory says that each 'day' should be understood as an 'age' or an 'epoch'. It is argued that this enables the order of events in Genesis 1 to be brought into agreement with the order of events according to conventional science. Actually, there is little agreement between the order of events in Genesis 1 and the order of events according to conventional science—the 'days' must be made to overlap with one another in order to produce any kind of harmony.[2] As an aside, it is perhaps worth noting that the day-age theory is not the same as the time dilation theory of Humphreys (see chapter 1). In the time-dilation theory, each creation day would have been of ordinary length to an Earth-bound observer. By contrast, the day-age theory equates the creation 'days' with millions of years of pre-human history from an Earth perspective.

3. The days of revelation theory

This theory says that the 'days' of Genesis 1 are not actually the days on which God created, but rather the days on which God revealed to the writer of Genesis what he had already done over long ages. In Genesis 1, however, there is no indication that we are reading a revelation or vision—the sense is rather of a straightforward historical narrative. Furthermore, the theory runs counter to Exodus 20:8–11, which tells us that God made (Hebrew *'asah*) 'heaven and earth, the sea, and all that in them is', in six days.[3]

Others take a straightforward view of the length of the creation days, but suggest that there may have been an indefinite time gap between Genesis 1:1 and Genesis 1:2. This view allows the creation of the universe and the Earth to have taken place long ago, while verse 2 onwards is seen as describing events occurring on the Earth, or as they would be observed from the Earth—including the 'appearance' (rather than the creation) of the Sun, Moon and stars in the sky on the fourth day. However, this seems to be a rather unnatural interpretation of the text. It has been pointed out that if the author of Genesis had intended to teach us that the Sun, Moon and stars 'appeared' on the fourth day, then he would have used the Hebrew word for 'appear' (*ra'ah*). This is the word used to describe the appearance of the dry land from beneath the waters on the third day (Genesis 1:9). On the contrary, Genesis 1:16 says that the Sun, Moon and stars were made (Hebrew *'asah*) on the fourth day.

Furthermore, the creation of 'the heaven and the earth' in Genesis 1:1 is best regarded as a summary statement of all that follows, rather than something that *precedes* the events of verses 2–31. As one writer put it, 'By analogy we might say, "At the beginning of this year I built a garden shed. On the first day I laid the foundations. On the second day I erected the walls. On the third day I put the roof on. On the fourth day I installed the lights. On the fifth day I added some fish in a tank and some birds in a cage. On the sixth day I added some rabbits in a hutch. On the seventh day I rested."'[4] If this is the correct interpretation, there is no room for a gap of any duration between Genesis 1:1 and Genesis 1:2.

Questions we need to ask

In the rest of this chapter I will seek to explain my own understanding of the creation account by turning to the early chapters of Genesis and asking some important questions.

Firstly, *what kind of literature is Genesis?* This question is important because how we answer it will determine how we set about interpreting the text:

1. Is it *poetry*? No, for it lacks the defining characteristics of Hebrew poetry (e.g. balanced couplets or parallelism).[5]

2. Is it *an allegory*? No, for it does not have features consistent with allegory (e.g. a person who tells the story and interprets it).

3. Is it *myth*? No, for the Lord Jesus and the apostles clearly accepted the reality of the characters and events recorded here—including Adam and Eve (e.g. Matthew 19:1–6; Mark 10:2–9; Romans 5:12–21; 1 Corinthians 15:21–22; 1 Timothy 2:11–14) and Noah and the Flood (e.g. Matthew 24:37–39; Luke 17:26–27; 1 Peter 3:20).

What we find in the early chapters of Genesis are the characteristics we would expect of a *historical* account—and these chapters seamlessly connect with the history that follows. This suggests that our understanding of the 'days' of creation must be consistent with a historical interpretation of Genesis.[6]

The second question we must ask ourselves is this: *what is the normal meaning of the words used in Genesis 1?* In Old Testament Hebrew, the words for 'day' and 'days' are, respectively, *yôm* and *yāmîm*. These words have essentially the same range of meaning in Hebrew as in English. Although the words can be used to mean an indefinite period of time (e.g. 'the Day of the LORD'), they are mostly used to refer to a normal day, or the daylight portion of a day. This means that we would need strong evidence from the context of Genesis 1 to suggest that they have a non-literal meaning.

This brings us to our third question: *how are these words used in the context of Genesis 1?* There are four things to notice:

1. *Genesis 1:5 defines the word* yôm *for us*. It reads: 'And God called the light Day, and the darkness he called Night. And the evening and the morning were the first day.' In this verse, *yôm* is used to describe the daylight portion of a day and the entire light/dark cycle—in other words, a normal day.

2. *Each day of creation is given a number*. In the Hebrew the first

day has a cardinal number (i.e. 'day one') and the others
have ordinal numbers (that is, 'second', 'third', 'fourth', etc).
Elsewhere in the Old Testament, the words *yôm* and *yāmîm*
are used with a number 359 times, and, with no obvious
counter-example, the meaning is always a normal day.[7]

3. The days are said to consist of an 'evening and morning'.
    The words, 'evening' and 'morning' are combined with
    yôm nineteen times outside Genesis 1, and in each instance
    a normal day is meant.[8] Furthermore, when 'evening' and
    'morning' occur together without *yôm*, thirty-eight times
    outside Genesis 1, they always refer to a normal day.[9]

4. There are several other Hebrew 'time' words, including *ôlām*
    (meaning 'long time, duration'), which could have been
    used to convey the idea of long or indefinite creation days.
    However, none of these words is used in Genesis 1.[10]

Finally, we must also consider *what Exodus 20:8–11 tells us about
this subject*.[11] At the beginning of this chapter we referred to this
passage, which instructs us to remember the sabbath day and keep
it holy. This is one of the Ten Commandments written by the finger
of God on the tablets of stone brought down from Mount Sinai by
Moses (Exodus 31:18). It evidently equates the days of Genesis 1
with the days of our week.[12]

In summary, the Bible seems to teach that God created all things
in six ordinary days, similar to those we now experience. This
conclusion is supported by the historical nature of the Genesis
account, the normal meaning of the words, the context of Genesis
1 and the testimony of the Ten Commandments. Moreover, as we
shall see in the next section, the objections raised against this view
are not compelling when carefully examined.

Objections to the 'ordinary day' interpretation

Several objections are commonly raised to this understanding of
the 'creation days', and it would be appropriate here to think about
some of them. Let us consider them as a series of questions.

1. Doesn't the Bible teach that God's days are not our days?

Two verses in particular are mentioned in this respect. Psalm
90:4 says, 'For a thousand years in thy sight are but as yesterday
when it is past, and as a watch in the night.' 2 Peter 3:8 says, 'But,
beloved, be not ignorant of this one thing, that one day is with
the Lord as a thousand years, and a thousand years as one day.'
However, these passages teach only that God is not constrained
by time, not that one 'creation day' equals '1,000 human years'.[13]
Applying these verses to Genesis 1 would be to take them out of
context.

*2. How could there have been ordinary days before the Sun was
created?*

Some have argued that the first three 'creation days' could not
have been ordinary days because the Sun was not made until day
four (Genesis 1:14–19). However, this objection is based upon
a misunderstanding. The Sun is not needed to measure out an
ordinary day. All that is needed is for the Earth to rotate relative to a
light source. Genesis 1:3 tells us that God created such a light source
on the first day and that from then on there was a cycle of evenings
and mornings. This temporary light source—perhaps emanating
from God himself (see Revelation 22:5)—was apparently replaced
by the Sun on the fourth day.

3. Don't the events of the sixth day require more than twenty-four hours?

Another frequent objection is that too many events occurred on the sixth day of creation to fit into an ordinary-length day. It is sometimes said, for instance, that it would have taken Adam a long time to name 'all cattle', 'the fowl of the air' and 'every beast of the field', as described in Genesis 2:19–20. However, it can be shown that this task need only have taken a few hours. There is no requirement for the other events of the day to have taken long periods either.[14]

4. Isn't the seventh day continuing?

It has been suggested by some that the seventh day of Genesis 1 must be a long period because Hebrews 4:1–11 says that it continues to the present time. However, a careful study of Hebrews 4 reveals that it does not say that the *seventh day* continues—only that God's *rest* continues. In context, this 'rest' refers to the kingdom of God, not to the seventh day of the Creation Week.[15]

The family lists of Genesis 5 and 11

Assuming that we accept that the word *yôm* means an ordinary day in Genesis 1, we can begin to build a chronology (timescale) for the history of the world. Adam, the first man, was created on the sixth day (Genesis 1:26–31), which means that the Earth is only five days older than Adam. Confirmation of this is found in the words of the Lord Jesus Christ in Mark 10:6. Referring to Adam and Eve, he says, 'But from the beginning of the creation God made them male and female.' The phrase that the Lord uses here—'from the beginning of the creation'—refers elsewhere to the origin of the physical world (e.g. Mark 13:19; 2 Peter 3:4). The obvious meaning of Mark 10:6 is that mankind has been around for about the same length of time

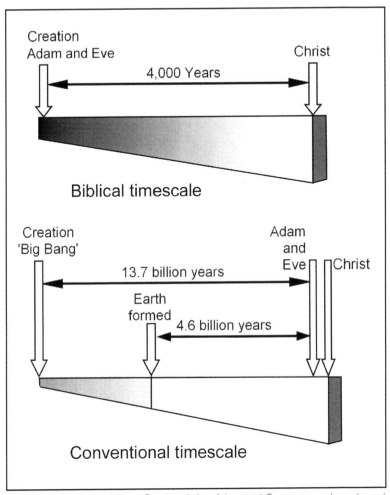

Creation
Adam and Eve

Christ

4,000 Years

Biblical timescale

Creation
'Big Bang'

Adam
and
Eve Christ

13.7 billion years

Earth
formed

4.6 billion years

Conventional timescale

In Mark 10:6, the Lord Jesus Christ said that Adam and Eve were made male and female 'from the beginning of the creation'. If there had been a long period of pre-human history, this statement would not be true..

as the world itself. In other words, if we can calculate when Adam lived, we will also know the age of the Earth.

In Genesis, we have two lists of family descent (genealogies): from Adam to Noah (Genesis 5), and from Noah to Abraham

(Genesis 11:10–32). The lists give us some important information. Genesis 5:3–5 is representative:

> And Adam lived an hundred and thirty years, and begat a son in his own likeness, after his image; and called his name Seth: and the days of Adam after he had begotten Seth were eight hundred years: and he begat sons and daughters: and all the days that Adam lived were nine hundred and thirty years: and he died.

Here we are given the age of Adam at the birth of his son, how long he lived after his son was born and how old he was when he died. The family list of Genesis 11 is similar, except that it does not give the age of the father at the time of his death. The probable reason is that the pattern has been set and we are expected to add the numbers up for ourselves!

So far, so good—but we will only be able to use these genealogies to work out a chronology if we can be sure that they are complete. If there are missing generations then we will not be able to calculate when Adam was created—at least not with any degree of precision. Since some genealogies in the Bible *are* incomplete, it has been suggested that there might be similar gaps in the Genesis lists. The reasoning runs as follows: since there are gaps in, say, the family line of Christ in Matthew 1, we may conclude that gaps are also likely in the Genesis family lists. If this is true, then any calculations based upon them will be inaccurate by an indeterminate number of years. However, this argument overlooks the strong evidence that the Genesis lists are unbroken and were intended to provide a chronology. Let us summarize some of this evidence.

1. There is an interpretive principle that says Scripture complements Scripture

In other words, what one book omits, another includes; what one writer says in full, another summarizes. When Matthew 1:8 tells us that Joram begat Uzziah he is missing out three generations—but we know this because the three names omitted here are found elsewhere in Scripture.[16] In the case of the genealogies in Genesis the 'missing' generations can only be speculative because they are not supplied or referred to elsewhere.

2. None of the lists with gaps mentions the age of the father at the birth of the next in line

The Genesis lists, on the other hand, do. Some have suggested that the relationships in the Genesis lists may be 'ancestor-descendant' rather than 'father-son'. But even if this is granted, the fact that the lists give the age of each 'father' when his 'son' was born means that they can still be used to build a chronology.[17] Consider, for example, the information provided in Genesis 5:9–11. Let us assume, for the sake of argument, that Cainan is actually the great-grandson of Enos. The text still says that Enos was ninety years old when Cainan was born—leaving the calculated chronology exactly the same as if he were his direct son.

3. In many places, cross-checks show that there is no gap[18]

Consider the following:

- Seth is a direct son of Adam because he was seen as a replacement for Abel (Genesis 4:25).
- Enos is a direct son of Seth because Seth named him (Genesis 4:26).
- In Jude 14, Enoch is said to be 'the seventh from Adam', which seems to rule out any missing generations between Adam and Enoch.
- Noah is a direct son of Lamech because Lamech named him (Genesis 5:29).
- Shem, Ham and Japheth were direct sons of Noah because they were with him on the ark (Genesis 7:13).

- Arphaxad was a direct son of Shem because he was born two years after the Flood (Genesis 11:10).
- Abram, Haran and Nahor were clearly the direct sons of Terah (Genesis 11:26–31).
- The Hebrew name Methuselah may mean 'when he dies it will come'.[19] If there are no gaps in the family lists, it is interesting to note that Methuselah would have died in the same year that the Flood began. Methuselah would, of course, have been named by his father Enoch, who, we are told, was a prophet (Jude 14).

4. The extra Cainan of Luke 3:36 is probably a copyist's error

In Luke's genealogy we have an 'extra' Cainan who is not mentioned in Genesis 11:12. Some say this is evidence that at least one generation is missing from the Genesis 11 list. However, the extra name does not appear in the oldest manuscripts of Luke's Gospel and early commentators do not refer to it. This strongly suggests that it is one of those rare copying mistakes that crept in long after Luke's Gospel was written. Note that it is *not* evidence of an error in the original Bible manuscripts—but neither is it evidence of a gap in the Genesis genealogy.[20]

The evidence strongly suggests that the genealogies of Genesis 5 and 11 were intended to give us a straightforward chronology from Adam to Abraham. However, even if we concede that these genealogical lists are incomplete, as some of my creationist friends have argued, the amount of time that can be inserted into them is very limited. Since the fathers listed in Genesis 11 had their sons at age thirty-five or less, about 300 missing generations would be needed to add even 10,000 years to this chronology. It is difficult to see how the chronology could be extended even by that amount without stretching the genealogies to their breaking point.

So how old is the Earth?

If we accept the foregoing arguments that the Genesis genealogies are complete, we can use them to work out how much time passed between Adam and Abraham (see chart overleaf). For these calculations I have chosen to use the Hebrew (Masoretic) text of Genesis. There are alternative texts of the Old Testament, such as the Greek Septuagint translation and the Samaritan Pentateuch, which give somewhat different numbers. Although some scholars prefer them over the Hebrew text,[21] it is most likely that they represent corruptions of the original reading. Even if we used one of the variant texts it would make no more than 2,000 years difference, at most, to our calculations.[22]

According to the Hebrew Masoretic text of Genesis, 1,656 years passed between the creation and Noah's Flood and 342 years between the Flood and the birth of Abraham—1,998 years in total.

Next we can use established historical dates to work backwards to find out when Abraham was born. We can begin with the building of Solomon's Temple in the fourth year of Solomon's reign, which has been reliably dated to 971/970 BC. 1 Kings 6:1 tells us that this was 480 years after the children of Israel came out of Egypt—suggesting a date for the Exodus of about 1450 BC. Exodus 12:40 tells us that there were 430 years between the descent of Jacob into Egypt and the Exodus, and we know that Jacob was 130 years old when he came to Egypt (Genesis 47:9). Jacob was born when his father, Isaac, was aged sixty (Genesis 25:26) and Isaac was born when his father, Abraham, was aged 100 (Genesis 21:5). Putting all this together, we conclude that Abraham must have been born about 2170 BC—which agrees well with the evidence from archaeology.

Finally we are ready to add up the numbers to give us the date of Adam's creation. I have used rounded figures:

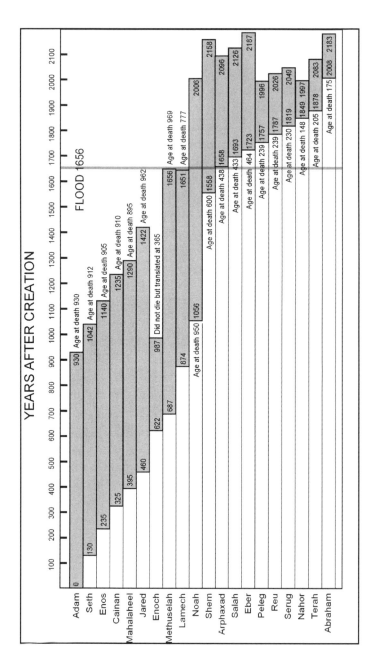

The patriarchs from Adam to Abraham. On the basis of the biblical genealogies, the time represented by this chart is just over 2,000 years

Adam to Abraham	2,000 years
Abraham to Christ	2,000 years
Christ to today	2,000 years
Total	**6,000 years**

So, if we have correctly understood the biblical text, Adam was created only 6,000 years ago—and the Earth has been around for about the same length of time. Indeed, this was the almost unanimous belief of the Christian world until well into the seventeenth century. It was the view held by most of the early Church Fathers (including Augustine) and the Reformers (including Luther and Calvin).[23] It was the view also of esteemed Christian scholars of the seventeenth century like James Ussher (1581–1656) and John Lightfoot (1602–1675).[24] Of course, to modern ears this seems an absurdly short chronology and there are two obvious objections to it.

The first concerns *the dating of civilizations like ancient Egypt,* which are said to have been in existence for much longer than the biblical dates allow. However, it should be noted that some scholars believe the Egyptian chronology to be in error by several centuries and that a thorough downwards revision is required. This would inevitably have a 'knock-on' effect with other civilizations, many of which are dated by correlation with Egypt. This is an immensely complex subject and the thorough treatment which it deserves is really beyond the scope of this book. However, readers who are interested in pursuing these ideas might like to begin with John Bimson's booklet *(When) Did It Happen? New Contexts For Old Testament History.*[25]

The second objection—and the one to which we shall devote more attention in this book—is that *6,000 years is about one million times less than the age of the Earth according to conventional science.* As we stated at the beginning of this chapter, we are faced with a seemingly enormous inconsistency between the chronology presented to us in the Bible and the chronology given to us by modern geology and astronomy. It would certainly be helpful for us to understand how this conflict arose because it will give us some insight into the philosophical presuppositions that lie behind the different perspectives. There is also a need to give some careful consideration to scientific dating methods and other evidence that has a bearing upon the question of the age of the Earth. These matters will therefore be examined in some detail in chapters 5, 6 and 7. In the course of our discussion we will be asking whether there is an alternative way—perhaps a better way—to understand the scientific evidence than to invoke long geological ages.

This is a big issue, and so we must tread carefully—the authority of Scripture and the credibility of our Christian witness are at stake. We will also try to deal with these issues graciously, recognizing that there are fellow believers who see these matters differently. Of necessity, we can only begin to examine the issues in this book, and readers may want to supplement their reading with other recommended books and articles. However, the next three chapters are intended to help us find a way forward.

5

Is the present the key to the past?

The conventional scientific view that the Earth is about 4.6 billion years old and that its geological development has been immensely long and gradual is now so deeply entrenched in our consciousness that it is difficult for us to conceive that the intellectual climate was ever different.

Nevertheless, until well into the seventeenth century most educated people in Western Europe believed that God had created the Earth in six days only a few thousand years ago, a conclusion based upon careful study of the biblical texts which we examined in the last chapter.

By the nineteenth century, however, all that had changed. While there was informed dissent,[1] belief in an old Earth had become the majority view. What brought about this radical change in thinking? In this chapter we will sketch out the critical steps in the acceptance of long geological ages and try to show that they had more to do with changing philosophical presuppositions than objective science.[2] Then we will consider the need for Christians today to develop a new approach to the history of the Earth based upon the Bible.

The pioneers of geological science

In the seventeenth century, most of the pioneering work in geology was conducted by scholars who had a respect for biblical history. A leading figure was Thomas Burnet (1635?–1715), who, in his *Sacred Theory of the Earth* (1681), brought together historical and scientific evidence in support of the events of Genesis 1–11. According to Burnet, the Earth's present-day topography was the result of fracture and collapse of the crust which occurred at the time of Noah's Flood.[3] Another theorist was John Woodward (1665–1728), a scholar with extensive first-hand knowledge of the natural world. In his *Essay toward a Natural History of the Earth* (1695), Woodward argued that the rock layers had been deposited by Noah's Flood and that the fossils enclosed in them represented creatures that had perished during the catastrophe.[4] These men, and others like them, helped to advance the geological understanding of their time. They held to a short biblical timescale and reserved a central place in their thinking for the cataclysmic processes associated with the Genesis Flood.

As time went on, however, it became less fashionable for scholars to base their geological thinking on the Bible. The belief that God had revealed himself separately in the natural world and in the spiritual world came to dominate scholarly thinking. Knowledge was divided into two compartments—the 'sacred' and the 'secular'—and there was little interplay between the two realms. Geology became increasingly divorced from biblical revelation, and speculative thinking came to the fore. Epitomizing this approach was the French naturalist Georges-Louis Leclerc, Comte de Buffon (1707–1788), who strongly criticized Burnet, Woodward and others for seeking a concordance between nature and Scripture.[5] Although Buffon did not deny that the biblical Flood had taken place, to all intents and purposes he ignored it in his thinking about Earth history. He argued that present-day physical processes were sufficient to explain the record of the rocks and fossils. In his *Epochs of*

Nature (1778), Buffon actually abandoned the biblical timescale altogether, proposing instead that the Earth had formed by the collision of a comet with the Sun and had taken at least 75,000 years to cool down from a molten state.

Buffon was only one of many scholars adopting a 'naturalistic' approach at that time. Others included Benoît de Maillet (1656–1738), who proposed an evolutionary theory for the origin of fossils, and Pierre Laplace (1749–1827), who, in his *Exposition of the System of the Universe* (1796), promoted the idea that the solar system had condensed from a gas cloud. Another influential thinker was the German mineralogist Abraham Werner (1749–1817), who proposed that the rocks and minerals of the Earth had been precipitated from a gradually receding 'universal ocean'. Long after this controversial theory had been rejected, Werner's students, who came from all over Europe, maintained his belief in vast geological ages.

Some naturalists of the period remained willing to acknowledge catastrophic processes at work in the history of the Earth, but even they developed their ideas independently of the scriptural framework. The best-known 'catastrophist' of the day was the French anatomist Georges Cuvier (1768–1832), who came to view the history of the Earth as long and gradual but punctuated by sudden changes which he called 'revolutions'. In developing this view, Cuvier proposed a theory of multiple catastrophes to explain the sequence of fossils observed in the Paris Basin in France. Some scholars, eager to retain some sort of connection with biblical history, however tenuous, identified the latest of Cuvier's 'revolutions' with Noah's Flood, although Cuvier himself did not explicitly do so.[6] Cuvier's own view seems to have been that the 'revolutions' were localized, not global, events.

There were evidently many scholars in the eighteenth and early nineteenth centuries developing theories about the origin and history of the Earth. However, it is equally clear that virtually all of them had abandoned the biblical record or were seeking, consciously or otherwise, to explain the natural world without any reference to God.

The rise of uniformitarianism

These trends in thinking ultimately paved the way for the complete break with the Bible that came with the 'Age of Enlightenment'. This period of intellectual history was marked by the wilful rejection of revelation as a source of knowledge and the triumph of 'scientific' rationalism.

James Hutton

The Scottish geologist James Hutton (1726–1797) was one of the champions of this new world view. In 1785 he published his *Theory of the Earth with Proofs and Illustrations* in which he argued for the necessity of very long geological timescales. Hutton had observed that in the present day the land was being worn down slowly and ocean sediments were building up gradually, and he came to insist that only those forces that could be seen to be currently acting should be invoked to explain the record of the Earth's past. Hutton was of the opinion that geological history must have been almost inconceivably long to accommodate the sequence of events which he believed could be 'read from the rocks'. Contemplating the Earth's past, Hutton famously concluded that he could see 'no vestige of a beginning, no prospect of an end'.7

In the nineteenth century, Hutton's views were taken up and

developed by Sir Charles Lyell (1797–1875) in his Principles of Geology.[8] Lyell apparently saw it as his geological mission to 'free the science from Moses'.[9] He is credited with developing one of the most fundamental geological principles, the principle of uniformitarianism, which can be summed up in the phrase: 'The present is the key to the past.' This principle built upon Hutton's belief that the same

Sir Charles Lyell

processes of erosion and sedimentation which can be observed today have always operated. However, Lyell went even further in assuming the strict uniformity of geological rates. Since most geological processes operate very slowly today, Lyell insisted that the same must have been true in the past. His popularization of this approach was enormously successful and the Lyellian dogma came to be adopted by virtually the entire geological community of his, and subsequent, generations.

Although in recent decades there has been something of a move away from this most rigid form of uniformitarianism towards a more open acknowledgement of the evidence for short-lived catastrophic events in the Earth's past, the modern geological community remains firmly wedded to the concept of long geological timescales. There has certainly been no return to belief in biblical creation and the global flood. On the contrary, scholarly thinking in the geological sciences is now completely divorced from the biblical record. The idea that Earth history has unfolded over a timescale of millions of years continues to dominate the science of geology today, as it has since the time of Hutton and Lyell.

Rethinking the geological history of the Earth

For Christian scholars who perceive the need to base their thinking on the Bible, there is an urgent need to re-evaluate the standard reconstruction of Earth history that is prevalent today. From a biblical perspective, there are serious problems with the uniformitarian philosophy underpinning most thinking in the geological sciences. Not only does this philosophy come into conflict with the short timescale derived from the biblical genealogies, but there is also the fact that, according to the Bible, the history of the Earth has not always been characterized by slow, gradual and uniform processes. The scriptural record reveals that the history of the Earth has been punctuated by decidedly non-uniformitarian events, in particular creation and the Flood. A New Testament passage that emphasizes this truth is 2 Peter 3:3–7:

> *Knowing this first, that there shall come in the last days scoffers, walking after their own lusts, and saying, Where is the promise of his coming? for since the fathers fell asleep, all things continue as they were from the beginning of the creation. For this they willingly are ignorant of, that by the word of God the heavens were of old, and the earth standing out of the water and in the water: whereby the world that then was, being overflowed with water, perished: but the heavens and the earth, which are now, by the same word are kept in store, reserved unto fire against the day of judgement and perdition of ungodly men.*

Here the apostle Peter warns his readers that in the last days unbelieving people will reject the idea that Jesus Christ will return as the Judge of the Earth. They will do so on the basis that 'all things continue as they were from the beginning of the creation'. This sounds remarkably like the principle of uniformitarianism that we have been discussing. However, Peter reminds us that the history of the world has been characterized by unique events that are not being repeated today. He explicitly mentions the creation of the world, which was originally covered by water (Genesis 1:1–2), and the global flood by which God judged the world in Noah's day (Genesis 7:6–8:19). Peter's sobering message is that rebellious men, in defiance of God, will deliberately reject these historical truths because they do not want to acknowledge that one day they must give an account to the Creator for their own lives.

Our review of the history of the last three hundred years shows that Peter's prophecy has come true. In these last days the idea of creation has been replaced by the theory of evolution and the concept of the Flood has been replaced by the idea of long ages of geological time. These significant events of biblical history have been wilfully forgotten, just as Peter said. However, if we are to make progress in reconstructing the true history of the Earth, we must give serious consideration to the accounts of creation and the Flood provided for us in God's Word. Scholarly thinking that does not give a central place to these revealed truths will inevitably come to incorrect conclusions about the Earth's past. The challenge for Christian scholars today is to reinterpret the data of geology in a way that is consistent with the history of the world revealed in the Bible. We need to develop an understanding of geological history that is rooted in biblical revelation.

In chapter 13 we will examine in some detail one of the scientific models that creationists have developed based upon the biblical account of the global flood. However, in this chapter we will take a broader perspective and examine some of the evidence that suggests that catastrophic processes have played a significant role in Earth history. There is a great deal of evidence suggesting that the ancient rock layers were formed at rates much faster than those we usually observe today. There are also aspects of the record which indicate that geological processes were different in the past from what they are today. Together, these evidences give us confidence that the Bible's framework of recent creation and a global flood will provide a fruitful approach to investigating the Earth's past—and so it is to these evidences that we now turn.

The catastrophic formation of sedimentary rock layers

Sedimentary rocks were once layers of sediment, such as mud, silt or sand, deposited by water. In most cases, these layers built up sequentially, one being laid on top of another in the manner of a multi-layer sandwich. Provided that earth movements have not disturbed the sequence, the oldest layer will be at the bottom of the pile.

Many of the Earth's sedimentary rock layers appear to have formed rapidly. Turbidites, for example, are sedimentary layers deposited by fast-moving and dense underwater currents.[10] These currents can deposit a layer covering hundreds of thousands of square kilometres in a few hours. They are very common in the geological record. Conglomerates and breccias are rocks made up of pebbles and boulders that have been cemented together. Some contain boulders so large that they have been called megabreccias.[11] Powerful water currents would have been needed to form these layers and it is thought that many were laid down during hurricanes or storms. Another sign of rapid deposition is cross-bedding. This is a type of inclined layering which is formed as sand dunes migrate across the sea floor under the influence of powerful water currents. Many of the cross-beds in the geological record are so large that they must have been formed by high-velocity water flows more powerful than those that are observed today.[12]

Another significant feature of the sedimentary rock layers is that they are often very widespread. Geologists study places where sediments are being laid down today, such as oceans, rivers and lakes, and then use this knowledge to try to

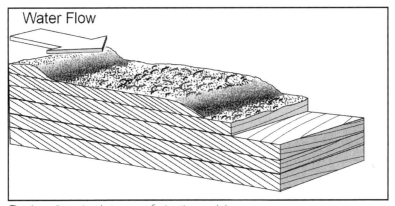

The three-dimensional structure of migrating sand dunes

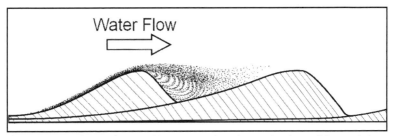

A cross section showing how sand is transported up the gentler slope of the sand dune and deposited on the steeper face as a series of inclined cross-beds

understand the environments in which the sedimentary rocks of the past were laid down. However, when we consider that some rock units can be traced for enormous distances, comparisons with modern environments seem very inadequate. We simply do not see sediments forming on this scale today. Take the Chalk formation, for instance—familiar to many people as the rock that makes up the famous White Cliffs of Dover, on the English south coast. Chalk is a type of limestone made up of tiny 'armour plates' from billions of ocean-dwelling algae. It underlies much of England and also appears on the Antrim coast and other parts of Northern Ireland. Across the English Channel it can be found in France, Germany, Sweden and Denmark. It can be traced across Poland, Bulgaria, Turkey, Egypt, Israel and the former

Soviet Union. It has even been recorded in Australia and North America.[13] There are no limestone deposits forming on this scale anywhere on the Earth today.

Furthermore, there are large-scale patterns in the sedimentary rock layers. For instance, by carefully studying the sedimentary layers, geologists can often work out the direction of the water currents that deposited them. One geologist, Arthur Chadwick, has collected half a million current direction measurements from fifteen thousand locations.[14] He has found that current directions are remarkably consistent across North and South America through great thicknesses of sedimentary layers. These layers are conventionally thought to have been laid down over hundreds of millions of years, but it is difficult to imagine how current directions could have remained constant for so long over the whole continent. Today, current directions are very localized and variable. This evidence indicates that the sedimentary layers were laid down by processes unlike those in operation today.

Evidence that the time between sedimentary layers was quite short

The evidence that the sedimentary layers were laid down rapidly seems to be very persuasive. However, there are undoubtedly gaps in the record when no sediments were being laid down, or when erosion removed sediments that had previously been laid down. Is it possible that large amounts of time could have passed during these gaps? In most cases the answer seems to be no—the time between the deposition of each layer appears to have been quite short.

To understand why this is the case, consider the lack of erosion that we find between many of the sedimentary layers. The top of each layer must once have formed the sea floor or land surface before it was covered up by the next layer. We know that if a layer forms an exposed surface for a substantial period of time

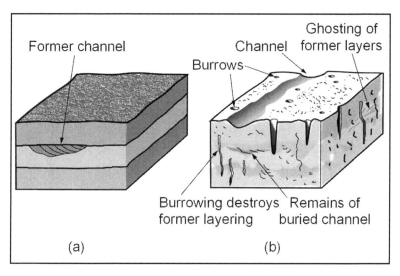

(a) The rapid deposition of successive layers tends to promote their preservation. Each layer is exposed at the surface for only a short period, so there is less opportunity for it to be disrupted by erosion or burrowing.

it is very vulnerable to damage. The next tide or rainstorm will begin to scour the sediment away. In most cases, however, there is little evidence of erosion between the layers.[16] For example, in the north face of Pen y Fan in the British Brecon Beacons there is a junction between two layers that supposedly represents a time gap of ten million years—but the contact is flat and smooth and there is little evidence of prolonged erosion.[17] This suggests that the time gap between the layers was actually quite short.

The fine preservation of many layers is another reason why the time between the deposition of each layer must have been short. The oceans teem with living creatures that burrow into sedimentary layers to build dwelling places or to feed. This is an extremely effective way of destroying layering in sediments. It is easy to find modern-day examples of this. Hurricane Carla laid down distinctive layers of sediment off the coast of Texas in 1961.[18] About twenty years later, geologists returned to these layers to find out what had happened to them. Most of the layers had been destroyed by living creatures burrowing into them and disturbing them—and where the layers could still be found they were almost unrecognizable.[19] It is difficult to imagine a layer of sediment surviving intact for more than a few centuries at the very outside. When we examine the sedimentary layers laid down in the Earth's past, however, we often find little evidence of disruption—even though the fossil remains of burrowing animals may be present. This suggests that the layers built up too rapidly for the animals to burrow into them.

Geological challenges

The evidence that we have considered so far supports the idea that the sedimentary layers were formed rapidly, and this is consistent with the short biblical timescale. It must be acknowledged, of course, that there are also challenges to this catastrophist interpretation of the geological record and we need to address them. Let us consider briefly a few features that pose apparent difficulties for the young-age view of Earth history.

1. Occasionally we find places in the geological record where sedimentation apparently ceased, the sea-floor became hardened, and burrowing and boring creatures like clams, worms or shrimps colonized the hardened surface. These surfaces seem to require time to develop. An in-depth evaluation of this problem has not been done by creationists, but it seems likely that the time represented by these surfaces is relatively short—certainly not thousands or millions of years.

2. Some geological formations contain repeating pairs of thin layers—called varves—which are said to represent a single year of deposition in an ancient lake. The total number

of such layers suggests that some geological formations must have taken millions of years to be laid down. However, varve-like sediments can build up rapidly under catastrophic conditions. One of the best examples is the laminated volcanic ash (almost eight metres, or twenty-five feet, thick) deposited by a hurricane-velocity surging flow at Mount St Helens on 12 June 1980.[20] Another example comes from a Swiss lake in which up to five pairs of layers were found to build up in a single year, deposited by rapid underflows of turbid water.[21]

3. In other sedimentary layers we find structures that resemble reefs. Modern reefs grow slowly by the activity of living creatures such as corals. If the buried reefs grew at similar rates, in the places where we now find them, it would suggest that the sedimentary layers containing them took a long time to form. However, some of these structures may not be true reefs at all. Others may be true reefs that grew somewhere else and have been washed into place by water. Each case needs to be studied carefully before firm conclusions are reached.[22]

Inevitably there are many unanswered questions about the geological record and how it might have formed by large-scale catastrophic processes. It is also usually the case that for every answer provided by research, a host of other questions are raised. That is the nature of scientific enquiry. We have never scientifically studied a catastrophe of the magnitude of the biblical Flood; we have limited knowledge even of many smaller-scale geological catastrophes that have taken place in the past. There are bound to be large gaps in our understanding about what such events are like and what they can accomplish. Nevertheless, the trend in geological research is towards consideration of increasingly catastrophic processes. It seems likely that this trend will continue and that further research will provide answers to many of the outstanding questions concerning geological features that appear, in our present state of knowledge, to require extended periods of time.

In the next chapter we will examine perhaps the most serious challenge to the biblical timescale—the multi-million-year 'ages' derived from the radiometric dating of rocks and minerals.

6

The clock that ran fast

Perhaps the most significant challenge to the idea of a young Earth comes from radiometric dating. First developed in the early twentieth century, radiometric dating uses naturally occurring radioactive elements to date rocks and minerals. These methods usually yield ages of millions or billions of years and seem so persuasive that many Christians have felt that they must reinterpret the early chapters of Genesis to accommodate these long time spans. In this chapter we will examine radiometric dating methods and ask how compelling they really are. Do they require the Earth to be billions of years old, or are there alternative ways to interpret the evidence?

By virtue of the subject matter, this chapter is inevitably somewhat technical, and many readers may find it more challenging than other parts of the book. It is, however, important that this subject is addressed at a serious level. Do not worry too much if you struggle with the detailed concepts explained here; the overall message will, I trust, be clear.

Understanding the radiometric 'clock'

To understand how radiometric dating works, we must first
consider the structure of atoms. The nucleus of an atom contains
positively charged particles called protons, and particles with no
electrical charge called neutrons. Orbiting the nucleus of an atom at
various distances are negatively charged particles called electrons.

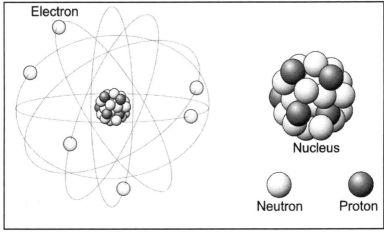

*Each atom consists of a nucleus of protons and neutrons surrounded by orbiting
electrons.*

Chemical elements are classified by the composition of their
nucleus. Each element has an atomic number, which is the
number of protons within the nucleus, and an atomic mass,
which is the number of protons plus neutrons. For an individual
element the number of protons is always the same; however, the
number of neutrons may vary. Forms of an element having the
same number of protons, but a different number of neutrons,
are called isotopes. For example, the element uranium has
three isotopes: uranium-238 (^{238}U with 92 protons and 146
neutrons), uranium-235 (^{235}U with 92 protons and 143 neutrons)

and uranium-234 (^{234}U with 92 protons and 142 neutrons). In each case the atomic mass is written as a superscript alongside the chemical symbol for uranium.

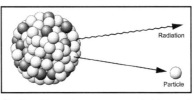

Radioactive atoms are unstable and spontaneously decay with the emission of a charged particle and electromagnetic radiation.

Most, though not all, isotopes are unstable and spontaneously decay over time by emitting a charged particle along with electromagnetic radiation. This process is called radioactive decay. There are two main types of radioactive decay. Alpha decay occurs by the emission of an alpha particle (two protons and two neutrons). Beta decay occurs when a neutron decays into a proton and an electron, with the emission of the electron as the beta particle. The original radioactive isotope is called the 'parent' and the new isotope that is formed is called the 'daughter'. The decay process continues until a stable, non-radioactive isotope is formed. Each parent isotope has its own characteristic half-life—defined as the time it takes for half of a given amount of parent to decay into daughter. If 100 atoms of a parent isotope are left to decay, after one half-life only fifty of the parent atoms will remain. It will then take the same amount of time to reduce the fifty remaining parent atoms to twenty-five and so on.

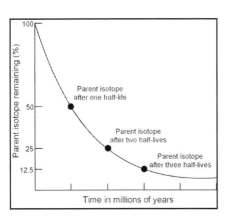

A graph illustrating the concept of radioactive half-life. After one half-life, 50% of the original parent remains. After another half-life, 25% is left. After a third half-life, only 12.5% of the original parent remains.

Principal parent and daughter isotopes used in dating			
Parent isotope (radioactive)	Daughter isotope (stable)	Radiation emitted	Half-life (billions of years)
Carbon-14 (^{14}C)	Nitrogen-14 (^{14}N)	β	0.000005730
Potassium-40 (^{40}K)	Argon-40 (^{40}Ar)	Electron capture	1.25
	Calcium-40 (^{40}Ca)	β	
Rubidium-87 (^{87}Rb)	Strontium-87 (^{87}Sr)	β	48.8
Samarium-147 (^{147}Sm)	Neodymium-143 (^{143}Nd)	α	106
Lutetium-176 (^{176}Lu)	Hafnium-176 (^{176}Hf)	β	35
Rhenium-187 (^{187}Re)	Osmium-187 (^{187}Os)	β	43
Thorium-232 (^{232}Th)	Lead-208 (^{208}Pb)	α	14.1
Uranium-235 (^{235}U)	Lead-207 (^{207}Pb)	α	0.704
Uranium-238 (^{238}U)	Lead-206 (^{206}Pb)	α	4.47

Most of these nuclear decays also emit gamma rays. All the half-lives are the presently measured values, given in billions of years. The decay of ^{40}K to ^{40}Ca is not used for dating, but the given half-life is for the parent isotope and includes decay both to ^{40}Ca and ^{40}Ar.

The table lists the most important isotope pairs used in the radiometric dating of rocks and other materials.

This decay process is used as a type of 'clock' to estimate the age of rocks. The method works something like this. When molten rock is erupted from a volcano, or injected into other rocks below the Earth's surface, it begins to cool. As the molten rock cools, crystals begin to form, and these crystals contain radioactive parent isotopes. The parent isotopes decay into daughter isotopes and, when the rock cools below a certain temperature, the crystals begin to accumulate daughter at the expense of parent. Theoretically we can use the simple accumulation of daughter products to work out the age of a rock or mineral sample—called 'the model age'—so long as we know three things:

- That the rate of decay of parent to daughter has been constant over time

- That the rock or mineral contained a known amount of daughter in the beginning

- That the amounts of parent and daughter have not been altered during the history of the rock or mineral except by radioactive decay

An obvious question to ask is how well these three assumptions of the 'model age' method fare under analysis. The first assumption, the constancy of decay rates, is usually regarded as robust. Many experiments have been conducted over the years to try to modify rates of radioactive decay. Radioactive atoms have been subjected to extremes of temperature, pressure, chemical alteration, magnetism and electrical fields. The results show very little change in half-lives, usually a few per cent or less. However, the second assumption concerning 'initial conditions' and the third assumption concerning the 'openness' of the isotope system to disturbance have proved more problematic. The amount of daughter that a sample contained when it first formed is often uncertain. Indeed, modern-day lava flows often give very old ages because they contain daughter products from the very start.[1] Furthermore, it is well known that the amounts of isotopes in a rock or mineral can be altered by many processes besides radioactive decay. They can be moved around when water flows through the rocks or when the rocks are heated up. Evidence of this can be found in virtually all rock or mineral samples.[2]

Isochron dating

Recognizing these problems, geologists developed another technique called 'isochron dating'. This method seems to resolve the question of initial conditions and alteration of the amounts of parent and daughter isotopes associated with 'model age' calculations, and so it is the most commonly used dating technique today.

To explain how the isochron method works, consider the decay of rubidium-87 (^{87}Rb) into strontium-87 (^{87}Sr). There are three other isotopes of strontium (^{84}Sr, ^{86}Sr, ^{88}Sr) which are not produced by radioactive decay. However, these various isotopes are chemically identical so, when the minerals form in a rock, there is no way to include one of them preferentially over the others. As a result, the various strontium isotopes will be included in a set of *constant* proportions in relation to one another.

By contrast, rubidium and strontium are quite different from one another chemically and so each mineral in the rock will have a *different* proportion of rubidium to strontium. Some will have very small amounts of strontium but plenty of rubidium; some will have large amounts of strontium with very little rubidium; and others will have intermediate amounts of each.

What this means is that, although each mineral will start off with a different ^{87}Rb/^{86}Sr ratio, the ^{87}Sr/^{86}Sr ratio in each mineral will be the same. We can plot these starting conditions as a horizontal straight line on a graph which has the ^{87}Sr/^{86}Sr ratio as its vertical axis and the ^{87}Rb/^{86}Sr ratio as its horizontal axis.

Now consider what happens as time passes after the rock has formed. The amounts of ^{84}Sr, ^{86}Sr and ^{88}Sr (the isotopes not formed by the radioactive decay of ^{87}Rb) will remain constant, but the amount of ^{87}Sr will increase as ^{87}Rb decays. However, the amount of ^{87}Sr will increase at a different rate in each mineral because each of them started

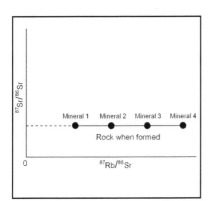

This graph plots isotope ratios (^{87}Sr/^{86}Sr versus ^{87}Rb/^{86}Sr) for four mineral samples taken from a rock, all of the same age. The points on the horizontal line represent the isotope ratios at the time the rock formed.

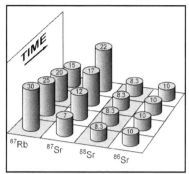

A chart showing the amounts of ^{87}Rb and the various Sr isotopes over time. As ^{87}Rb decays, the amount of ^{87}Sr increases in direct proportion to it. However, the amounts of ^{88}Sr and ^{86}Sr remain the same because they are not formed by the radioactive decay of ^{87}Rb. For simplicity, ^{84}Sr is not shown.[3]

with a different amount of ^{87}Rb. Another way of expressing this is to say that, in each mineral, the $^{87}Sr/^{86}Sr$ ratio will change in direct proportion to the $^{87}Rb/^{86}Sr$ ratio.

These changing ratios do something very interesting to our graph (see below). The ratios still form a straight line, but the line now has a slope. As time passes, the ratios change further and the steeper the slope of the line becomes. Geologists call this line an isochron, meaning 'equal time', and its mathematical slope provides the 'isochron age' of the rock sample. When the isotope ratios of rocks and minerals are plotted graphically, many of them have been found to yield 'straight line arrays' of this kind, and the isochron method is now very widely used.

One of the reasons for the popularity of isochron dating is that it seems to resolve some of the problems of standard radiometric dating techniques that we mentioned earlier. It does this in two ways. First, an isochron plot gives us information about the starting conditions, because the intersection of the isochron line

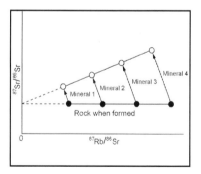

The same graph shown as on the facing page. However, in this case some decay of ^{87}Rb to ^{87}Sr has occurred, with the result that the points representing the isotope ratios have moved upwards to make a sloped line. This line is called an isochron.

with the vertical axis of the graph provides the initial $^{87}Sr/^{86}Sr$ ratio at the time the rock formed. Second, the fact that the data have actually fallen onto a straight line strongly suggests that the isotope system has remained 'closed' to disturbances throughout its history. If geological processes other than radioactive decay had removed or added either strontium or rubidium, it would seem that this method would reveal it at once, because the points would fail to lie on a straight line. The isochron method is therefore regarded as 'self-checking'.

We should note that two different types of isochron data can be plotted on a graph. The first involves the plotting of isotope ratios from different minerals obtained from a single rock. The resulting date is called 'the mineral isochron age'. The second involves plotting isotope ratios from several whole rock samples without any separation of individual mineral constituents. However, the samples are all taken from a single rock unit and are therefore assumed to have formed at about the same time. This graph results in what is called 'the whole-rock isochron age'.

There has been a lot of radioactive decay

The multi-million-year ages derived from radiometric dating are not the only evidence that large amounts of radioactive decay— millions of years' worth at present-day rates—have occurred in the Earth's past. There is also physical evidence of decay which can be seen under the microscope in the form of minute spheres of radiation damage in minerals. These areas of damage, called radiohalos, are produced by alpha particles emitted by decaying radioactive atoms. A large number of alpha particles are needed to form a mature radiohalo, typically about 500 million. At present-day rates this amounts to about 100 million years of decay of an isotope like uranium-238. The existence of radiohalos is therefore consistent with the idea that a great deal of radioactive decay has occurred.[4]

Additional evidence comes from the study of fission tracks. When an unstable atom, such as uranium-238, spontaneously splits (or 'fissions') into two smaller atoms, the fragments fly apart at high speed, leaving a trail of damage. Microscope studies reveal large numbers of fission tracks in many mineral samples, consistent with millions of years' worth of decay at present-day rates.[5]

Furthermore, of all the radioactive isotopes not currently being produced in the natural environment, only those with half-lives greater than about eighty million years occur in nature. This distribution is consistent with an Earth whose age is 4.6 billion years, but inconsistent with an age much younger, assuming that decay rates have stayed the same through geological time.[6]

Questioning the results of radiometric dating

It is obvious that radiometric dating presents a significant challenge to the idea that the Earth is only thousands of years old. It is difficult to escape the conclusion that large amounts of radioactive decay have occurred in the past—millions of times more than can be accounted for in 6,000 years at today's decay rates. But is that the end of the story? Must we abandon the short biblical timescale in the face of these data? Or is there another way to look at the evidence?

In 1997 the Institute for Creation Research (ICR) and the Creation Research Society (CRS) boldly responded to the challenge of radiometric dating by taking the decision to investigate the problem thoroughly from a biblical creationist perspective. They convened a team of seven scientists with expertise in geology, geophysics and physics. The team's brief was to conduct several major research projects over an eight-year period, daring to ask the difficult questions and looking for an alternative explanation of the radiometric dating results.[7] The project, one of the most ambitious creationist research initiatives ever undertaken, became known as RATE, which stands for Radioisotopes and the Age of The Earth.

In 2005, the main phase of the project was drawn to a conclusion and the technical results published in a major 818-page book.[8] A lay-person's summary was also made available.[9] The RATE results have shed a whole new light on the matter of radiometric dating and have provided powerful support for the biblical young-Earth timescale.

We do not have space here to describe all that the RATE project achieved, but I will attempt to draw out some of the main conclusions. One focus of investigation was the consistency of radiometric dating results. When multiple dates for a rock or mineral sample agree with one another they are said to be concordant; when they disagree they are said to be discordant. To study the agreement between dating methods, the RATE team collected fresh rock samples from ten different locations in New Zealand, Australia and the USA and applied multiple radiometric dating methods to them. The four methods used were potassium-argon, rubidium-strontium, samarium-neodymium and lead-lead—the latter being a variation on the uranium-lead technique in which only the isotopes of lead are measured. The results showed that different methods routinely gave *different* 'dates' for the *same* rock and mineral samples. This is not what we would expect if the radiometric methods were reliable. Consider the following examples:

1. Beartooth Mountains, Wyoming (USA)

RATE collected a sample from a rock unit conventionally thought to be 2,790 million years old and applied the four isotope dating systems to both the whole rock and its constituent minerals. The results showed a wide range of dates.[10] In some cases the whole rock age was greater than the age of the minerals, whereas for others, the reverse was true. The potassium-argon mineral ages ranged between 1,520 and 2,620 million years. The rubidium-strontium mineral isochron gave an age of 2,515 million years, while the samarium-neodymium isochron for the same minerals gave an age of 2,886 million years.

2. Bass Rapids, Arizona (USA)

The Bass Rapids rock unit, which occurs in the central part of Arizona's Grand Canyon, is conventionally dated as 1,070 million years old. However, the four isotope systems applied during the RATE study showed strong discordance.[11] The lowest age was 841.5 million years (potassium-argon whole rock age) and the highest was 1,379 million years (samarium-neodymium mineral isochron age). There is a 537.5 million-year difference between these two dates.

These results were found to be typical. All ten RATE studies revealed similar patterns of discordance between different dating methods.[12] The interesting question is 'Why?' What is the explanation for these discordant dates? The RATE team thinks it has the answer. The clue is in the fact that the discordances are not random—they are systematic. There seems to be a distinct 'pecking order' of dates. The oldest ages are usually given by samarium-neodymium, followed by uranium-lead, then rubidium-strontium, with the youngest ages coming from potassium-argon.[13] There is an identifiable pattern here: the isotopes which decay by alpha emission tend to give older dates than the isotopes which undergo beta decay, and the isotopes with longer half-lives seem to give older dates than those with shorter half-lives. These trends should not exist if radioactive isotopes have always decayed at a constant rate and provide accurate rock and mineral ages. However, this pattern *can* be explained if the standard assumption of constant decay rates is brought into question.

Let us imagine for a moment that radioactive decay rates were 'accelerated' at some time in the Earth's past. Considerations from theoretical physics suggest that the amount of acceleration would depend on the type of decay involved (alpha versus beta decay) and the length of the half-life of each parent isotope.[14]

This would result in precisely the kind of systematic differences between dating results observed by the RATE team. Indeed, the RATE scientists have argued that the *only* explanation for the observed trends is that radioactive decay rates have undergone one or more episodes of acceleration in the Earth's past. This is undoubtedly a radical departure from conventional thinking, but one that seems to be warranted by the systematic nature of the dating discordances.

However, the systematic discordances were only one piece of the jigsaw puzzle. In the course of their research, the RATE team uncovered multiple lines of evidence that independently supported the hypothesis of accelerated radioactive decay.

More evidence for accelerated radioactive decay

Another impressive piece of evidence came from a study of helium in the rocks of the Earth's crust. Each time an atom of uranium-238 decays to an atom of lead-206, eight alpha particles are emitted. An alpha particle consists of two protons and two neutrons and is, in effect, a helium nucleus. Many of these helium nuclei 'grab' an electron from their surroundings and become helium atoms. Thus, helium gas is formed as a by-product of uranium decay.

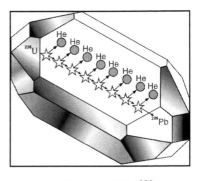

Two decades ago, there were reports of surprisingly high amounts of helium in tiny zircon crystals in granite-type rocks in New Mexico, USA. According to radiometric

An atom of uranium-238 (^{238}U) in a zircon crystal emits eight alpha particles as it decays through various intermediate isotopes to lead-206 (^{206}Pb). Each alpha particle is a helium-4 (^4He) nucleus, consisting of two protons and two neutrons.[15]

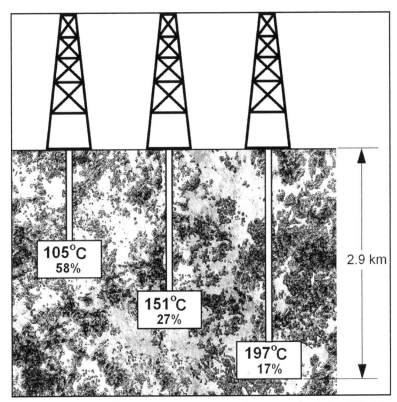

Predictions of helium diffusion rates compared with the experimental data. Diffusivity is plotted against temperature. The predictions based on the creation model (upper squares) and the uniformitarian model (lower squares) are shown. There is a 100,000 fold difference between the predictions, making this a good test of the two models. The experimental data are shown as black circles. Note the close fit between the actual measurements and the creation model.[19]

dating, these rocks are about 1.5 billion years old. Indeed, up to 58% of the helium expected as a by-product from 1.5 billion years of decay was found to be still in the zircon crystals.[17] However, this was a very puzzling discovery. Helium atoms are small and mobile and it was thought that they would escape relatively quickly from the crystals and leak into the Earth's atmosphere. Why was so much of the helium still in the zircon crystals? What was needed was an actual measurement of the rate at which the helium was escaping from these crystals.

In the year 2000, samples of the New Mexico zircons were sent by the RATE scientists to a state-of-the-art laboratory where measurements could be made of how fast the helium was escaping. The measurements confirmed that helium was able to leak out of these crystals quickly over a wide range of temperatures. In fact, the results showed that the helium could not have been escaping from these rocks for more than about 6,000 years.[18] It is easy to see why the RATE team was excited by these results. On the one hand, these rocks contain large amounts of helium—consistent with the radiometric age of 1.5 billion years. On the other hand, the helium should long since have escaped from the rocks if they were really that old. Both observations can be explained, however, if the helium was generated during a burst of accelerated radioactive decay within the last 6,000 years. This would have produced large quantities of helium rapidly, but, because the event occurred in the recent past, there would not have been time for most of the helium to have escaped since it was produced.

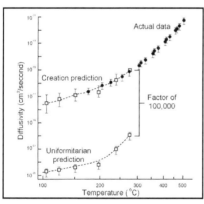

Predictions of helium diffusion rates compared with the experimental data. Diffusivity is plotted against temperature. The predictions based on the creation model (upper squares) and the uniformitarian model (lower squares) are shown. There is a 100,000 fold difference between the predictions, making this a good test of the two models. The experimental data are shown as black circles. Note the close fit between the actual measurements and the creation model.[19]

Further evidence of accelerated decay came from the study of radiohalos, the minute spheres of radiation damage in minerals that we mentioned earlier. Dr Andrew Snelling of the RATE team conducted a survey of over 40,000 radiohalos in more than 100 granite samples collected from Finland, Australia, the USA and the UK.[20] These granites, which formed by the cooling of molten magma deep underground, contain radioactive uranium-238. Uranium-238 decays by a series of steps, producing a radiohalo consisting of eight concentric 'rings', each ring representing a different step in the uranium decay chain. The last three of the rings in a uranium radiohalo are produced by short-lived isotopes of an element called polonium. However, in many granites we find apparently 'parent-less' polonium halos—isolated polonium halos that are not part of a uranium halo. The origin of these parent-less polonium halos has long been a mystery. The conclusion that they must have formed very rapidly, in only hours or days, seems inescapable because the isotopes of polonium that produced them have such a fleeting existence. Polonium-210 has a half-life of 138 days, polonium-218 a half-life of 3.1 minutes and polonium-214 a half-life of only 0.000164 seconds!

What seems to have happened is that, as uranium decayed to produce polonium, some of the polonium was separated from the uranium and transported a short distance by hot, flowing water. This polonium became concentrated into a new radioactive centre where it then decayed to form the parent-less polonium halos. But the implications of this are astonishing. In order to form, the polonium halos require an abundant supply of polonium—equivalent to millions of years' worth of uranium decay at present-day rates. However, all this polonium had to be separated from the parent uranium very quickly before it could decay away. In fact, millions of years' worth of uranium decay had to take place in just a matter of days—millions of times faster than the same amount of decay would take to occur at presently measured rates![21] This is yet more evidence that radioactive decay rates must have been greatly accelerated at some time in the Earth's past.

The RATE research has strongly supported the young-age timescale derived from the Bible and suggests that radiometric dating methods vastly overestimate the *true* age of rocks and minerals. Of course, the hypothesis of accelerated radioactive decay raises other questions that must remain a matter for future research. For example, when did the episodes of accelerated decay take place? The RATE team believes that they are most likely to have occurred during the Creation Week and the global flood of Noah's day. Another unresolved question is the disposal of the excess heat that would have been generated by accelerated radioactive decay.[22] At least one mechanism for removing the heat has been suggested, although this and other possibilities need to be explored further. Investigations into the physical mechanisms that might have been responsible for accelerated decay[23] and the protection of animal and human life while it was occurring[24] are also part of this ongoing work. Nevertheless, despite the unresolved questions, the hypothesis of accelerated decay appears to be well supported by the data.

It seems that the Earth is young, after all.

7

A youthful creation

The RATE research has shown that radiometric dating methods, which are usually regarded as supporting the conventional timescale, can be interpreted in a way that is consistent with a young age for the Earth's rocks and minerals. Creationists are also developing other arguments pointing to a young age for the Earth and our solar system. In this chapter we will explore some of these 'young-age' evidences.

As we study these evidences, we should remember that all scientific dating methods involve assumptions of one kind or another, for example about the rates of past processes. This cannot be avoided, but we should be aware that the conclusions we draw are only as good as the assumptions that we make. We have already seen that this is the case with radiometric dating methods, but it is equally true of methods that suggest younger ages. Even our best attempts at reconstructing the past will have a subjective element to them and we must be honest enough to face this issue squarely.

Another important proviso we must make is that several of the methods we will discuss here give *maximum limits* on age, but not necessarily the *actual* age. The actual age may be anywhere between zero and the maximum age—but it cannot exceed the upper limit. The significant thing about these methods is that the biblical age of

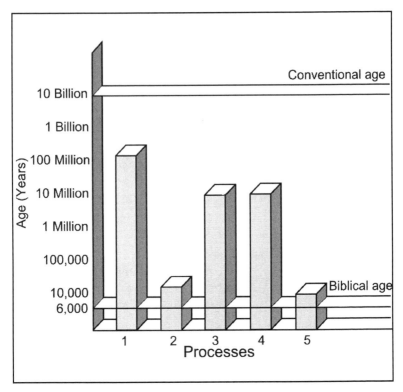

The concept of maximum limits on age. In this chart there are five hypothetical processes with upper age limits ranging from about 10,000 years to about 100 million years. The lower limit in each case is zero. The biblical age falls within the range defined by each process, but the uniformitarian age is excluded by all of them.

the world falls within the estimated age range, but the conventional evolutionary age does not.

With these cautionary comments in mind, let us consider some examples of dating methods that seem to yield ages much younger than those suggested by radiometric dating. These methods imply that the creation may not be as old as is usually supposed. We will begin by examining the age of our solar system.

The age of the solar system

As we noted in chapter 3, our solar system is conventionally thought to be 4.6 billion years old. However, there are several processes that seem to constrain its age to younger values.

1. The lifetime of short-period comets

Comets are mostly made up of ice and dust and have been described as 'dirty snowballs'. According to conventional theory they are the same age as the solar system. However, each time a short-period comet orbits close to the Sun, it loses so much of its material that it could not survive much longer than about 10,000 years.[1]

Usually, astronomers explain this discrepancy by assuming that the solar system is replenished from a belt of comets, just beyond Neptune, called the Kuiper Belt. Several hundred faint objects have been discovered in this region of the outer solar system.[2] They have the right kind of orbits and seem to be made of the right material to be the source of new short-period comets. However, recent searches show that the Kuiper Belt contains far fewer objects than previously estimated.[3] In fact so few objects exist in that region that it could not sustain the short-period comet population for billions of years.[4] The simplest explanation as to why we can still see short-period comets is that the solar system is young.

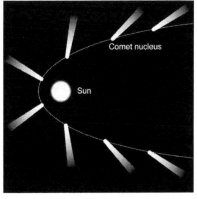

Short-period comets orbit the Sun every 200 years or less. Each time they pass close to the Sun, they lose about five to ten percent of their mass. The 'tail' represents material being vaporized from the nucleus of the comet.

2. The extinction of interplanetary dust

The disintegration of comets and collisions between asteroids are thought to supply a large quantity of microscopic dust to the solar system. Over time, however, the smaller particles of dust are ejected from the solar system by the outward pressure exerted by solar radiation, and the larger particles spiral downwards into the Sun. In this way the solar system is 'swept clean' of dust. Evolutionary scientists assume that the production and destruction of the dust are equally balanced to maintain the observed dustiness of the solar system for billions of years. However, creationists have argued that the 'dust extinction rate' exceeds the 'dust production rate' and have presented calculations suggesting that the solar system is too dusty to be any older than tens of thousands of years.[5]

3. The heat output of the gas-giant planets

Another argument for a young solar system is provided by observations of the heat output of the gas-giant planets. All the gas giants,[6] with the probable exception of Uranus,[7] give off more heat than they receive from the Sun. Jupiter radiates nearly twice as much heat as it receives. Saturn radiates half as much power as Jupiter, but it is only 30% as massive, which means that it produces nearly twice the energy per unit mass compared with Jupiter. The problem is that these planets cannot have been radiating heat for billions of years or they would have cooled down long ago. Evolutionary scientists assume that they have an internal source of energy that has maintained their output for billions of years, but identifying this energy source has proved to be rather difficult. The most common explanation is that the gas giants are contracting under the influence of gravity and that this process is generating the heat. However, even the most optimistic studies suggest that this is contributing far too little heat to solve the problem.[8] Another suggestion, concerning Jupiter, is that nuclear fusion reactions inside the planet might be generating the heat.[9] But the core of Jupiter would need to be very hot to sustain nuclear fusion reactions, and this is not thought to be the case. An obvious explanation for the heat output of the gas giants is that they are young and have been hot ever since they were created.

4. The heat output of Jupiter's moon, Io

Io is one of the four moons of Jupiter discovered by Galileo in 1610; the others are Europa, Ganymede and Callisto. Modern exploration of the solar system has revealed Io to be one of the most volcanically active bodies in it; some of the hottest spots on Io's surface are thought to reach temperatures well above the boiling point of sulphur. Planetary scientists have had great difficulty, however, in accounting for the vast amount of heat which is being continually radiated from Io's surface. The reason is that this moon ought to be cold and dead if it is billions of years old. Most astronomers suppose that Io is being internally heated by the tidal forces acting upon it from Jupiter and its other moons. Just as tides are raised on the Earth by the gravitational pull of our Moon, so, it is claimed, gravitational interactions cause Io to distort and stretch—a process which generates heat through internal friction. The problem is that the amount of heat thought to be generated by tidal friction is considerably less than the amount of heat being radiated from Io's surface.[10]

There are other problems with the tidal-heating theory. These tidal effects should cause measurable, long-term changes in the orbit of Io. The moon should be drifting slowly away from Jupiter over time. Yet studies indicate that if there is any change in Io's orbit, it is too small to measure.[11] Another conundrum is that there is no volcanic activity on Ganymede, though some have argued that tidal heating should affect this moon too.[12] Although tidal heating probably accounts for some of the heat output of Io, it does not appear to provide a complete explanation. The high heat-flow of Io suggests that it may be younger than the conventional billions of years.

5. Planetary rings

Also youthful by comparison with the conventional age of the solar system are planetary rings, such as those beautifully displayed around Saturn. The rings are composed of dust and ice particles orbiting the planet in a flat disc-shaped region. For some time it was believed that Saturn's rings had persisted virtually unchanged for billions of years since the solar system formed. However, during the last few decades delicate ring systems have been discovered around the other gas planets and observations suggest that they are decaying so rapidly that they cannot possibly have lasted for billions of years. Furthermore, in 1980 the Voyager 1 mission revealed that Saturn's rings were much more finely structured than previously realized, which implies that they too are short-lived features. Today, many astronomers believe that Saturn's rings were formed relatively recently when a moon was torn apart by tidal forces or during a collision with another object. As a result, the estimated age of Saturn's rings has been steadily revised downwards—from billions of years to only tens of millions of years.

Some attempts have been made to minimize this downward revision of age by appealing to the 'shepherding' effects of small moons orbiting near the outer edges of the rings or within gaps in the rings. These 'shepherd moons' are said to maintain the structure of the rings over long timescales by deflecting stray particles back into the ring system. However, many of these shepherd moons are themselves rapidly disintegrating, and only a few out of the hundreds of thousands of ringlets have nearby moons that can be interpreted as shepherds. Without this shepherding mechanism, the maximum lifetime of Saturn's rings may be closer to tens of thousands of years.[13]

6. The gradual movement of the Moon away from the Earth

Tidal friction causes angular momentum to be transferred from the Earth to the Moon and, as a result, the Moon accelerates in its orbit and recedes from the Earth. The current rate of recession is about four centimetres (1.6 inches) per year, but this would have been even greater in the past when the Moon was closer to the Earth. We know that the Moon could never have been closer to the Earth than 18,400 kilometres (11,500 miles), known as the Roche Limit, because the tidal forces would have caused the Moon to break up. But even if the Moon had originally been touching the Earth, it would only have taken 1.37 billion years to reach its present distance.[14] This seems to place an upper limit on the age of the Moon that is much lower than the conventional age of 4.6 billion years.

One attempt to solve this particular problem proposes that the present-day distribution of the Earth's continents results in an unusually large tidal drag and, therefore, an abnormally high rate of lunar recession. If in the past the Earth had a single land mass, centred on either the poles or the equator, the tidal bulge of the oceans would have been able to sweep around the Earth unimpeded. Tidal drag would have been reduced and, consequently, the rate of lunar recession would have been lower.[15] This model gives an age for the Earth-Moon system that is consistent with conventional astronomy; however, it has been challenged as contrived, designed so as to obtain the 'correct' solution. The model assumes an Earth with a single supercontinent located at the poles or the equator and, although this may have been the case for part of Earth's history, there have also been times of continental dispersal.

Others have said that tidally laminated sediments (rhythmites) in the geological record also indicate that the Moon was moving away from the Earth more slowly in the past. However, the interpretation of rhythmites is itself a matter of considerable controversy.[16] A study of sedimentary rocks in South Africa suggests that the tides were not unusually strong at the time they were laid down (3.2 billion years ago by conventional dates), implying that the Moon's orbit must have been similar to that seen today.[17] Although an in-depth re-evaluation of the data is needed, our current understanding suggests that the problem for the multi-billion-year timescale remains.

The age of the Earth

When we turn to the Earth itself, we discover more processes that seem to pose a problem for conventional timescales. We will consider some examples.

1. The accumulation of sodium (salt) in the oceans

Over 450 million tons of sodium are transported annually to the oceans by rivers and other sources. Only 27% of this sodium leaves the oceans each year; the remainder simply accumulates over time. If the sea contained no sodium to start with, it could have accumulated its present amount in less than forty-two million years at today's input and output rates. This is inconsistent with the conventional age of the oceans of more than 3.5 billion years.

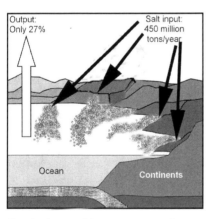

On the basis of best estimates of input and output rates, if the oceans were billions of years old they should be much more saturated with salt than they are today.

The usual response is to suggest that past sodium inputs must have been lower and outputs greater. However, calculations which are as generous as possible in both respects still give a maximum age of only sixty-two million years—fifty times younger than the conventional age of the oceans.[18] Remember what was pointed out in the introduction to this chapter: this is an *upper limit* on the age of the oceans, rather than their actual age. It tells us that the oceans cannot be older than sixty-two million years, but they could be much younger (for example, if they were created already salty).

Recently, an appeal has been made to the formation of the sodium-bearing mineral albite on the ocean floor in an attempt to resolve this discrepancy. This process, called 'albitization', removes sodium from sea-water. It is certainly true that albite forms near the mid-ocean volcanic vents where sea-water reaches high temperatures. However, the process of sea-floor spreading (see chapter 13) eventually moves the albitized ocean floor away from the mid-ocean vents and into cooler sea-water. When the albite gets into cooler water, it decomposes into the mineral chlorite and releases the same amount of sodium back into the sea-water. That is why significant amounts of albite are found only at the mid-ocean ridges and nowhere else. The net effect on sodium in the ocean water is zero.[19]

2. The accumulation of sediment on the ocean floor

This is another well-studied process. Most of the sediment is carried into the ocean by rivers. Estimates of how much sediment is transported into the oceans annually vary considerably. A conservative estimate is about twenty billion tons per year.[20] At this rate the oceans could have been filled with sediment nineteen times over in 3.5 billion years.[21] Yet the average thickness of the sediment on the ocean floor is less than 400 metres (1,300 feet).[22]

A number of explanations have been offered as to why there is so little sediment in the ocean basins. One suggestion is that the continents were smaller in the past and produced less sediment. But this explanation would only work if the continents had been extremely small, and most geologists agree that they have been at about their present size for most of their history.[23] Another idea is that some of the sediment is taken down and 'recycled' when moving ocean plates dive into the Earth's interior along subduction zones (see chapter 13). However, this process is thought to remove only one billion tons of sediment per year,[24] not enough to resolve the discrepancy.

3. Rates of erosion

The rate at which the continents are being eroded is also indicative of young age. By sampling the amount of sediment being carried along major river systems, geologists can estimate the rate at which the continents are being worn down by water and wind. An average estimate for the USA is sixty-one millimetres (2.4 inches) of erosion per 1,000 years.[25] Measured against the human life span, this seems very slow, but at this rate North America could have been worn down to sea level in only ten million years. According to the conventional timescale, the continents have been around for over 3.5 billion years; in that period, the continents could have been levelled more than 340 times.

Rates of erosion are even greater in areas of high relief such as mountains. For example, the Himalayas are being eroded at a rate of about 1,000 millimetres (thirty-nine inches) per 1,000 years.[26] With such high erosion rates, it is reasonable to ask how mountain ranges believed to be hundreds of millions of years old, such as the Caledonides of Western Europe and the Appalachians of eastern North America, could have survived to the present day. Even with a very low average erosion rate of about one millimetre (0.04 inches) per 1,000 years, no continent should have remained above sea level after a few hundred million years.

It has been suggested that mountains still exist because they are being constantly renewed by uplift from below. However, sedimentary layers of various ages seem to be well represented in mountainous regions, whereas we would expect the erosion associated with millions of years of continual uplift to have eradicated them. Another suggestion is that rates of erosion are uncharacteristically high today because of the effects of agriculture and other human activities. It is true that farming practices have increased erosion rates by about two to two and a half times,[27] but the increase would have to be several hundred times greater than that to resolve the discrepancy. Another idea is that erosion rates were much slower in the prehistoric past as a result of much drier climatic conditions. Yet the abundance of lush vegetation in the fossil record suggests that there were also periods when conditions were much wetter than they are today. Moreover, present-day erosion rates in hot, dry lowlands are not sufficiently low to provide the answer, unless we envisage such conditions applying across unrealistically large areas of the Earth's surface for a significant proportion of geological history.

4. *The evidence from carbon-14 dating*

It is appropriate here to include some discussion of carbon-14 (^{14}C) dating. There is a common misconception that ^{14}C supports a very old age for the Earth. However, this is not the case because ^{14}C has such a short half-life (about 5,730 years) that it can only be used to date objects that are thousands of years old. Any samples that were truly old—millions or billions of years—would not contain any ^{14}C because it would long since have decayed away. In fact, measurable amounts of ^{14}C are routinely found in samples of fossil materials, including coal and oil, which are supposed to be millions of years old.[28] The RATE project, introduced in the previous chapter, commissioned measurements of ^{14}C in ten coal samples, conventionally dated between thirty-four million and 311 million years old. Even though great care was taken to avoid contamination, traces of ^{14}C were found in all ten samples. The RATE scientists also obtained twelve diamond samples for ^{14}C analysis. These were the first measurements of their kind because diamonds are conventionally thought to be very ancient (more than a billion years old) and, therefore, are assumed to be entirely free of ^{14}C. As with the coal specimens, however, ^{14}C was found in every diamond sample. These results strongly suggest an age of only a few thousand years for these samples.[29]

The age of mankind

So far we have been thinking about the age of the solar system and the age of the Earth, but to conclude this chapter we now turn to the age of mankind. Population growth estimates can shed some light on how long it has been since man made his first appearance on the Earth.

The world population today is estimated to be about 6.5 billion people, and the current growth rate (measuring the net number of births over deaths) is thought to average about 1.14% per year. This means that for every 100 million people, 1.14 million are added annually. Now according to evolutionary theory human beings originated at least 1.5 million years ago. Calculations have shown, however, that an average population growth rate of only 0.5%—less than half the current rate of growth—is sufficient to generate the present world population from just two people in a mere 4,000 years.[30] This seems to point to a recent origin of the human population just a few thousand years ago.

There is evidently a substantial disagreement between population growth estimates and the evolutionary timescale. If man has been around for 1.5 million years, it is reasonable to wonder why it took so long for the world population to reach its present size. The usual explanation is that the human population remained very small for much of its history because numbers were limited by man's 'hunting and gathering' lifestyle. Then, a few thousand years ago, agriculture was developed for the first time and the human population underwent an 'explosion'. But this surely raises the question: why did man, with all his resourcefulness and creativeness, take so long to develop agriculture?[31] It seems difficult to believe that human beings took hundreds of thousands of years to work out that seeds placed in the ground would yield plants for food! The number of people alive on the Earth today suggests that man has not been around for the time proposed by evolutionary theory.

The evidence we have discussed in this chapter tends to confirm the short timescale implicit in the Bible. Collectively these data indicate that the solar system, the Earth and mankind are young—thousands rather than millions of years old—just as the book of Genesis suggests.

Part III:

Life—Past and present

8

The origin of life

In the last few chapters we have been focusing upon the origin and age of the physical world. In this section we turn to the origin and history of living organisms—the field of biology.

When we begin to consider the scientific study of living things, however, we are faced with a surprising problem. Strange as it may seem, it is not at all easy to define what life actually *is*. We usually distinguish living things from non-living things by what they *do*—living things move, respond to stimulation, grow, reproduce and expend energy—although it is possible to find examples of non-living things that share at least some of these attributes.

There is, however, one characteristic that seems to set living things apart from all non-living things, and that is their complexity. Even an introductory biology course is sufficient to persuade most people that living things are bewilderingly complex, far beyond anything we see in the non-living world. How is such complexity to be explained? How did it come into existence? Was it the result of design and purpose, or of chance and necessity?

The Bible reveals to us that all life comes from God and is preserved by him (Nehemiah 9:6). God alone 'hath life in himself' (John 5:26). He is the only self-existent being, and all other life is derived from, and dependent upon, him. As Acts 17:25 puts it, 'He giveth to all life, and breath, and all things.' In the beginning, it was the Lord who commanded the land to produce vegetation (Genesis 1:11), the water to teem with living creatures (Genesis 1:20), the sky to be filled with birds (Genesis 1:20) and the land to be populated by herds of animals (Genesis 1:24). It was God who breathed life into the first man (Genesis 2:7) and in whom 'we live, and move, and have our being' (Acts 17:28). In other words, according to Scripture, all created life has its origin in the plan and purpose of God and all living things continue to be upheld and sustained by him.

A 'warm little pond'

By contrast, most biologists today believe that life originally arose from non-living matter by solely natural processes. This idea is called 'abiogenesis' and it is an inevitable outworking of the theory of evolution which seeks to explain how all living things came into being without the direct involvement of a Creator.

Although evolutionary ideas have a long pedigree, the modern theory originated with Charles Darwin, a Victorian naturalist, who set out his ideas in a revolutionary book published in 1859. The full title of Darwin's book was *On the Origin of Species by Means of Natural Selection, or the Preservation of Favoured Races in the Struggle for Life*, often abbreviated simply to *The Origin of Species*. Although the book was an attempt to explain how all living things had descended from a common ancestor,[1] it did not address the problem of the origin of life. But Darwin did speculate upon the matter in a letter to the botanist Joseph Hooker. He suggested that 'in some warm little pond' proteins might form and then undergo 'still more complex changes' until the first cell appeared.[2] In 1924, a more detailed scenario was proposed by the Russian biochemist Alexander Oparin. He envisaged a series of reactions that would allow a cell gradually to assemble itself from simple precursor chemicals.[3] This led to the concept that life had arisen from a 'primordial soup'—an ancient pond or ocean rich in organic (carbon- and hydrogen-based) compounds.

The first experimental support for these ideas was published by Stanley Miller in 1953. He attempted to reproduce the conditions believed to have existed on the Earth billions of years ago. His laboratory apparatus was quite simple: a flask of hot water (representing the oceans), connected by a pipe to a flask of gases (representing the atmosphere). Today's air was replaced with

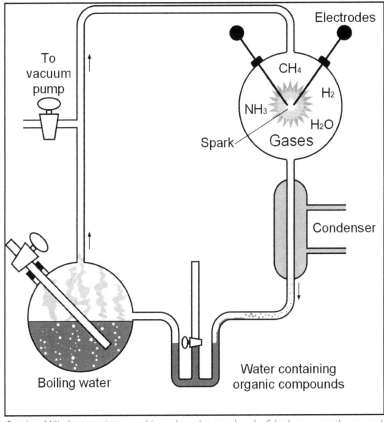

Stanley Miller's experiment subjected an 'atmosphere' of hydrogen, methane and ammonia to electrical discharges, and the reaction products were collected and analysed. These products included amino acids.

the gases he thought would have been present in the atmosphere of the early Earth—hydrogen, methane and ammonia. Miller sent sparks through this mixture using electrodes, to replicate the effects of lightning. As the hot water in the flask evaporated and entered the 'atmosphere', chemicals began to form. These products were collected in a trap to be analysed. The analysis revealed that amino acids—the building blocks of proteins—had formed.[4]

Doubts about the 'primordial soup' theory

Ever since 1953, Miller's experiment has been hailed as evidence that the compounds necessary for life could have spontaneously formed on the early Earth. However, the problems with Miller's experiment, and others that have followed its approach, are often overlooked. Let us consider a few of the difficulties.

1. The complexity of the 'simple' cell

At the time of Darwin, scientists thought that explaining the origin of life would be fairly straightforward. Living cells were regarded as simple blobs of jelly that could be made by the interaction of chemicals such as carbon dioxide, oxygen and nitrogen.[5] But we need only peruse a contemporary textbook on molecular biology to discover how mistaken that idea was. The lowliest living things capable of independent existence are the bacteria.[6] Each bacterium is a microscopic factory comprising a multitude of molecular machines working in an integrated way to perform the functions of the cell. It has an outer membrane that allows materials to be selectively transported in and out of the cell. Complex metabolic systems harness food and use it for energy and growth. There are intricate assembly lines manufacturing proteins. There is a system of replication, enabling information to be passed from one generation to the next. The Miller experiment produced the building blocks,

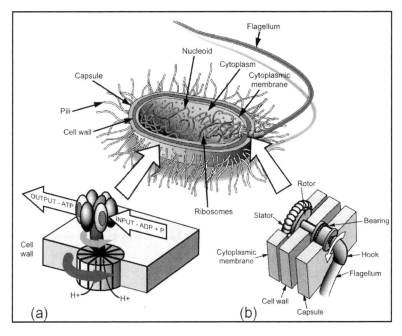

Each bacterial cell comprises a multitude of molecular machines. Two examples are shown here: (a) the ATP synthase enzyme, which makes adenosine triphosphate (ATP) from adenosine diphosphate (ADP) plus inorganic phosphate and (b) the bacterial flagellum, which operates like an outboard motor to propel the bacterium along.

but there is no experimental evidence showing how these building blocks formed larger molecules, let alone the simplest of living cells. Surely the staggering complexity of living things is a testimony to the greatness and power of the God whose 'understanding is infinite' (Psalm 147:5).

2. The narrow window of time for life to get started

According to conventional science, the Earth, for the first few hundred million years of its existence, was being pounded by giant meteorites which melted the crust, boiled away the oceans and made life impossible.[7] However, chemical traces of life have been found in rocks thought to have formed even before the end of this episode of meteorite bombardment.[8] For those who accept abiogenesis and the standard geological dates, this is a serious obstacle, for it suggests that the first cells must have arisen from non-living matter in an uncomfortably short time.

3. The composition of the Earth's atmosphere

A key feature of the Miller-type experiments is that they exclude oxygen. The reason is straightforward: if oxygen is present, any organic molecules that form are rapidly broken down. However, Miller's assumptions about the early atmosphere are difficult to justify. It has been argued that gases such as carbon dioxide, nitrogen and water vapour predominated in the early atmosphere—not methane, ammonia and hydrogen.[9] Furthermore, there is evidence that significant amounts of oxygen were present in the early atmosphere.[10] For instance, the chemical weathering of rocks and minerals conventionally dated up to 3.5 billion years old appears to have taken place in oxygen-rich conditions.

4. The concentration of the primordial soup

Energy is needed to form simple organic chemicals, and in Miller's experiment this was provided by electrodes. However, energy is a double-edged sword: it builds complex molecules out of simpler parts, but it can also break up developing molecules. In the atmosphere and the oceans, destructive processes would have diminished the amounts of organic molecules available for further interactions, and perhaps would have destroyed them altogether. It is difficult to see how a concentrated soup could have formed even in lakes, pools and lagoons.[11]

5. 'Left-handed' amino acids and 'right-handed' sugars

Many molecules that are necessary for life exist in two forms: we call them 'right-handed' and 'left-handed'. They are chemically

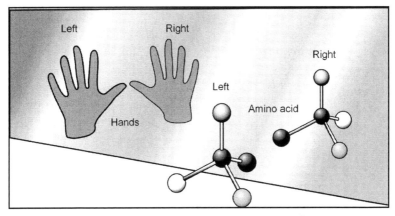

Many organic molecules exist in 'right-handed' and 'left-handed' forms, which are the mirror image of one another.

identical but mirror images of each other. It is an intriguing fact that most amino acids in proteins are left-handed and most sugars in DNA are right-handed. However, Miller-type experiments produce a 50:50 mixture of right- and left-handed varieties. Those who believe that life originated in a primordial soup must explain how one form came to predominate over the other. Despite much work, abiogenesis researchers have not come close to finding a satisfactory solution to this problem.[12]

The molecule with a message

We can see that researchers face many great difficulties in trying to explain how life arose naturally from non-living materials. However, we have yet to consider the most serious objection to these types of scenario—the problem of information. All living things contain information. Consider the molecule of heredity, DNA, which has a structure somewhat like a long spiral staircase. The 'steps' of the staircase are made of pairs of molecules called bases. There are four bases in DNA—adenine (A), thymine (T), cytosine (C) and

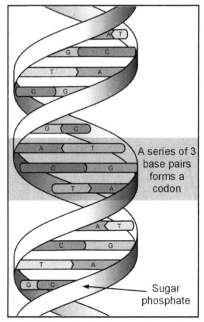

A series of 3 base pairs forms a codon

Sugar phosphate

The DNA molecule has a spine, or long axis, made of sugar and phosphate units. Attached to each sugar along the spine are chemicals called bases (the four types represented here by A, T, C and G), the sequence of which encodes the information for building proteins.

guanine (G)—and they can be thought of as the 'letters' from which the language of life is put together.

The language of life (the aptly-named 'genetic code') is made up of 'words' that are three letters long: CGT, AAA, TCC and so on. Each three-letter word codes for one amino acid—the building blocks of proteins which make up the bodies of living organisms. By reading the code along the DNA molecule, translating it and using its instructions to make proteins, the cell uses DNA as a template to build the chemicals of life. Each protein that is manufactured in this way is a precise sequence of several hundred amino acids. Given that three letters 'equal' one amino acid, a sequence of one or two thousand letters on the DNA gives the code for one protein. Getting the sequence right is vitally important because chemical interactions between the amino acids in the chain determine the way that the protein will fold—and, ultimately, the shape of the protein will determine its function.

In this way, a precise sequence of letters on the DNA molecule is translated into a precise sequence of amino acids, which in turn determines the usefulness of the protein that is produced. In just the same way that human language conveys information, so the precise sequencing of letters in the DNA molecule conveys information. But where did this information come from? Information is not a property of matter—there are no physical or chemical laws that compel the DNA bases to line up in the way that they do. There are not even any chemical bonds between the bases running along the spine of the DNA molecule.[13] We can also rule out the notion that the bases lined up the right way by pure chance because it is simply too improbable. One writer estimated that the probability of randomly building a chain of 100 'left-handed' amino acids is roughly one chance in 10^{60} (i.e. effectively zero, even assuming conventional geological timescales).[14] The most reasonable explanation is that the bases were arranged in meaningful sequences that code for useful proteins *by some external agent*—which points us to an intelligent designer behind living things.

An everyday illustration may help us here. Suppose you were walking along a beach one day and came across a message etched into the sand: 'Good morning'. Even though the message is a very simple one, I am sure you would realize that natural laws were not responsible for it. You would recognize that the actions of wind and waves do not normally compel sand particles to arrange themselves into meaningful English phrases! I think you would also dismiss chance as an explanation because it would be so unlikely for sand particles to 'just happen' to line up this way. Instead, you would quickly conclude that there must have been a writer—an intelligent mind—behind the message. You would come to this conclusion even if you had never met the writer and had not seen the message being written. This is precisely the same kind of reasoning which we have applied to the DNA in living cells to conclude that it, too, must have had an intelligent designer.

Significantly, in the Gospel of John we read this:

In the beginning was the Word [Greek, logos], *and the Word was with God, and the Word was God. The same was in the beginning with God. All things were made by him; and without him was not any thing made that was made* (John 1:1–3).

In this passage Jesus Christ is set before us as the eternal Creator. How apt that the living Word of God—the eternal Logos— has seen to it that all the living things on Earth are based upon information! Surely the genetic code, which is the language of life, points us beyond nature to the one who is the very author and originator of life.

Other origin-of-life theories

Frustration with the failures of the primordial soup idea has led to several other theories being developed, but they have not proved any more successful in explaining the origin of life. In many ways they represent a counsel of despair. Here are a few of them:

1. Panspermia

This is the theory that life arose elsewhere in the universe and was carried to Earth on comets and meteorites. Supporters of panspermia have included some well-known names, such as Francis Crick (co-discoverer of the DNA 'double helix')[15] and Fred Hoyle (a former Cambridge astrophysicist).[16] Nevertheless, many scientists regard panspermia as a 'cop-out'. It does not really solve anything; it simply moves the problem to another location.

2. Hot-spring theory

In the 1970s, exploration of the floor of the Pacific Ocean revealed fissures along which very hot water was bubbling up. Some scientists began to speculate that life might have arisen in these extreme conditions. However, the water temperature around the vents can reach 350°C—more than enough to rapidly break down any complex molecules that may form. Although there have been suggestions that the first living cells might have formed in tiny cavities near the vents—where they could be protected from the heat—no detailed explanation has yet been developed.[17]

3. Self-reproducing clays

The difficulty of forming the complex molecules used by living organisms today has led some to suggest that life was originally based on different chemicals. Graham Cairns-Smith of Glasgow University has proposed that life began with clay minerals.[18] The first self-reproducing system was started when defects in clay crystals were 'inherited' by newly-forming crystals. Later the system was 'taken over' by organic compounds. The problem is that the theory lacks supporting evidence; no one has shown that clays can replicate themselves in this way.

Commenting on the various origin-of-life theories that have been proposed, the science writer Andrew Scott, has written:

> Despite the great debates that rage *within* the relatively small circle of scientists researching into the origins of life, their fundamental belief that organic life did originate spontaneously and rather directly on the newly formed Earth is virtually unshakeable. I choose to describe it as a 'belief', because many scientists seem to have a faith in this outline of our origins as firm as the beliefs of any religious devotees. In their more public pronouncements some of them behave rather like the creationist opponents they so despise—pretending to have firm answers which they have not got at all, and glossing over the many great mysteries that remain.[19]

What motivates the search?

Some years ago, a documentary programme was broadcast on British television evaluating the various competing theories.[20] The programme title said it all: *Life Is Impossible!* There were some revealing contributions by the scientists who were interviewed for the documentary. One lamented that this is a field 'where there is an underabundance of understanding and probably an overabundance of big egos and it's not surprising that there's acrimony'. Another said that the search for the origin of life is really 'a kind of religion'. It seems evident that this line of investigation continues to be pursued tenaciously because it is motivated by more than scientific considerations. Andrew Scott, quoted previously, has also perceptively commented:

> Most scientists *want* to believe that life could have emerged spontaneously from the primeval waters, because it would confirm their belief in the explicability of Nature—the belief that all could be explained in terms of particles and energy and forces if only we had the time and the necessary intellect.[21]

This is the real impetus behind origin-of-life research—the belief that natural processes alone are sufficient to explain how everything came to be. However, today, a purely natural explanation for the origin of life seems as elusive as ever. Positive results are thin on the ground. Two well-known researchers, Carl Woese and Gunter Wächtershäuser, reviewing 'the state of the art' in 1990, lamented:

> In one sense the origin of life problem today remains what it was in the time of Darwin—one of the great unsolved riddles of science. Yet we have made progress. Through theoretical scrutiny and experimental effort since the nineteen-twenties many of the early naive assumptions have fallen or are falling aside—and there now exist alternative theories. In short, while

we do not have a solution, we now have an inkling of the magnitude of the problem.[22]

With this in mind, the biblical view—that God is the source of all life—seems ever more reasonable.

9

Diversity by design

Anyone who has studied biology will have been amazed by the rich diversity of life. About 1.7 million species of plants, animals, fungi, microbes and other forms of life have been identified and named by biologists, but estimates of the total number of species on Earth vary greatly, from ten million to 100 million. From ants to apes, bacteria to blue whales and corals to cats, living things come in a spectacular array of shapes, sizes and designs. As we think about this extraordinary diversity, we ask ourselves some important questions. How did this diversity originate? Is there a pattern to life? If so, what is it?

According to evolutionary theory, the main pattern of life can be summed up in one word—*continuity*. Evolutionary theory asserts that all living things have arisen from a single common ancestor. In other words, life is one big set of genetic interrelationships. We

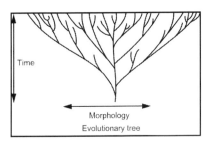

The evolutionary tree, depicting the relationships between living organisms proposed by evolutionary theory. In this view, all living things are interrelated and have descended from a common ancestor.

can depict this view as a single evolutionary tree—and every organism that has ever lived has a place on it somewhere.

However, the Bible points to a very different pattern of life. Genesis 1 tells us that God made living things in the course of a single week—they did not arise by natural processes operating over millions of years. Furthermore, the Creator made different groups on different days—the plants on day three, the birds and sea creatures on day five and the land creatures on day six. This suggests that *discontinuity*— not continuity—is a major characteristic of life, a conclusion also supported by other Scripture passages. We can depict this view as an orchard of trees, each tree representing a distinctly different group of organisms made by God.

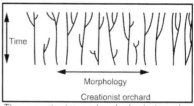

The creationist orchard, depicting the relationships between living organisms proposed by creation theory. In this view, many basic types were separately created in the beginning and diversification has taken place within the groups.[1]

A foundation for creation biology

Thus the Bible teaches that God created the major groups of organisms separately, and upon this foundation a creationist theory of biology can be built. An early contribution was made by a biologist called Frank Lewis Marsh (1899–1992), who concluded that God had made organisms in groups called 'kinds'. In 1941, he introduced the concept of the *baramin*—taken from the Hebrew words meaning 'created kind'.[2]

The 'created kind', or baramin, is not the same as the modern species. The category of 'species' is somewhat artificial and not always easy to define. In deciding whether two creatures belong to the same species, scientists consider such things as similarities in appearance, behaviour and distribution and the ability to interbreed and produce fertile offspring. However, Marsh regarded each baramin as a broad group probably encompassing many species.[3]

While each baramin had been created separately, Marsh suggested that a great deal of variation was possible within the created group. Consider, for instance, the different varieties of dogs. On the basis of reproductive isolation, modern science regards wolves, coyotes, jackals, dingoes and domestic dogs as separate species. But Marsh considered all these dogs to be members of a single baramin. He based his conclusion upon their overall similarity in appearance and the ability of some of these species to cross-breed and produce hybrid offspring.[4] In fact, Marsh regarded the ability of two organisms to hybridize (cross-breed) as important evidence that they belonged to the same baramin.

Basic-type biology

Many creation biologists have taken up Marsh's ideas and endeavoured to build upon them. In recent years, this has led to the development of 'basic-type biology'.[5] This field of study, pioneered by Siegfried Scherer and his colleagues in Germany, seeks to identify the original created kinds using hybridization studies. One group that has been studied in this way is the Anatidae—the group of birds that includes ducks, geese and swans.[6] The group is quite diverse, ranging from the small Mandarin Duck (weighing only 400–500 grams, or fourteen to eighteen ounces) to the large Mute Swan (weighing up to fifteen kilograms, or thirty-three pounds). Within the group there are 148 species, and 126 of them are connected directly or indirectly through hybridization. Based on this information, Scherer has suggested that the entire family represents a basic type (what Marsh would have called a baramin).[7] This approach has been applied to a number of other groups— including bryophytes,[8] grasses,[9] roses,[10] spleenwort ferns,[11]

The family Anatidae—ducks, geese and swans. Hybridization studies suggest that the members of this family belong to the same created kind.

pheasants,[12] falcons,[13] finches,[14] dogs,[15] horses[16] and primates.[17] Up to twenty-five basic types have been proposed so far, and work continues to identify others.

Despite the usefulness of the hybridization approach, however, it also has some limitations.[18] For example, it is impossible to know whether two extinct organisms known only from fossils would have been able to cross-breed. Also, hybridization does not apply to organisms like bacteria that do not reproduce sexually. Another problem arises when it is not practical or desirable for organisms to hybridize, for example when a species is endangered (e.g. the giant panda). Furthermore, the failure of two organisms to hybridize is not definitive—there are many reasons why organisms may not be able to interbreed successfully even though they belong to the same baramin. Finally, hybridization is a complex process and there are different levels of 'success'. Most would agree that a sterile cross (e.g. a mule) is a hybridization success, and perhaps also the production of a foetus which does not survive to birth. But what about failure at an earlier stage of development? There is no universally agreed definition of success.

The development of baraminology

Recognizing the limitations of hybridization, a different method of identifying and classifying the created groups was proposed by palaeontologist Kurt Wise.[19] He called it 'baraminology'. As with basic-type biology, this has developed into an exciting field of creation studies with its own conferences and publications.[20] Baraminology uses many different criteria, not just hybridization. The idea is to 'home in' on the created kinds by looking not only for similarities, but also for differences. Baraminology does not try to identify each baramin in one go; rather, it works by successive refinement. Larger groups are split up and smaller groups are added to, until all the members of the baramin have been identified. Several groups have been studied using the methods of baraminology—including grasses,[21] sunflowers,[22] sunfish,[23] turtles,[24] snakes,[25] salamanders,[26] cats,[27] horses,[28] deer,[29] camels,[30] primates,[31] whales,[32] as well as a host of animals and plants of the Galápagos Islands.[33] Encouragingly, a number of studies with other organisms are also awaiting publication.

Designed to diversify

One exciting conclusion from these latest studies in creation biology is that many baramins were apparently created with the potential for very significant change. It seems that God designed these baramins with the ability to bring forth many new species and varieties. This process has been called diversification.[34] This in-built ability to adapt can be seen as a provision of the Lord to enable the baramins to survive in a changing world—especially after the global restructuring that took place at the time of Noah's Flood.

At the time of the Flood, each baramin of birds and land animals was represented on the ark by a single pair (in the case of the 'unclean' animals) or seven individuals or seven pairs (in the case of the 'clean' animals). From these survivors has come the diversity that we see in their descendants in the world today. Let us consider the implications of this with three examples.

1. The cat family

It seems likely that all members of the cat family—including lions, tigers, leopards, pumas, lynxes and domestic cats—have arisen from an original pair of 'cats' that were taken on board Noah's ark. Many modern cat species can produce crosses—strong evidence that they belong to the same baramin.[35] For example, lions can cross-breed with tigers, leopards and jaguars; leopards can interbreed with jaguars and pumas; and lynxes can cross-breed with domestic cats.

2. The camel family

This family includes six modern species—the Old World camels (the dromedary and the Bactrian) and the New World camels (the llama, the alpaca, the guanaco and the vicuña). There are also 200 fossil species. The successful crossing of a dromedary camel with the guanaco indicates that the Old and New World species belong in the same baramin.[36]

3. The horse family

About 150 species of horses lived after Noah's Flood; we find their fossil remains buried in sediments laid down in post-Flood times. A recent study suggests that these species belong to the same baramin,[37] which means that they probably arose from one pair of 'horses' which Noah took on board the ark.

Rapid change after the Flood

So the latest research by creation biologists suggests that the baramins diversified to produce many new varieties and species after the Flood. Even more remarkable, however, is the speed at which these changes seem to have taken place. We know from the Bible that many modern species were around within a thousand years or less from the time of Noah's Flood—including lions (Job 4:10–11; 10:16; 28:8; 38:39), camels (Genesis 12:16) and donkeys (Genesis 12:16). This means that the baramins must have diversified very quickly after their ancestors stepped off the ark. Following the Flood there must have been a period of explosive change—unlike anything we observe going on today.

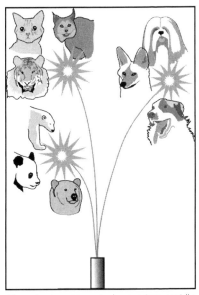

New species appear to have arisen rapidly after the Flood in a burst, or series of bursts, of diversification.

This raises an obvious question—and one that is the subject of much discussion by creation biologists. How could so much change have happened so quickly? One possibility we have already hinted at is that God may have created living things with the inbuilt ability to adapt. This can be illustrated by the analogy of a Swiss army knife.[38] Just as the knife has 'hidden' tools ready to be accessed as needed, so God may have created 'hidden' adaptations in organisms that could be expressed when needed. In fact, this concept has led creation biologist Todd Wood to develop a completely new theory of biological change. He calls it 'the AGEing process'.[39]

The AGEing process

It has been known for several decades that some pieces of DNA are able to independently replicate themselves and move around. These pieces of DNA have become known as mobile genetic elements. Today, most biologists regard mobile genetic elements as harmful parasites, but Todd Wood has suggested that these pieces of DNA originally had a beneficial function. He has therefore proposed a new name for them, 'Altruistic Genetic Elements', or 'AGEs'. (Altruism is the principle of living or acting for the good of others.) The AGEing theory proposes that these mobile genetic elements were originally designed by God to co-operate with the genes of living organisms to produce diversity.

There are a number of ways in which AGEs could have done this. For example, we know that some of these mobile elements are able to promote or inhibit the activity of genes—even 'switching on' inactive genes and 'switching off' active genes. They can also cause genes to recombine into new arrangements. Furthermore, because these pieces of DNA are mobile, they can take complete genes and move them around *within* an organism—or even *between* organisms![40] Altering the genetic make-up of organisms in this way has the potential to produce substantial change in a very short amount of time.

Of course, most biological change taking place today is happening much more slowly than this, and so another obvious question presents itself. If mobile genetic elements caused organisms to change rapidly in the past, why are they not doing so today? In fact, there is an understandable reason for this. Harmful mutations—random genetic 'copying mistakes'—occur in these mobile elements when they replicate themselves, causing damage which accumulates over time. This damage would eventually have led to the beneficial function of the mobile elements being lost or reduced. As a result of this degeneration, most AGEs are currently inactive and some are actually harmful.

The AGEing theory has only recently been proposed and, like any new scientific theory, it presents us with many as yet unanswered questions. Nevertheless, it seems promising because several features of living organisms seem to be better explained by the AGEing theory than by any other. Like other new ideas, the AGEing theory also suggests some exciting possibilities for future research. Perhaps creation biologists will find evidence of the past activity of AGEs by studying the genomes of different creatures. They may find latent genes that were never switched on, or previously active genes that have been switched off. The AGEing theory may lead to new insights into some of the so-called 'junk DNA' which does not code for proteins. The organization of DNA is turning out to be far richer and more complex than we could ever have expected. This is a humbling reminder that we have much to learn about the mechanisms that generated diversity within the baramins.

How is this different from evolution?

Perhaps some readers, unused to thinking of such a dynamic history for living organisms, are wondering how the biological changes we have been considering are different from those proposed by evolutionary scientists. Indeed, there is a widespread misconception that the Bible teaches the 'fixity' of species, the idea that each species was created in precisely the same form and geographical location that we find it today. This mistake was even reflected in an exhibit, now closed, in London's Natural History Museum which said, 'Before Charles Darwin, most people believed that God created all living things in exactly the form that we see them today. This is the basis of the doctrine of creation.' Actually this is not the basis of the creationist view because the Bible nowhere says this. On the contrary, the Bible suggests that living things have had a very dynamic history. When we consider the implications of the historical events recorded in the book of

Genesis, it seems certain that there must have been a great deal of change within the created groups or baramins.

Nevertheless, for those readers who may be concerned that what we have been describing in this chapter sounds similar to the theory of evolution, let me point out at least three important differences:

1. According to evolutionary theory, all living things can be traced back to a single common ancestor, but in creation theory each baramin had a *separate* ancestry.

2. According to evolutionary theory, the changes in organisms were brought about by unguided natural processes, but in creation theory living organisms were *designed* to change.

3. According to evolutionary theory, diversity is generated by random genetic accidents (mutations) acted upon by natural selection, but in creation theory the potential for variety was *already present, though latent*, within organisms.

It seems that the Creator, in his providence, equipped organisms from the beginning to survive in a fast-changing world. What is exciting for the modern-day creation biologist is that the latest research is providing insights into how this process of diversification may have come about.

10

Similarities and relationships

In the Garden of Eden, the first job that Adam was given was to name the animals and birds that God had made:

And out of the ground the LORD God formed every beast of the field, and every fowl of the air; and brought them unto Adam to see what he would call them: and whatsoever Adam called every living creature, that was the name thereof (Genesis 2:19).

Adam appears to have performed this task intuitively—God did not have to teach him how to do it.[1] This suggests that the ability to name and classify things is an integral part of being human.

But have you ever wondered *why* God delegated the naming of the animals and birds to Adam? After all, God himself gave names to the stars (Psalm 147:4; Isaiah 40:26). Two main reasons suggest themselves:

1. The naming of the animals was designed to arouse in Adam an awareness of his loneliness (Genesis 2:18–20) and was followed immediately by the creation of Eve from Adam's side (Genesis 2:21–22).

2. Adam was made to be a steward of God's creation (Genesis 1:28), and the naming of the animals was a way of Adam expressing his rule over them.

However, there may be a third, less obvious, reason. We established in chapter 1 that the creation is an expression of God's own nature and that, by studying the works of God, we get to know him better (Romans 1:20). Perhaps God gave this task to Adam in order to reveal himself—as Creator—to the man.[2] It may be that, as we study the Earth's living creatures, we, like Adam, learn something about the God who made them. This thought provides a high motivation for many Christian students of the natural world.

Groups within groups

Like Adam, we continue to name and classify living organisms. Scientists who specialize in this field—called taxonomy—usually place species in groups according to their shared similarities. They observe, for example, that a leopard is more similar to a lion than to a domestic cat. So they place the leopard and lion in the same genus (*Panthera*), but the domestic cat in a different genus (*Felis*). However, leopards, lions and domestic cats have more in common with one another than any one of them has with, say, dogs. Thus, the cats are grouped in one family (Felidae) and the dogs in another (Canidae). And so it goes on—the families are grouped in orders, the orders in classes, the classes in phyla, the phyla in kingdoms. As a result, the conventional classification scheme arranges living organisms in a series of groups within groups—a pattern of similarities that is called a 'nested hierarchy'.

One of the basic questions facing biologists is why this pattern of similarities exists. Most biologists think that this pattern is a consequence of the evolutionary history of living organisms. According to evolutionary theory, new species are produced by

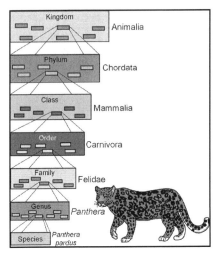

The taxonomic hierarchy of the leopard, Panthera pardus.

The species pardus *is nested within the genus* Panthera, *the genus* Panthera *within the family* Felidae, *the family* Felidae *within the order* Carnivora, *the order* Carnivora *within the class* Mammalia, *the class* Mammalia *within the phylum* Chordata, *and the phylum* Chordata *within the kingdom* Animalia.

a series of branching events. An ancestral species splits into two descendant species—each of which forms a new branch on the evolutionary tree. Each of these branches may then divide to give rise to other branches. Any new characteristic that arises in a particular branch is passed on to all the descendants of that branch. The evolutionary biologist Douglas Futuyma illustrates it like this:

> Thus, for example, the four-legged condition evolved in amphibians, and is retained by most of their descendants. Among these, the ancestors of the mammals evolved a single-boned lower jaw. Among some of their descendants, the rodents developed gnawing incisors, and so on. There is a nesting of groups within groups, as a consequence of common ancestry.[3]

The idea that life is arranged in a nested hierarchy has been so pervasive that, until recently, it was assumed to be true even by creationists. As a result, there have been attempts to explain this pattern in terms of creation rather than evolution.[4] For instance, it is possible to classify man-made objects in a nested pattern—and we know that they did *not* evolve from a common ancestor! Here is how palaeontologist Kurt Wise put it:

> Humans have designed a large number of different types of teaspoons. Some are made of stainless steel, others of silver. Some have monograms on them, others do not. Some have artistic designs engraved on their handles, others do not. Yet they are all classifiable as teaspoons. And though there are many types of tablespoons, many types of soup spoons and many types of serving spoons, all these types of spoons can be classified together as spoons. The wide variety of spoons can be classified with the wide variety of forks and the wide variety of knives as silverware; and the silverware can be classified with plates, bowls and cups as tableware. Tableware can be classified with furniture and appliances as housewares, and so on. Humans, without so intending, create objects that are distributed in character space in a nested hierarchy of form.[5]

In other words, it can be argued that even *designed* objects can be classified in a nested pattern. However, the evolutionary argument goes one step further than this. It does not simply say that it is possible to classify living organisms in a series of nested groups. It says that there is *only one true nested pattern*—the one that reflects the series of branching events that took place during the evolutionary history of life. Evolutionary biologists point out that, while it is possible to classify cutlery in a nested hierarchy according to function, it can be classified equally persuasively according to materials, size, weight, colour or country of manufacture.[6] This, they claim, is *unlike* the pattern of relationships between living things which is described by a *unique* nested hierarchy. The uniqueness of this hierarchy is said to provide strong evidence in support of the evolutionary explanation for shared similarities.

Questioning the single nested pattern

Recently, however, creation biologists have started to question whether there really is only *one* nested pattern that properly describes the relationships between living organisms. In fact, this seems not to be the case. It turns out, for example, that *multiple* nested hierarchies can be constructed for the same set of organisms. Scientists use computer programs to construct 'evolutionary trees' of relationship, and in fact it is common for these programs to produce *thousands* of alternative 'trees' for the *same* set of organisms. Various assumptions are then made to decide which of the many trees is 'the right one'. This shows that the same group of organisms can actually be arranged in more than one nested pattern—multiple nested hierarchies are possible.[7]

The reason for this is that there are many similarities that do not readily fit the treelike pattern. Whichever tree the evolutionary biologist chooses as the right one, there are invariably similarities between organisms that contradict the chosen tree. In evolutionary thinking, these tree-contradicting similarities cannot have been inherited from a common ancestor and so must have arisen independently in different lineages. Evolutionary biologists refer to these as 'convergent similarities'. Here are two examples that illustrate the point:

1. Bats

Biologists recognize two groups of bats: the microbats and the megabats. Both groups have the same wing structure, and this similarity unites them. However, the megabats have a pattern of nerve connections in the brain that they do *not* share with the microbats. Instead, they share this complex arrangement of nerves with the primates (lemurs, monkeys, apes, etc).[8] Most biologists think that all bats evolved from a common ancestor—but, if so, the megabats must have evolved a primate-like brain independently of the primates. A small number of biologists have argued that the megabats have a primate-like brain because they are, in fact, flying primates—but, in that case, the megabats must have evolved their wings independently of the microbats.

2. Whales

There has been an ongoing debate among evolutionary biologists about which group of mammals is most closely related to the whales. Until recently, this honour went to a group of extinct mammals called mesonychids which shared many features with the whales, including the form of the teeth.[9] However, most evolutionary biologists now think that a group of mammals called artiodactyls are the closest relatives of the whales, because 'early' whales and artiodactyls both possess a 'double-pulleyed' heel bone, and the mesonychids do not have this feature.[10] If the whales were descended from the artiodactyls, however, that must mean that the mesonychids evolved whale-like teeth independently of the whales. Alternatively, if the whales are descended from the mesonychids, it would mean that the 'early' whales evolved an artiodactyl-like heel independently of the artiodactyls.

In both examples, there are similarities that contradict whichever tree the evolutionary biologist chooses to adopt. The abundance of these tree-contradicting similarities weakens the argument that there is a *unique* nested hierarchy that describes the pattern of life. Indeed, creation biologists are encouraged by these observations to explore non-evolutionary explanations for the similarities shared between living organisms.

A non-evolutionary network

If the similarities that we observe in living organisms are not arranged in an evolutionary treelike pattern, then how are they arranged? What is the pattern of life? Creation biologists are free to consider various possibilities. More recently, Kurt Wise has suggested that life is a complex network rather than a single nested hierarchy. From this perspective, each basic type or baramin is a unique combination of traits (characteristics) that might be shared individually with members of other groups. This suggests that individual traits are distributed among living organisms in a way similar to that in which coloured tiles are distributed in a mosaic.

There are many examples of creatures that illustrate this mosaic pattern. The duck-billed platypus, for instance, has features of both mammals (hair, milk production) and reptiles (egg-laying). Perhaps the best-known fossil example is the bird *Archaeopteryx*,

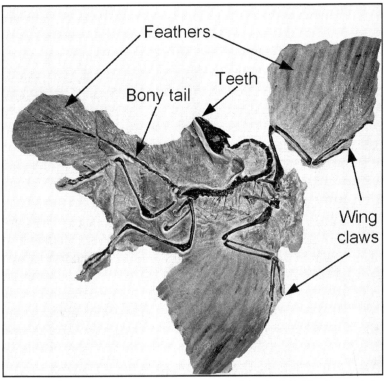

The famous fossil Archaeopteryx *is a curious mosaic. It has both birdlike characteristics (such as asymmetric flight feathers) and characteristics resembling those of reptiles (such as teeth, claws on the forelimbs and a long, bony tail).*

which combines feathers with teeth and wing claws. Another example is *Psarolepis*, a fossil fish discovered in China, which combines characters found in at least four different groups.[11] Kurt Wise has given these mosaic creatures a name; he calls them 'chimeromorphs'.[12] Evolutionists often interpret these mosaic creatures as evolutionary intermediates linking major groups. However, Wise makes the following important point about such mosaics:

> Although the entire organism is intermediate in structure, it's the *combination* of structures that is intermediate, not the nature of the structures themselves. Each of these organisms appears to be a fully functional organism full of fully functional structures.[13]

Evolutionary theory might lead us to expect examples of intermediate *structures*, but in these mosaic organisms the structures are fully developed and highly complex. What is unusual is their combination in a single creature. The existence of these curious mosaics, which share similarities with two or more other groups, seems to support the creationist view that life is *not* singularly nested.

Further evidence that the pattern of life might be better described as a complex network has come from the discovery of similar genes in 'distantly related' organisms. For a decade or more it has been known that certain bacteria (single-celled organisms) may share genes even though they are not thought to be closely related in evolutionary terms. This has led to speculation that organisms on different branches of the evolutionary tree swapped genes between themselves—in a process called horizontal gene transfer—early in the history of life.[14] Many evolutionary biologists have reacted to this discovery with consternation because it means in effect that 'the history of life cannot properly be represented as a tree'.[15] The popular magazine *Scientific American* even published an article on this subject with the title 'Uprooting the tree of life'.[16] Researchers are increasingly using terms like 'ring'[17] or 'net'[18]—rather than 'tree'—to describe these relationships.

The underlying message is that the familiar 'tree of life', a popular evolutionary icon ever since the time of Charles Darwin, simply does not apply to all organisms. It fails as a description of the emerging pattern of life. However, what we observe seems to be consistent with the mosaic pattern of similarities suggested by creation biologists.

A creation basis for shared similarities

There is one final question that we ought to address here. If life has been created, rather than evolved, why should there be any similarities between organisms at all? Creation biologists point to at least three *non-evolutionary* reasons why there are shared similarities among living things.

1. They are necessary for a functioning creation

Virtually all living things share profound similarities in metabolism—the chemical reactions which provide energy for the vital processes of life. For instance, similar proteins do similar jobs in humans and yeast. There are remarkable consistencies in the structure of blood-serum proteins, haemoglobin and the cytochrome system (proteins used in respiration). Such similarities are essential for the creation to operate; otherwise it would not be possible for organisms to share an environment and interact with each other as they were designed to do.[19]

2. They result from an economy of design

Human beings often use the same design element in many different objects—for instance, similar motors are used in washing machines, tumble dryers, dish washers and vacuum cleaners. We

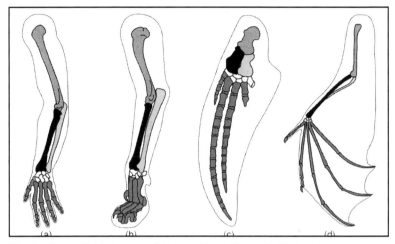

The forelimbs of (a) humans, (b) dogs, (c) whales and (d) bats have the same arrangement of bones but modified for different purposes.

see something similar in living organisms. The arrangement of bones in the vertebrate limb provides a striking example. Our own forearm illustrates the general pattern: we have a single bone in the upper arm, two bones in the lower arm, a cluster of bones in the wrist and hand, and the five fingers. This same pattern is found in the amphibians, reptiles, birds and mammals. However, we see the basic pattern modified for different purposes: grasping, walking, running, digging, swimming or flying. One study looked at possible alternatives to this design and found that variations which moved away from it appeared not to work.[20] This may explain why the Creator chose to use this arrangement in so many different organisms.

3. They point us to a common Creator

1 Corinthians 8:6 says, 'There is but one God, the Father, of whom are all things' (see also Deuteronomy 6:4; 1 Kings 8:60; 1 Timothy 2:5). One of the purposes of creation is to direct people to this one true God who made all things, and shared similarities help

to achieve this. Imagine if different groups of organisms had little in common—we might arrive at the incorrect conclusion that there had been many different creators. As it is, despite the great diversity of living organisms, there is an underlying unity.[21] For instance, virtually all organisms operate using the same genetic language and machinery.[22] This fundamental similarity suggests a common origin and, thus, a common Creator.

11

Defects and degeneration

Throughout the Creation Week, God expressed his satisfaction with the things he had made by stating six times that they were 'good' (Genesis 1:4, 10, 12, 18, 21, 25), and upon completing his work God crowned it all with an even stronger declaration—that the finished creation was 'very good' (Genesis 1:31). The works of God's hands reflected something of his own perfection.

However, as we look at the world around us today, we find that it is not always good. In fact it is full of messy contradictions. There is beauty but also ugliness, pleasure *and* pain, health *and* sickness, happiness *and* sorrow, life *and* death. As Romans 8:22 puts it, 'The whole creation groaneth and travaileth in pain together until now.' Something has gone wrong with God's 'good' creation and, as a consequence, it has become 'subject to vanity' and is under the 'bondage of corruption' (Romans 8:20–21). In this chapter, we will look at what went wrong and the implications for our understanding of the natural world.

The Fall of Adam

When God made the first man, Adam, he placed him in a paradise setting (Genesis 2:8). The place of Adam's residence was a garden planted by God especially for him. Adam was given the task of tending and keeping the garden (Genesis 2:15). He was provided with a helper, his wife Eve, and together they enjoyed God's presence (Genesis 2:18). There was everything here that they could possibly need—and only one restraint:

> And the LORD God commanded the man, saying, Of every tree of the garden thou mayest freely eat: but of the tree of the knowledge of good and evil, thou shalt not eat of it: for in the day that thou eatest thereof thou shalt surely die (Genesis 2:16–17).

Here, surely, was a test of Adam's obedience to God. How would he respond? Would he listen to his Creator and obey him, or would he choose to go his own way? In Genesis 3, we read the wretched account of Adam's rebellion against God. Satan, in the guise of a serpent, deceived Eve into eating the forbidden fruit, and she gave some to Adam, who also ate (Genesis 3:1–6). In this way, Adam wilfully disobeyed God's clear instruction and, as a result, stirred up God's righteous anger against sin.

The Curse was pronounced

The magnitude of Adam's transgression is brought home to us when we consider the penalty that God pronounced. The whole creation—everything over which Adam had been given dominion—was placed under judgement.

First, *the serpent*, the creature that Satan had used to beguile Eve, was cursed (Genesis 3:14–15). By condemning the serpent to crawl on his belly and eat dust,[1] God has given us a vivid reminder of sin's effects. Note that God cursed the serpent 'above all cattle, and above every beast of the field'. The implication is that the other animals were cursed also; we shall see later that this is supported by what Scripture says about their original diet.[2]

Next, *Eve* was punished (Genesis 3:16). Two aspects of the curse on Eve are explicitly mentioned. First, there is pain in childbearing and, second, there is conflict between the woman and her husband. Both the bringing forth of children and the marriage relationship ought to have brought great joy, but they became spoiled by sin.

Last of all *Adam* was dealt with (Genesis 3:17–19). There are three aspects to his punishment. First, the ground was cursed for his sake—it would bring forth thorns and thistles. God had given Adam the Earth as his home, but now his very home was cursed. Secondly, and as a consequence of the ground being cursed, Adam's life from now on would be one of sweat, sorrow, hardship and toil. His work, which once would have been a pleasure to him, would become hard and wearisome. Thirdly, he was subjected to death. God had warned Adam that eating from the tree of the knowledge of good and evil would surely bring about his death. And that is precisely what happened. The Hebrew of Genesis 2:17 says, literally, 'Dying you will die.' From the moment that Adam disobeyed God, his death became a certainty, and 930 years later Adam returned to the dust from which he had been taken (Genesis 2:7; 3:19; 5:5).

The implications for biology

The fall of Adam has far-reaching implications for the study of biology. The Curse brought about, directly or indirectly, many changes to living things. Let us consider some of them.

The first, and perhaps most obvious, of these changes was *the introduction of physical death for human beings*. Adam and Eve were created to live for ever, and death was introduced as a judgement upon Adam's rebellion. Romans 5:12 says that 'By one man sin entered into the world, and death by sin; and so death passed upon all men, for that all have sinned.' Adam stood as the head of the human race and, in Adam, *we* sinned; therefore we also are subject to death. Genesis 5 provides a list of Adam's descendants up to the time of Noah, and each entry in the list, with the sole exception of godly Enoch, ends with the words, 'and he died'. This awful refrain serves as a bleak reminder of sin's curse upon mankind.

The second thing we note is the apparent absence of *carnivorous (meat-eating) animals* before the Curse. The animals, like Adam and Eve, were created to be vegetarian:

> *And God said, Behold, I have given you every herb bearing seed, which is upon the face of all the earth, and every tree, in the which is the fruit of a tree yielding seed; to you it shall be for meat* [i.e. food]. *And to every beast of the earth, and to every fowl of the air, and to every thing that creepeth upon the earth, wherein there is life, I have given every green herb for meat* [i.e. food]: *and it was so* (Genesis 1:29–30).

Carnivory does not appear to have been part of the natural order at the beginning. This is consistent with the vision of Isaiah 11:6–8, which speaks of the future restoration of all things by the Messiah. At that time, says Isaiah:

> *The wolf also shall dwell with the lamb, and the leopard shall lie down with the kid; and the calf and the young lion and the fatling together; and a little child shall lead them. And the cow and the bear shall feed; their young ones shall lie down together: and the lion shall eat straw like the ox. And the sucking child shall play on the hole of the asp, and the weaned child shall put his hand on the cockatrice' den. They shall not hurt nor destroy in all my holy mountain: for the earth shall be full of the knowledge of the* LORD, *as the waters cover the sea.*

The third point is that people and animals would apparently not have perished from *disease* before the Curse. The absence of death in the original creation implies that disease was also unknown at that time. Many diseases are caused by mutations—errors in the copying of genetic information from one generation to the next. A well-known example of a genetic disease is sickle-cell anaemia, in which a mutation causes the red blood cells to change their shape and work less efficiently. Originally, there would have been no mutations in living organisms, but after the Curse the number of mutations would have built up in human and animal populations. Some organisms also cause disease—we call them pathogens. An example is the bacterium *Bacillus anthracis* that causes anthrax.[3] Those organisms that have harmful effects today must once have been beneficial. Even today, less than one per cent of all microbes and viruses are pathogenic.[4] Most play an essential role in decomposing plant litter, cycling elements and water in the environment, secreting vitamins, assisting in digestion, and so on.

Fourth, *the struggle for survival* apparently started with the Curse. In today's fallen world, more offspring are produced than the environment can support and there is competition between organisms. This leads to natural selection, the process by which nature 'selects' those individuals that are better suited to survive in a particular environment. Natural selection plays a vital role in maintaining the health of populations by weeding out diseased and unfit organisms. Although we associate the concept of natural selection with the founder of evolutionary theory, Charles Darwin, the idea did not originate with him. It had been proposed in 1835 by a creationist, Edward Blyth, for whom natural selection was merely a way of filtering out unhelpful variations from a population.[5]

Finally, we note that *thorns and thistles* were brought forth from the ground because of the Curse (Genesis 3:18). Today, plants develop thorns and prickles by a modification of the growth process of stems and leaves. In a cursed world it is necessary for plants to protect themselves and the possession of thorns and prickles is one of the ways in which they do this.

What about the 'death' of plants?

It seems clear that there were many changes in the natural world as a result of Adam's fall into sin—including the origin of physical death.[6] Nevertheless, some have argued that physical death must have been a part of the world *before* the Curse because, at the very least, plants would have 'died' when they were eaten. However, the Bible itself seems to make a theological distinction when it comes to the plants.[7]

1. In the Old Testament, the word *nephesh* is one of the most commonly used words for 'living', but it is never used in connection with plants.

2. Similarly, plants are never said to contain 'the breath of life' (*chay* or *chayyah*) or 'spirit' (*ruach*).

3. Neither are plants classified as having muscle or flesh (Hebrew *basar*), as are animals and men. (See also 1 Corinthians 15:39, which speaks of different kinds of flesh, but refers only to animals).

4. Leviticus 17:11–14 says that the life of a creature is in the blood. There is a clear link between sin and bloodshed throughout the Bible (e.g. Hebrews 9:22). Although some plants have root systems that contain a type of haemoglobin (an iron-rich molecule found in blood), they do not have a true blood system.

It appears that physical death, *as defined in Scripture*, does not encompass plants. Therefore, the eating of plants before Adam sinned is consistent with the teaching that there was no death before the Curse.

How did these changes come about?

The biblical record raises many fascinating questions for biologists. If such imperfections as carnivory and disease arose as a consequence of the Curse, what processes and mechanisms were involved? The Bible does not give us exhaustive information. We must make reasonable inferences based on what it does tell us, coupled with the information we can glean from a study of the living world. Various possibilities may be considered.

Some imperfections may have come about by *a simple change in habitat or behaviour*. For example, many types of bacteria live in the intestines of people and animals—with mutual benefit. But if these bacteria become displaced (e.g. by getting into a supply of drinking water) they may cause illnesses such as diarrhoea.[8] Many natural poisons and toxins can also be thought of in this way. Virtually all chemical substances can be harmful if they are used in the wrong place or in the wrong amounts.[9]

Other imperfections may be the result of *degenerative changes* since the Curse. Genetic diseases such as sickle-cell anaemia and cystic fibrosis, which are caused by harmful mutations, would fall into this category. Another example is the Ebola virus. There are various strains of Ebola; some cause a severe infection which usually leads to death, but others produce no symptoms at all. It is probable that degenerative changes have led to the emergence of virulent strains from closely related non-virulent strains.[10]

The third category of imperfections is perhaps the most challenging to explain. It includes those structures that seem to be beautifully designed, but are used to harm or kill. Consider the pit vipers of the New World.[11] These snakes have a pair of pits, between the nostril and the eye, which are sensitive to heat. They act as thermal sensors, guiding the snake towards its prey.[12] The snake's skull is so designed that the long fangs fold up like switchblades inside the mouth and extend only when the jaws are opened. Venom from special glands is injected into the prey through the fangs, which are hollow, rather like hypodermic

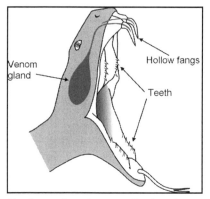

The fangs of pit vipers are like hypodermic needles, and appear to have been designed for killing.

needles.[13] The venom contains many complex and specific chemicals that attack the blood and blood vessels of the victim, causing it to die by internal bleeding. The details are horrible, but grimly fascinating. How did such a system arise? It is difficult to think of a benign use for this arrangement and it is so complex and well designed that it seems unlikely to have arisen by degenerative changes (e.g. mutations) since the Curse. A possible explanation is that some organisms were *designed* with the genetic information for structures and behaviour that were unexpressed until sin came into the world. This idea seems to be consistent with what we know of God's sovereignty and foreknowledge (Acts 2:23; Romans 8:29; 11:2; 1 Peter 1:1–2; Revelation 13:8). Of course, we may yet discover that even these structures, or modifications of them, had benign uses before Adam's fall into sin.

Creation biologists are also interested to know over what timescale these imperfections were introduced. Some may have come about immediately at the time of the Curse; others probably arose over a period of time as the creation degenerated. Even today, new diseases and pathogens are emerging. The Ebola virus is a case in point—the first cases were reported in 1976. This fits the biblical picture of a creation that is continuing to deteriorate as a result of the Curse.

Insights into the 'lost world'

It is, of course, difficult for us to imagine what the world must have been like before the Fall. The world around us has been cursed because of sin. We see the struggle for survival, aggressive meat-eaters, death, suffering and bloodshed—and we find it hard to conceive that the world was ever different. Even so, on occasions our study of the natural world gives us intriguing clues to how things might have been before the Curse. Here are a few examples:

1. A vegetarian crocodile

In 1995, scientists reported a fossil crocodile from China that had molar-like teeth, suggesting that it was a herbivore.[14]

2. Jellyfish that do not sting

The *Mastigias* jellyfish in a saltwater lake in the Pacific Republic of Palau do not sting, but harvest their own food from sunlight using algae that they carry with them.[15]

3. A bird of prey that eats nuts

The Palm Nut Vulture of Africa (*Gypohierax angolensis*) feeds almost exclusively on husks of the fruit of the oil palm or, less frequently, the *Raphia* palm. It eats meat only when its usual diet is not available.[16]

4. A piranha relative that eats fruit

The pacu is a South American river fish closely related to the fearsome piranha. However, the pacu mostly eats aquatic plants and fruit falling from trees.[17]

As we study the natural world from a biblical perspective, we must always bear in mind that its original perfection has been spoilt because of Adam's sin. What we see around us is not the world as it was in the beginning. The creation has been cursed, bringing death and bloodshed to mankind and the animals placed under man's care. If we are to develop a fully biblical understanding of the world and its creatures, we will need to consider the far-reaching implications of Genesis chapter 3.

12

Embryos and vestiges

It takes only nine months, from conception to birth, for a single fertilized egg to develop into a fully formed human infant. Thanks to the latest scientific and technological advances, we can even observe this remarkable transformation take place. We marvel at photographs and ultrasound images of the unborn baby in the womb and the extraordinary process of development that they reveal. But even more amazing is the realization that we all began life in this way.

The Bible tells us that, like our first parents, Adam and Eve, each of us was made in the image and likeness of God (Genesis 1:26–27; 9:6; James 3:9). That was already true when each of us was a single fertilized egg; even then, we were image-bearers of the Almighty. For this reason, the Bible places great value on human life from the time of conception onwards.

At conception, a new human being comes into existence—not a *potential* life, but an *actual* life. The idea that the human embryo is simply a 'mass of tissue', or an extension of the mother's body, is foreign to Scripture. On the contrary, the Bible applies personal language to the unborn and even gives evidence of a personal relationship between God and the unborn child. As Psalm 139:14–16 reminds us, it is God who forms us, and we are not hidden from his eyes even in the womb:

I will praise thee; for I am fearfully and wonderfully made: marvellous are thy works; and that my soul knoweth right well. My substance was not hid from thee, when I was made in secret, and curiously wrought in the lowest parts of the earth. Thine eyes did see my substance, yet being unperfect; and in thy book all my members were written, which in continuance were fashioned, when as yet there was none of them.

Evolution and the sanctity of human life

Tragically, this high view of human life is being undermined today by a tidal wave of anti-life legislation, including legal abortion, embryo experimentation and human cloning. It is estimated that twenty-six million babies are legally aborted worldwide every year.[1] More than forty million abortions have taken place in the USA alone since 1973. In England and Wales there are about 187,000 abortions a year and another 12,000 in Scotland.[2] This is about 550 every day—nearly six million since abortion was legalized in Britain in 1967. Similar statistics are available for many other countries around the world. This constitutes a moral meltdown of enormous proportions, and surely the Lord must be angry with these nations for allowing it to happen. Evolutionary thinking has contributed to this disaster by downgrading humans to little more than 'naked apes'. There are even those today, such as bioethicist Peter Singer, who contend that the life of a mentally impaired infant is of less value than the life of a pig, a dog or a chimpanzee.[3] In his *Writings on an Ethical Life*, Singer frankly admits that he bases his system of ethics on the theory of evolution:

If you look at the book of Genesis, you see there the idea that humans are special, that God created humans in his own image and gave them dominion over the other animals. Since Darwin, at least, we've known that that's factually false, and now we've got to draw the moral implications of understanding that it's factually false.[4]

Embryos and 'evolution'

It is perhaps not widely appreciated today that the study of embryos played an important part in the development of evolutionary thinking. Nevertheless, the science historian Robert Richards has argued that the modern idea of evolution can be traced back to much earlier ideas concerning the development of embryos.[5]

In fact, the word 'evolution' was originally used in the seventeenth century to refer to a theory of embryo development called 'preformism'. According to preformism, 'The embryo from the very beginning existed as a "miniature adult" that simply unfolded or "evolved" during gestation.'[6] This theory seems to have originated with the Dutch entomologist Jan Swammerdam (1637–1680) and to have been based upon his observations of insect larvae. Soon, the preformists became divided into two camps, some believing that the 'miniature adult' resided in the female egg and others that it resided in the male sperm.

By the late eighteenth century, however, the theory of preformism had given way to other ideas. The growth of an embryo was no longer regarded as the unfolding of an already formed adult of its own species, but rather as the unfolding of a series of miniature adults of 'more primitive' species. At the time there was a common belief that living things could be ranked in a linear fashion from 'lower' to 'higher' species, with insects at the bottom and man at the top. This idea, derived from Aristotelian philosophy, was known as 'the Great Chain of Being'. It became fashionable to believe that the developing embryo was 'passing through'—or recapitulating—the hierarchy of species below it.[7] The most sophisticated form of this recapitulation principle was developed by the German anatomist Johann Friedrich

Meckel (1724–1774). Among other things, he tried to show that the heart and vascular system of embryonic mammals resembled what could be found in frogs, salamanders, lizards and various insects.

Influenced by Meckel's ideas, many biologists eventually came to believe that the embryo, as it developed, was retracing the actual evolutionary history of its ancestors. However, Meckel's theory of recapitulation was not universally accepted. One prominent critic was Karl Ernst von Baer (1792–1876), who advanced several objections to the theory.[8] He did not dispute that the embryos of all vertebrates—fishes, amphibians, reptiles, birds and mammals—started off looking very similar and then gradually diverged in appearance. However, in his view this was simply a process of differentiation—a change from a more generalized to a more specialized form—and nothing to do with the ranking or development of species.

Then, in the mid-nineteenth century, along came Charles Darwin, the father of modern evolutionary theory. Darwin was very familiar with the writings of those advocating recapitulation and other embryological theories. His notebooks, essays, unpublished manuscripts, letters and books make that clear. What Darwin did was to merge the ideas of Meckel with those of von Baer. While denying that embryos recapitulated the adult stages of 'lower' animals, he endorsed the idea that the embryos of closely related organisms would pass through similar stages. In *The Origin of Species* Darwin wrote:

> In two groups of animal, however much they may at present differ from each other in structure and habits, if they pass through the same or similar embryonic stages, we may feel assured that they have both descended from the same or nearly similar parents, and are therefore in that degree closely related.[9]

In this way, the concept of recapitulation became the bridge that linked the older theory of 'evolution', that of embryo development, with the modern theory of 'evolution', that of species descent with modification.

It was not long before Darwin's evolutionary ideas about embryos were picked up and popularized in a somewhat exaggerated form by the German biologist Ernst Haeckel (1834–1919). It is Haeckel whose name is most often associated with the theory of recapitulation today. However, Haeckel was not, as he is sometimes mistakenly portrayed, the originator of the theory. Rather, he was an aggressive promoter of ideas whose origins could be traced back at least a century.

Doubts about the recapitulation theory

Today, most evolutionary biologists acknowledge that the recapitulation theory is, at best, greatly oversimplified. Although there is a *general* similarity between an organism's development and its proposed evolutionary history, there are many differences in detail. For example, it is true that, at various stages, the embryonic human heart has one chamber (as in the worm), two chambers (as in the fish), three chambers (as in the frog) and four chambers with a connection between the two sides (as in the reptile). But they appear in the wrong order: the human heart starts with two chambers which fuse into one for a time.[10] This reverses the supposed evolutionary sequence.

In fact, virtually all the specific examples of embryo recapitulation break down upon close examination. Take, for instance, the claim that the human embryo passes through a fishlike stage during which it possesses gill slits.[11] It is undoubtedly true that midway through development the human embryo has a series of folds in the throat that resemble gill slits. However, the resemblance is superficial.[12] The folds develop into parts that have nothing to do with respiration—namely, the tonsils, thyroid, parathyroid, thymus and tongue—and so it is inaccurate to call them 'gills'. Moreover, except for a very brief period, the folds do not perforate the throat,

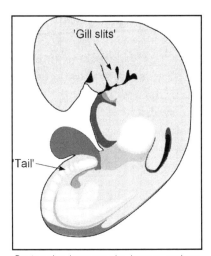

During development, the human embryo has throat folds that superficially resemble gill slits and a protruding coccyx that looks a little like a tail.

and this means that they cannot properly be referred to as 'slits'.

Another claim concerns the covering of downy hair—the lanugo—which the human embryo develops at about seven months and which is still present in some premature babies. This is sometimes said to be a vestige from our apelike ancestors.[13] In fact, the 'hairy' embryo has no more hair than a newborn baby or an adult. It is simply a different type of hair. The lanugo hair is fine and colourless but quite long—which is why it is so obvious. It is replaced by vellus hair which is also fine and colourless, but quite short. This is the type of hair on our neck, ears and face. Terminal hairs, like those on our heads or in a man's beard, are thicker and pigmented. When, in later life, a man 'loses' his hair he actually has as many hairs as he has always had; the terminal hairs are simply replaced with vellus hairs. There is no 'hairier' stage in human development that can be seen as a remnant of our evolutionary past.[14]

Still others have claimed that the human embryo has a tail.[15] It is true that, at four weeks, the base of the spine (the coccyx) sticks out a little like a tail (see illustration above). However, this is because different parts of the embryo grow at different rates, and by eight weeks the coccyx is enclosed within the body. The coccyx is an important part of the body; it is an anchor point for muscles that allow us to stand upright and control the elimination of waste from the body. It is not a leftover from a time when our ancestors had tails. Occasionally, a baby is born with a short tail-like growth near the end of the spine. Some have suggested that these growths are 'throwbacks' to an earlier stage of evolution.[16] Unlike true tails, however, the growths are fleshy and not connected to the spinal column. They are simply a type of birth abnormality that superficially resembles a tail.

It seems that God has designed the process of development in such a way that embryos go from simple to complex and from a more generalized form to a more specialized form. Since this is also the path that evolution is said to have taken, it is unsurprising that there are some *general* similarities between the two processes.[17] However, the abundant differences of detail suggest that evolutionary theory is not the best explanation. Creation theory, on the other hand, is able to explain both the similarities *and* the differences.

Embryos and dormant genes

A more sophisticated argument in favour of evolution concerns the existence of dormant genes in embryos. For instance, experiments have shown that the leg bones of chicken embryos can be made to develop in a reptile-like arrangement. This seems to be consistent with the evolutionary idea that birds evolved from reptiles millions of years ago. A reptile's lower leg is made up of several bones: the tibia, the fibula and a group of ankle bones called tarsals. A chicken leg has fewer bones because the tarsals are fused together with the tibia into a single structure (called the tibiotarsus). However, when a sheet of mica (a rock mineral that splits into thin sheets) is placed between the tibia and fibula of a young chick embryo, the 'reptile' arrangement of bones develops instead.[18]

According to evolutionary biologists, this experiment shows that chicken embryos have dormant genes—genes that are not normally expressed but which have been inherited from a reptile ancestor. However, this leaves the problem of how these dormant

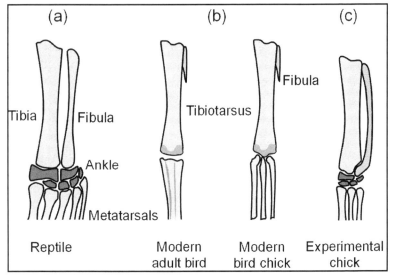

The arrangement of bones in (a) the leg of a reptile, (b) the leg of a bird (adult and chick) and (c) the leg of a chick after the experimental separation of the tibia and fibula.[19]

genes have managed to survive for tens of millions of years. Surely natural selection ought to have eliminated them long ago? As biologist Leonard Brand explains:

> It seems very unlikely that an unused assemblage of genes for producing reptile bones would remain intact for over 100 million years without serious mutational damage to those unneeded genes. It seems more plausible that birds and reptiles have a common set of 'instructions' for making legs and that regulatory genes control the specific application of these for making the structure appropriate for each animal.[20]

If this explanation is correct, then the 'reptile' arrangement of bones in the chicken embryos represents a disruption of the plan that God designed, but it tells us nothing about evolutionary ancestry.

Another interesting experiment suggests that chicken embryos have the ability to develop teeth. Although no modern birds have teeth, tissue from the jaw of a chicken embryo can be made to produce teeth by laying it over tissue from the jaw of a mouse embryo.[21] The teeth develop from the chicken tissue, but receive the 'instructions' to do so from the mouse tissue. We know from fossil evidence that many extinct birds possessed teeth and this experiment suggests that modern birds may retain the genes for teeth even though they are not expressed today. This is consistent with the idea that we explored in chapter 9—that God designed organisms with a great deal of 'hidden' genetic information that would allow them to diversify. These dormant genes may provide insights into how God equipped organisms to do that.

What about 'vestigial organs'?

A related argument for evolution concerns the existence of 'vestigial organs'. Evolutionary theory says that, as living things change, organs may take on a reduced function—and perhaps even lose their original function altogether. Biologists point to many examples of such organs or structures in humans and animals. However, persuasive though this argument appears, there are a number of problems with it.

1. Some vestigial organs are probably not truly vestigial

Take the appendix, for instance—the pouch located at the point where the small intestine meets the large intestine. In some animals (e.g. rabbits) the appendix is where tough plant material is broken down. Humans also have an appendix, but it is not involved in digesting plant material. Thus, for many years, it was thought to be a functionless vestige of our evolutionary past.[22] However, more recent research suggests that the human appendix plays a role in establishing and maintaining the body's defences, especially in infancy.[23] This shows how difficult it is to be certain that an organ has lost or changed its function. While an evolutionary biologist might conclude that the human appendix had changed its original function (digestion) for a new one (defence), a creation biologist might conclude that it was designed for defence in humans in the first place.

2. Some vestigial organs are expected by creationists

Earlier in this book we suggested that there has been tremendous diversification within the baramins, or created kinds, since creation. One result of this diversification process may have been the loss, or partial loss, of structures. We must also remember that the creation is imperfect today because it has been cursed—and this has led to degeneration. For both these reasons, we might anticipate true vestigial structures in living things. Here are some examples:

1. There are many varieties of cave-dwelling fish with non-functional, malformed or absent eyes. However, there is strong evidence that these blind fish were descended from sighted ancestors. In some cases the eyeless and eyed forms even belong to the same species and can successfully interbreed.[24]

2. The splint bones of modern horses may be remnants of the side toes of a multi-toed ancestor because there is evidence that horses with different numbers of toes belong to the same baramin.[25] During the burst of diversification after the Flood, these toes were reduced or lost to produce the single hoof of the modern horse.

3. Leg bones in whales are occasionally reported. These are said to be 'genetic throwbacks'—evidence that the ancestors of modern whales once possessed hind limbs.[26] It is possible that some whales were created with hind limbs—there are fossil

whales which apparently had them. Perhaps they were originally used for swimming or as sexual claspers.[27]

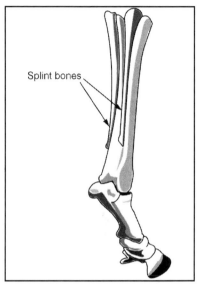

The leg of a horse showing the splint bones, which may represent reduced side toes.

4. Human beings have wisdom teeth that often become impacted and must be removed by surgery. A possible reason is that our jaws have changed in shape and size over time, causing crowding of our teeth.[28] This may have happened because of changes to our diet and the age at which we reach maturity.[29]

3. There are no obvious examples of organs coming into being

If evolution was happening, we ought to find organs that are appearing or gaining functions, as well as organs that are disappearing or losing functions. As Kurt Wise has pointed out:

> The absence of such organs would seem to argue that although we have evidence of degeneration from an earlier, more optimal design, we lack evidence of a move toward a new optimal design.[30]

This is consistent with the type of changes that creationists expect on the basis of the Bible's account of the history of living things.

In 1895, the German anatomist Robert Wiedersheim (1848–

1923) identified at least eighty-six vestigial organs in the human body.[31] With the benefit of modern research, we can see that he was mistaken.[32] It is now known that many of these 'vestigial organs' are functional. Some play a crucial role in the embryo, though not in the adult. But even the existence of some *truly* vestigial structures does not favour evolutionary theory, because creationists also expect the loss or partial loss of some structures as a result of changes within the created groups since their origin.

With this chapter we conclude our survey of creation-based biology. Next we will return to the subject of geology to examine the dramatic events that took place during the global flood of Noah's day and in the centuries following.

Part IV:

The Flood and its aftermath

13

Global catastrophe

Earlier in this book, we outlined the way in which the principle of uniformitarianism—'The present is the key to the past'—took hold in the science of geology. We considered the unbiblical roots of this principle and the need for Christian scholars to rethink Earth history from a biblical perspective. We now return to this theme with a detailed look at the events surrounding the Flood in the days of Noah. Genesis 7:11 says:

> In the six hundredth year of Noah's life, in the second month, the seventeenth day of the month, the same day were all the fountains of the great deep broken up, and the windows of heaven were opened.

Much discussion has focused upon the identification of the 'fountains of the great deep'. Biblical usage suggests that they were water sources distributed across the Earth's surface, both on the continents and in the oceans.[1] Noah's Flood began when all these fountains were broken up on a single day. The Hebrew phrase 'broken up' is used elsewhere in the Old Testament to describe faulting or cleaving of the Earth's surface (e.g. Numbers 16:31; Judges 15:19; Psalm 78:15; Isaiah 48:21; Micah 1:4; Zechariah 14:4). The implication seems to be that the Flood was initiated by some kind of upheaval involving the breaking up of the Earth's crust.

The Flood must surely count as the most devastating geological event in the whole of history. According to the apostle Peter, it brought about the total destruction of the former world (2 Peter 3:6). In fact, the English word 'flood' does not really convey the enormity of what took place. In Hebrew the word is *mabbûl* and, apart from the Flood narrative in Genesis it is used in only one other place in the Old Testament (Psalm 29:10), where the deluge of Noah is also in the writer's mind.[2] Similarly, the Greek New Testament refers to this event with a unique word, *kataklusmos*, from which we derive our English word 'cataclysm'. The fact that unique words are used to refer to Noah's Flood in both the Old and New Testaments indicates that this was an event unparalleled in history.

The geographical extent of the Flood

Indeed, the text of Genesis makes it clear that this was not merely a local or regional inundation—it was a *global* catastrophe. Consider, for instance the following points:

1. The purpose of the Flood

The intention of God in sending the Flood was to wipe mankind 'from the face of the earth' (Genesis 6:7). This was on account of man's great wickedness—'the earth also was corrupt' and 'filled with violence' because of him (Genesis 6:11–13). Thus, the Flood was to be universal in scope, and Noah and his family were the only human survivors (1 Peter 3:20; 2 Peter 2:5).

2. The depth and duration of the Flood

The Flood covered the tops of the highest mountains to a depth of more than twenty feet, or six metres (Genesis 7:19–20) and the waters prevailed for ten months (Genesis 8:5). No local flood could possibly fit this description.

3. The need for an ark

It makes no sense for God to have instructed Noah to build such a huge ark (Genesis 6:14–16) if the Flood were only regional in extent. If that were the case, it would have been more sensible for Noah simply to migrate out of the area or to higher ground.

4. The water was on 'the face of the whole earth'

This phrase, found in Genesis 8:9, is used in the book of Genesis four times outside the Flood account and always in the universal sense (Genesis 1:29; 11:4, 8–9).[3]

Noah's ark, based upon reconstructions by mechanical engineer Tim Lovett.[4] The ark was about 450 feet (137 metres) long, seventy-five feet (twenty-three metres) wide and forty-five feet (just under fourteen metres) high (depending on the cubit measurement used).

5. All the high hills 'under the whole heaven' were covered

The words 'all the high hills' in Genesis 7:19 might be understood to include only those hills within the geographic knowledge of the writer—except that any possible ambiguity is removed by the addition of the phrase 'under the whole heaven'. This phrase occurs unqualified five other times in the Old Testament and is used in the universal sense in each case (Deuteronomy 4:19; Job 28:24; 37:3; 41:11; Daniel 9:12).[5]

6. God's promise

God declared unequivocally that he would never send another flood like this one and he sealed his promise with the sign of the rainbow (Genesis 9:11–16). If Noah's Flood were only a local flood, then God has broken his promise repeatedly.

7. The testimony of Christ and the apostles

The Lord Jesus, Peter and the writer to the Hebrews spoke of the Flood in universal terms, as a picture of the judgement to come (Luke 17:27; Hebrews 11:7; 1 Peter 3:20; 2 Peter 2:5; 3:6).

Moreover, many nations worldwide have traditions of a great flood which destroyed all mankind. These stories are similar to the Genesis account in too many respects to be simply coincidence; it is much more reasonable to believe that these accounts had a common origin in real history. The same basic elements (ark provided, destruction by water, human seed saved) are present in almost all these stories.[6]

The rise of modern Flood geology

And yet, despite the biblical testimony and worldwide traditions, by the mid-twentieth century belief in a global flood of geological significance had almost entirely died out. Uniformitarian thinking seemed to have triumphed, even in the minds of Christian people.

In the providence of God, however, two men were to be raised up to challenge this consensus. In 1961, theologian John Whitcomb and hydraulic engineer Henry Morris published a hugely influential book called *The Genesis Flood.*[7] In it, they expounded the biblical case for a global, world-transforming deluge and set about reinterpreting the geological record in accordance with that idea.

The publication of *The Genesis Flood* is widely perceived to have been a landmark in the history of creationism. Although not all the ideas in the book have stood the test of time, Whitcomb and Morris are rightly regarded as pioneers for provoking serious thought among Christian scholars concerning the geological implications of the Flood. Today, many creationists, building upon the foundational scriptural insights of these men, are seeking to reinterpret the geological record—with its sedimentary rock layers and enclosed fossils—as a record of events taking place in biblical Earth history.

Since the 1960s, a number of scientific models of the Flood have been proposed.[8] In this chapter I want to focus upon perhaps the most promising model proposed to date. It is called the Catastrophic Plate Tectonics model, or CPT for short, and it was put forward by a group of three geologists and three geophysicists at the Third International Conference on Creationism in 1994.[9] It is essentially a modification of the modern theory of plate tectonics, which seeks to describe and explain the motion of the plates that make up the Earth's crust. According to CPT, the Flood involved the catastrophic resurfacing of our planet in the space of a few months. While much work remains to be done to refine the model, CPT seems able to explain many otherwise puzzling features of the Earth and offers an intriguing reconstruction of what the global flood may have been like.

Introducing the theory of plate tectonics

To understand CPT, we need to understand the essentials of *conventional* plate tectonic theory. Let us begin with the internal structure of the Earth.

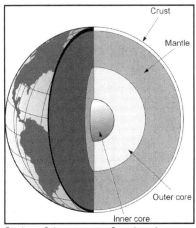

Although scientists cannot study the Earth's interior directly, they can draw some inferences about it based on the bending of earthquake waves as they travel through the Earth. These studies suggest that the Earth has a layered structure consisting of a core, mantle and crust. The core is metallic (composed of iron and nickel) and has a liquid outer layer and a solid inner portion. The mantle is a thick rocky layer (composed of silicates), which, although solid, has the extraordinary ability to flow in a plastic fashion under certain conditions of stress.

Studies of the passage of earthquake waves indicate that the Earth's interior is composed of a metallic core, a rocky mantle and a thin outer crust.

The crust is the thin outer layer and is divided into two types: oceanic and continental. Oceanic crust is made of a dense rock called basalt, which 'sits' lower in the Earth's mantle and forms the ocean basins. The continental crust is composed of a lighter rock called granite, which 'floats' higher in the mantle and forms the world's land masses. The crust is broken into a series of rigid plates which are able to move relative to one another. Most geological activity is focused along the margins of the plates, of which there are three main types:

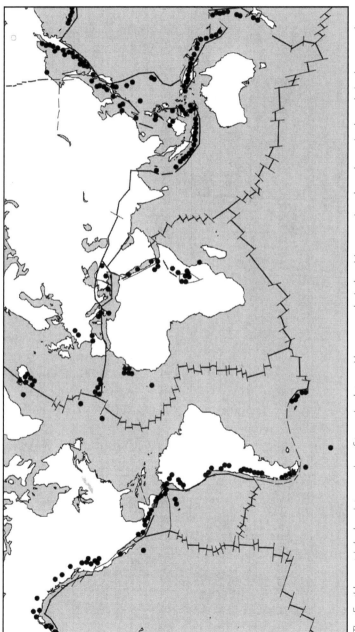

The Earth's crust is broken into a series of tectonic plates, with most geological activity occurring along the active boundaries between the plates. The black circles indicate the location of major volcanoes and earthquakes.

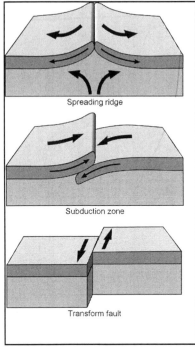

Spreading ridge

Subduction zone

Transform fault

The main types of plate boundary

1. *Spreading ridges*, where plates are moving apart and molten rock is rising up to add new ocean-floor material in between.
2. *Subduction zones*, where plates are moving towards one another and one plate is sinking under the other and being consumed.
3. *Transform faults*, where two adjacent plates are slipping past one another, without the addition or destruction of plate material.

One of the first to propose that the Earth's crust was made up of rigid plates that moved with respect to one another was Antonio Snider-Pellegrini. In a little-known work published in 1859, Snider proposed that the horizontal movements of the Earth's plates had occurred rapidly during Noah's Flood.[10] However, Snider's views were largely ignored and soon forgotten. He was living at a time when the uniformitarian views of Hutton, Lyell and Darwin were in the ascendant and catastrophic ideas were very unfashionable. Indeed, for the next century the science of geology was dominated by the belief that the continents were fixed and immobile. By the time that studies of earthquakes and the deep ocean floor had forced geologists to rethink the 'fixity' of the continents, gradualism had become an integral part of the theory. Virtually all scientists now accept that the present-day continents were once joined in a single supercontinent which broke apart; however, they believe that the plate motions that brought about the break-up took place extremely slowly over a timescale of tens to hundreds of millions of years.

Catastrophic plate tectonics: a global Flood model

The CPT model revives the catastrophic scenario of Snider by proposing that Noah's Flood began with the rapid break-up of the Earth's tectonic plates.

It seems that, before the Flood, the surface of the Earth was divided into oceanic and continental crust just as it is today. This is inferred from Genesis 1:9–10, which says that the seas and the dry land were brought into being on the third day of creation. From geological evidence, it also appears that the Earth's land masses were united in a single supercontinent which scientists have called Rodinia (from the Russian word for 'motherland'). In the CPT model, however, the original ocean crust was cooler and denser than today, and it was sitting on top of a warmer, less dense mantle.

In these circumstances, it would not have taken much to set the tectonic plates in motion. Some have suggested that the impact of an object or objects from space (such as an asteroid or comet) may have acted as the 'trigger'. Others have argued that no special intervention would have been required and that the catastrophe was the natural outcome of the conditions established within the Earth by God during the Creation Week.[11] Whatever the cause, the CPT model suggests that three things happened *simultaneously* as the Flood began.

Firstly, *the ocean crust broke loose from the continental margins and started to plunge into the Earth's mantle.* This is the process that geologists call subduction. In conventional geology, the standard assumption is that a descending plate can only pass through the mantle very slowly because the mantle material is strongly resistant to flow. However, one of the CPT researchers,

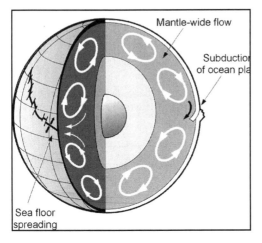

Mantle-wide flow

Subduction
of ocean plate

Sea floor
spreading

During the Flood-related episode of catastrophic plate tectonics, three things happened simultaneously: (a) the pre-Flood ocean floor was rapidly subducted into the Earth's interior, (b) causing widespread flow throughout the mantle, while (c) hot material welled up along the spreading ridges to form new sea floor.

geophysicist John Baumgardner, has demonstrated that when a certain threshold is overcome, something called 'thermal runaway' occurs.[12] It works like this. Friction from the plunging slab causes the mantle around the slab to heat up. As a result, the mantle's resistance to flow decreases and the plunging slab accelerates. As the speed of the slab increases, additional frictional heating takes place, causing a further decrease in resistance to flow around the slab. Computer simulations demonstrate that, under these runaway conditions, the descending slab reaches speeds of metres per second—billions of times faster than the usual rate. In this manner, virtually all the original ocean floor was rapidly 'recycled' into the Earth's mantle during the Flood—and the continents attached to the ocean plates were 'pulled' along with them causing the break-up of the pre-Flood land mass.[13]

Secondly, at the same time that the cold slabs of ocean floor were descending through the mantle, *the surrounding hot material was being 'pushed' out of the way.* The computer simulations conducted by Baumgardner suggest that the entire depth of the mantle underwent large-scale flow. This has been confirmed by seismic studies, which use earthquakes to reconstruct the interior of the

Earth. These studies have revealed the presence of 'cool' slabs of material—apparently remnants of the former ocean crust—located beneath subduction zones and extending deep into the mantle.[14]

Meanwhile, *as the cold ocean crust was diving into the Earth's interior, it was being rapidly replaced by hot mantle material welling up along the mid-ocean ridges where the plates were separating.* As this hot material came into contact with cold ocean water, the water was vaporized and propelled high into the atmosphere. The effect may have been something like the geysers we see today in volcanic areas such as Yellowstone National Park in Wyoming, but on an altogether more spectacular scale. The CPT model suggests that these geysers, erupting along thousands of kilometres of mid-ocean ridge, were among the 'fountains of the great deep' mentioned in Genesis 7:11. The ocean water that was caught up by these supersonic jets eventually fell back to the Earth as an intense global rain. This may have been the primary source of the rain that fell from the 'windows of heaven' for forty days and nights (Genesis 7:4,11).

The Earth's magnetic field 'flips'

The catastrophic movement of the plates also had consequences for the Earth's magnetic field, which is generated by electrical currents in the Earth's outer core.

As the descending ocean crust piled up on the boundary between the core and the mantle, it rapidly cooled the liquid in the outer core so that it began to circulate. Physicist D. Russell Humphreys has shown that these fluid flows would have caused the Earth's magnetic field to undergo a series of 'reversals'—in which magnetic north became magnetic south and vice versa.[15] On the Earth's surface, these 'reversals' were recorded by magnetic minerals within cooling lava flows. As the magnetic minerals crystallized out of the lava, they aligned themselves with the prevailing magnetic field. When the lava flow solidified,

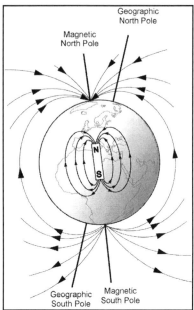

Geographic
North Pole

Magnetic
North Pole

N
S

Geographic   Magnetic
South Pole   South Pole

The Earth possesses a magnetic field generated in the liquid outer core. It is almost as though the Earth has a giant bar magnet at its centre. The magnetic poles of the Earth are offset from the geographic poles by about 11.3 degrees.

the magnetic minerals became 'frozen' in place, recording the alignment of the field at the time the lava flow formed.

In conventional plate tectonics, each magnetic reversal is thought to have taken a long time to occur (a few hundred thousand years)—much longer than it takes for an individual lava flow to cool (a few days to weeks). Conventional geologists do not, therefore, expect to find *individual* lava flows that record magnetic field reversals. However, in CPT the field reversals are thought to have happened so rapidly that there may have been the opportunity to 'capture' them within a single lava flow. In 1986, Humphreys predicted that if the 'rapid reversal' theory was correct then it might be confirmed by finding a thin lava flow that had cooled within a few weeks, but which recorded a reversal in progress.[16] Confirmation came in 1989 when a lava flow at Steens Mountain, Oregon, was found to record an extraordinarily large change in the magnetic field that had taken place in about a fortnight.[17] Subsequently, this find was not only confirmed, but it was realized that the transition took place even faster than was at first thought.[18]

Similar evidence has also been found in the lava flows forming the new ocean floor along the spreading ridges. In this case, the sea floor was moving laterally away from the ridge, and so the reversals

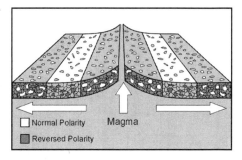

The symmetrical pattern of 'magnetic stripes' parallel to the mid-ocean ridges. Note the locally 'patchy' nature of the stripes which suggests that both the magnetic reversals and sea-floor spreading rates must have been rapid.

were recorded in the rocks as a series of 'magnetic stripes' parallel to the ridge. However, studies of the ocean floor reveal that the lavas are magnetized in a 'patchy' fashion, with small pockets of reversely magnetized lava within the 'stripes'.[19] This is just what we would expect if the reversals and the ocean-floor spreading rates were both rapid.

'All the high hills, that were under the whole heaven, were covered'

Most crucially for a scientific theory of the Flood, the CPT model is able to explain how the continents came to be inundated with water. As we have already seen, the model proposes that the cold, dense ocean floor from before the Flood was rapidly replaced with new, warmer ocean crust along the mid-ocean ridges. This new ocean floor was less dense and more 'buoyant' than the old ocean floor and, therefore, 'rode' higher in the Earth's mantle. As a consequence, the level of the ocean floor was raised significantly, causing the ocean basins to become shallower and displacing water onto the continents. A similar effect, though on a much smaller scale, was experienced when the coast of Sumatra was struck by an earthquake on 26 December 2004. On that occasion, the vertical flexing of the ocean floor was only about thirteen metres (forty feet), but it was enough to create a catastrophic tsunami wave that spread out in all directions.[20] The wave devastated many

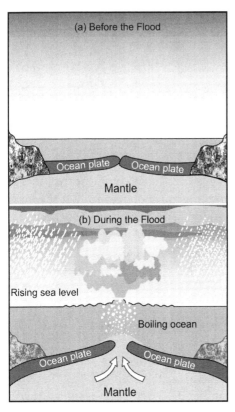

(a) Before the Flood

Ocean plate   Ocean plate

Mantle

(b) During the Flood

Rising sea level

Boiling ocean

Ocean plate   Ocean plate

Mantle

(a) Before the Flood, the crust making up the ocean floor was cooler and denser than today. There were high continents and ocean basins.

(b) During the Flood, the cool ocean crust was replaced by warmer material from the Earth's mantle. This caused the ocean floor to expand and rise, displacing sea-water onto the continents. The oceans also boiled, propelling water vapour high into the atmosphere which fell as an intense global rain.

towns and cities around the coasts, including Banda Aceh, and hundreds of thousands of people perished. Imagine how much more devastating Noah's Flood would have been. Sea level would have risen several kilometres over its pre-Flood level, sufficient to flood the continents and cover the tops of even the highest pre-Flood mountains.[21]

Of course, this also helps us to explain one of the most puzzling features of the geological record: the existence of widespread marine sediments on the continents. During the Flood, the rising and advancing ocean waters would have driven sediments onto the continents in a 'conveyer-belt' fashion. This process would have been assisted by earthquake-generated sea waves and ordinary tides. Strong currents would have been generated above the flooded continents.[22] We have here a mechanism for producing many of the widespread geological features we described back in chapter 5.

Eventually, the Flood was brought to an end by the complete replacement of the 'old' ocean floor. Since the new ocean crust was relatively warm, it had less of a density difference with the underlying mantle and, therefore, less of a tendency to sink back into the Earth's interior. The process of subduction slowed down and eventually came to a virtual stop. This, in turn, brought an end to the overturn of the mantle and the process of rapid sea-floor spreading. The 'fountains of the great deep' were closed up and the global rain ceased. As the new ocean crust cooled and subsided, the waters drained off the continents and back into the deepening ocean basins. The Flood finally came to an end.

While many of the details remain to be worked out, catastrophic plate tectonics is a very promising scientific theory. It is able to explain the same things that are explained by conventional plate tectonics—such as the familiar 'jigsaw fit' of the continents and the magnetic stripes on the ocean floor. However, it is also able to explain other things that are currently left unexplained by conventional plate tectonics—such as the locally patchy nature of the ocean-floor magnetic stripes. It also seems to be consistent with the biblical details concerning the Flood, such as the 'fountains of the great deep', the forty days and nights of rain and the flooding of the continents. No doubt future research in this field will shed further light on the nature of the geological events associated with the global flood.

In the next chapter we will see that the biblical account of the Flood also helps us to explain the millions of fossils buried and preserved in the sedimentary rock layers.

14

Understanding the fossil record

For thousands of years, people have been intrigued and fascinated by fossils. We know that 'Stone Age' people must have taken notice of them, because archaeologists have found flint axes with fossils incorporated into their design.[1] Legendary animals of antiquity, such as the griffin and the Cyclops, may even have been based on the discovery of fossil bones and eggs.[2]

Today, we understand that fossils are the remains or traces of animals and plants that lived in the past. Most are the hard parts of animals, such as shell or bone, although in special circumstances soft parts, such as skin or muscle, can be preserved too. Fossilized footprints, burrows and droppings can give us additional clues about life in the past.

The study of fossils is a major academic discipline (palaeontology) and thousands of professional scientists now work in this field. In addition, there are large numbers of amateur fossil-hunters. Anyone who has successfully tried their hand at this pursuit will know the thrill there is in breaking open a rock and finding a fossil inside!

Fossils provide a fascinating record of ancient life. But what story do they tell? In this chapter we will be thinking about fossils and what they reveal about the history of the Earth.

The fossil record as evidence for evolution

Most scientists interpret the fossil record from an evolutionary perspective. They believe that the rock layers, with their enclosed fossils, document the evolution of life over long eras of time. This understanding of Earth history can be summarized as follows.

The *Precambrian* rocks are considered to be the oldest rocks on Earth, deposited between 3,800 and 542 million years ago. Most Precambrian fossils are micro-organisms resembling today's bacteria and blue-green algae. Dome-shaped structures called stromatolites, thought to have formed when sediment became trapped by sticky algal mats, are abundant in Precambrian sediments.[3] Towards the end of the Precambrian, the first complex animals are thought to have evolved—represented by some strange segmented and frond-like organisms first discovered in the Ediacara Hills of South Australia.

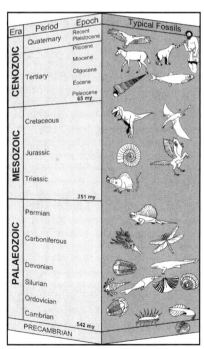

The *Palaeozoic* ('early life') rocks follow the Precambrian and are said to have been deposited between 542 and 251 million years ago. The beginning of the Palaeozoic Era was marked by the sudden appearance of many hard-bodied animals, including sponges,

The standard geological column representing the history of life on Earth according to evolutionary theory. Fossil organisms typical of each geological era are shown ('my' stands for 'millions of years ago').

brachiopods ('lamp shells') and trilobites. By the middle of the Palaeozoic Era, fish had become numerous in the oceans, and plants and animals had begun to invade the land. By the end of the era, the first large reptiles and modern plants (conifers) had developed.

The *Mesozoic* ('middle life') rocks are thought to have been deposited between 251 and sixty-five million years ago. This was the 'age of the reptiles'. Life on the land was dominated by the dinosaurs, in the skies by flying reptiles called pterosaurs, and in the oceans by aquatic reptiles such as ichthyosaurs, plesiosaurs and mosasaurs. Ammonites, squidlike creatures in coiled shells, were also common in the warm, shallow seas. The mammals, birds and flowering plants (angiosperms) also made their first appearance during this time.

The *Cenozoic* ('recent life') rocks are said to have been deposited between sixty-five million years ago and the present day. During the Cenozoic, the flowering plants diversified into a great array of trees, shrubs and vines. This was also the era in which most of the modern groups of birds and mammals evolved, and man emerged from his upright-walking, apelike ancestors.

Doubts about the evolutionary interpretation

We hardly need to say that this interpretation of the fossil record provides a stark contrast with what the Bible tells us about the history of the Earth and its organisms. The Bible, straightforwardly understood, does not allow for the passage of eras or periods of geological time. Neither does it allow for the gradual evolution of life over long ages. We should also note that there are several scientific problems with this evolutionary interpretation of the fossil record.

1. The rarity of 'transitional forms'

These are organisms that must have developed, according to evolution, as one major group evolved into another. Transitional forms would stand morphologically (i.e. in body form) between the ancestral and descendant groups. They would also be expected to lie between their ancestors and descendants in the vertical sequence of rock layers.[4] Since every group of organisms is thought to have evolved from an earlier group, transitional forms *between* groups ought to be common. However, convincing examples of such transitional forms are rare; there are far fewer than evolutionary theory would predict. This seems especially true of the most easily preserved groups in the fossil record—shallow marine invertebrates such as molluscs and brachiopods. From an evolutionary perspective this is counter-intuitive because these are precisely the groups that would be expected to yield the most convincing series of transitional forms. As we shall see later in this chapter, even the handful of claimed transitional forms may be better explained by creation theory than by evolutionary theory.

2. The fossil groups do not seem to occur in the order that evolutionary theory predicts

Evolutionary biologists seek to establish how groups of organisms are related by studying the shared characteristics they are thought to have inherited from a common ancestor.[5] From this, they can determine the order in which they think the groups diverged from one another and, therefore, the order in which they ought to appear in the fossil record. However, when the *actual* order of first appearance of the major fossil groups is compared with the order in which they are *expected* to have appeared, there seems to be little correspondence. In a study by palaeontologist Kurt Wise, only five out of 144 test cases showed a significant agreement between the fossil order and the predicted evolutionary order.[6] The sequence of the fossils does not seem to fit the expected evolutionary pattern.

3. The sudden appearance of many disparate groups in the fossil record

You may recall from chapter 10 that living organisms are traditionally classified into 'nested' groups: species within genera, genera within families, families within orders, orders within classes, classes within phyla, and phyla within kingdoms. According to evolutionary theory, the 'higher' groups (kingdoms, phyla, classes, orders) have emerged by the splitting of the 'lower' groups (species, genera, families). If this is true, there ought to be fewer higher groups at the beginning of the fossil record with more appearing gradually over time. We can visualize this as a tree which becomes broader at the top as new branches develop. However, what we actually see in the fossil record is something quite different. In the earliest Cambrian sediments (conventionally dated as about 542 million years old) we see the geologically sudden appearance of many different animal groups. At least nineteen, and possibly as many as thirty-five, different phyla—out of a total of forty—make their first appearance in the fossil record at that point.[7] In evolutionary terms, it is as if the base of the 'tree of life' is already very broad. Evolutionary theory has no obvious explanation for

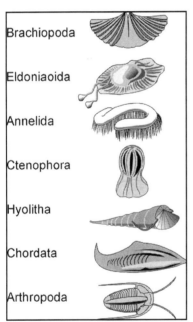

Brachiopoda

Eldoniaoida

Annelida

Ctenophora

Hyolitha

Chordata

Arthropoda

Representatives of seven of the major animal groups that make an abrupt appearance in the lowermost Cambrian sediments.

the sudden appearance of so many disparate groups so early in the fossil record.

Flood geology and the fossil record

Creationists propose a very different interpretation of the fossil record based upon the historical events described in the book of Genesis. As we saw in the last chapter, the most geologically significant event in the history of the Earth was the global flood of Noah's day. This suggests that the fossil record may be divided into three parts: a part formed *before* the Flood, a part formed *during* the Flood and a part formed *after* the Flood.

There is still a great deal of debate among creationists about which parts of the fossil record correspond to which episodes in biblical history. Most, though by no means all, accept that the Palaeozoic and Mesozoic sediments were deposited by the Flood.[8] In this view, the fossils in these sediments represent communities of organisms that were successively inundated during the catastrophe. The Flood appears to have been a transgressive event, proceeding from the oceans onto the land. As the flood waters advanced, communities of organisms would have been 'picked off' in the order in which they were encountered. The resulting sequence of fossils would therefore reflect the ecological distribution of organisms before the Flood, rather than evolution over long ages.

This idea, first proposed in 1946 by Harold Clark (1891–1986), has come to be known as the ecological zonation theory. It suggests that the fossil record can help us to reconstruct what the world was like before the Flood. The sequence of the fossils is highly ordered, indicating that the world back then was much more highly organized into ecological zones than it is today. Clark proposed a series of ecological zones varying in altitude from the deep ocean to the high mountains.[9] More recently, his theory has been modified to propose a series of adjacent—

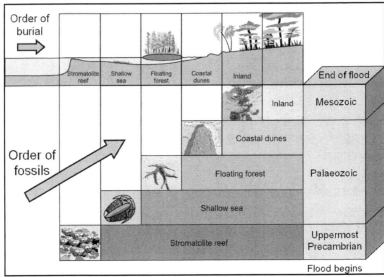

According to the ecological zonation theory, the order of burial of adjacent ecological zones by the encroaching flood waters produced a vertical sequence of rock layers containing characteristic fossils.[10]

rather than elevational—provinces. Some of the ecological zones that have been reconstructed are very different from those found on the surface of the Earth today. We shall look at some examples.

1. A stromatolite reef community

The fossils buried in the Precambrian sediments have been reconstructed as a community of organisms living in a hydrothermal ('hot spring') environment around the margins of the pre-Flood continents.[11] This may have consisted of stromatolite mounds forming a kind of 'barrier reef' protecting a deep-water lagoon in which the strange 'Ediacaran' animals lived. Nearer to the shore may have been an extensive shallow ocean with trilobites and other marine animals—represented today by the fossils of the lowermost Palaeozoic sediments.

2. A floating forest community

The unfamiliar plant and animal fossils of the Palaeozoic sediments may represent the remains of a huge 'floating forest' community.[12] This would have been something like a modern 'quaking bog' but on a much larger scale, growing out over the ocean. Around the edges of the floating forest would have been small, water-dependent plants. Towards the centre of the forest, the mat of vegetation may have been thick enough to support treelike ferns, seed ferns, club mosses and horsetails. During the Flood, the floating-forest community was broken up and destroyed, with the central part being buried to form the extensive Palaeozoic coal seams.

3. A dinosaur community

In the Mesozoic sediments we find abundant fossils of many types of dinosaur, along with some unusual mammals. Most of these mammals are small, although there have been recent discoveries of larger types.[13] These animals appear to have shared the same habitat before the Flood and to have been buried together as a community.[14] The dominant plants found in these sediments are 'naked seed' plants, such as cycads, ginkgos and conifers—probably the main food source for the plant-eating members of this unique community.

Oddly, most mammals, birds and flowering plants are missing from the Flood sediments—as is all evidence of human life. These organisms seem to represent another pre-Flood community but one which was not preserved in the fossil record like the others. It is intriguing to speculate why this was so.[15] One suggestion is that these organisms were living near a subduction zone that became activated during the Flood. You will recall that subduction zones are places where the ocean floor plunged into the Earth's interior—causing an almost unimaginable geological upheaval. If the mammals, birds and humans were living beside one of these zones, it is possible that their remains were completely destroyed by it. Another possibility is that the streams which watered the region around Eden (Genesis 2:6,10) might have been fed by one of the 'fountains of the great deep' which broke open during the Flood. If the mammals, birds and humans were living in this region, then the break-up of this spring may have resulted in their total destruction. The precise reason for the absence of this particular community from the Flood sediments awaits further insights from our research.

One strength of the ecological zonation theory is that it helps to explain some features of the fossil record that might otherwise be thought to support evolutionary theory. Earlier we referred to a study by Kurt Wise which found a significant agreement between the fossil order and the predicted evolutionary order in only five out of 144 test cases. But what about the five cases—one series of plants and four series of arthropods—in which there *was* agreement? Notably, in all five cases, the organisms were ordered in such a way that the sea-dwellers appeared 'lower' in the fossil sequence and the land-dwellers 'higher' in the fossil sequence. A global flood which

began in the ocean and then progressively overwhelmed the land would help to explain why some fossil organisms are found in this 'sea-to-land' order.

The ecological zonation theory also suggests alternative explanations for the handful of claimed 'transitional fossils'. For example, in the Palaeozoic sediments we find creatures that look like intermediates between fish and land animals.[16] They may well have been organisms living in pools and other watery environments associated with the 'floating forest' community— an environment that was

The fishlike tetrapod Acanthostega, and other similar animals, may have lived in shallow pools associated with the margins of the pre-Flood floating forest.[17]

itself intermediate between the sea and the land. Another classic example is the fossil series said to show a gradual transition from 'primitive' reptiles to the first mammals. This series may represent an ecological transition in the pre-Flood world from a reptile-dominated community to a mammal-dominated community—with the so-called 'mammal-like reptiles' living in between. The 'transitional sequence' in this case would be an artefact of the successive burial of these adjacent communities during the Flood.

The redistribution of organisms after the Flood would have led to much more mixing between different communities and competition for resources. Today's ecological zones appear not to be as well-defined as those that existed before the Flood. Furthermore, many fossil communities preserved in the Flood sediments are now partially or entirely absent from the modern world. These include the once-extensive stromatolite reef community, now represented by a few relics in salty pools or bays, and the dinosaurs, which have become extinct altogether. The floating-forest community also appears to have been unable to regrow in the much stormier seas of the post-Flood world. Our modern-day environments are ecologically impoverished when we compare them with the diversity of habitats that existed before the Flood.

A testimony to rapid burial

Another significant feature of the fossil record that is consistent with the Flood theory of geology is the pervasive evidence that fossils were formed rapidly. In modern environments, sediments are typically laid down too slowly to preserve fossils, but the abundance of well-preserved fossils in older sediments suggests that they must have been laid down quickly.[18] Here are some examples.

1. Fish

Experiments show that fish decay and become dismembered

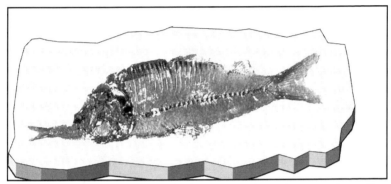

A fish fossilized while eating another fish. Specimens similar to this one are known from the Green River Formation of Wyoming, USA, and the Old Red Sandstone of Great Britain.

by currents and scavengers in a matter of days or weeks, even in oxygen-poor conditions. Yet the geological record contains many layers with millions of well-preserved fossil fish. A famous example is the Old Red Sandstone of Scotland.[19] It is sometimes suggested that these fish died in large numbers as a result of toxic conditions in the environment, but that does not explain how they also came to be buried and preserved. There are even specimens of fish that were fossilized in the middle of a meal.[20] In other cases, fish have been buried and fossilized so rapidly that even the delicate soft tissues have been preserved. The Santana Formation of Brazil contains fish whose gills and muscles are so perfectly preserved that geologists believe they were fossilized within five hours of death.[21]

2. Marine reptiles

The Jurassic sediments at Holzmaden in Germany are famous for their complete skeletons of sharks, fish and marine reptiles such as ichthyosaurs. Many of these skeletons have their skin preserved as a black carbon film. Hundreds of specimens of the ichthyosaur *Stenopterygius* have been found here, sometimes with stomach and intestine contents. There are even female ichthyosaurs fossilized while giving birth to young.[22]

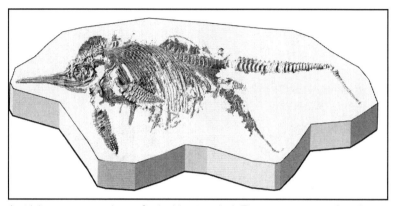

An ichthyosaur captured as a fossil while giving birth. This specimen came from Jurassic sediments near Holzmaden in the Württemberg region of Germany.

3. Whales

Hundreds of fossil whales have been found in layers of diatomite near Lima in Peru. Diatomite is a sedimentary rock composed mainly of microscopic algae called diatoms. In normal conditions, diatomite accumulates at a rate of only a few centimetres per thousand years. In this case, however, the whale carcasses must have been buried within a few weeks, or months, to account for the excellent state of preservation. Furthermore, the fossil whales are found at many levels throughout this diatomite deposit, not just a few 'mass kill' horizons, and this strongly suggests that the entire formation was laid down rapidly.[23] There are no known examples of diatomite accumulating so fast and in such quantities anywhere on the Earth today.

4. Dinosaurs

An expedition to Mongolia in 1971 made an extraordinary find of two dinosaurs, a *Velociraptor* and a *Protoceratops*, apparently fossilized in the middle of a fight.[24] The excavation revealed that the *Velociraptor* was in a typical attack posture and the *Protoceratops*

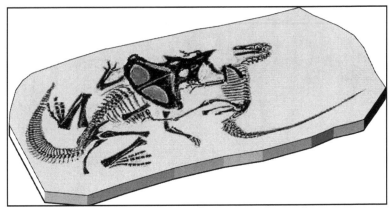

Two dinosaurs buried during a fight: the small plant-eating dinosaur, Protoceratops, was being attacked by the predatory dinosaur, Velociraptor, when both died together.

had been biting the right wrist of the *Velociraptor*. Remarkably, both animals were buried and preserved in this position.

5. Trilobites

More evidence of rapid burial comes from the study of fossil trilobites, an extinct group of marine arthropods. Trilobites look superficially like woodlice, and some species were able to roll up in a similar way for protection.[25] Many trilobites are found fossilized in this position, indicating that these animals were buried alive while trying to protect themselves.

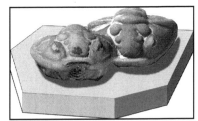

Two enrolled trilobites (Flexicalymene) from Ordovician sediments near Cincinnati, Ohio in the USA.

6. Crinoids

Well-preserved fossil crinoids (sea-lilies) also provide excellent evidence for rapid burial. Crinoids have a stalk, a body and long

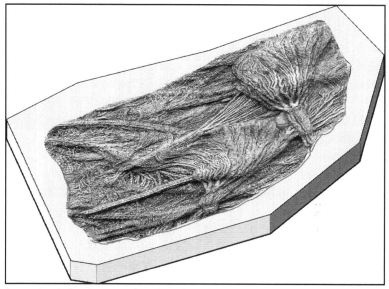

Intact crinoids like these must have been buried rapidly while the animal was still alive or soon after death.

'arms' made up of small calcium carbonate plates, called ossicles. When the creature dies, the soft tissues quickly decay and the ossicles begin to break apart. Experiments and observations of modern crinoids show that dead sea-lilies completely break up in a matter of days, even in still water.[26] Intact, or nearly intact, crinoids, such as those found in the Jurassic rocks of Dorset in southern England, must have been buried in sediment while the creatures were still alive or very soon after death.

7. Trees

There are countless examples of tree trunks fossilized in upright positions and sometimes penetrating multiple sedimentary layers.[27] They are especially common in coal-bearing sediments, such as those exposed in the north of England. Geologists explain the preservation of these trees by the rapid accumulation of sediments around them before the normal processes of decomposition could take place. Often, as in the case of the 'petrified forests' of Yellowstone National Park in Wyoming, USA, there is evidence that the fossil trees are not in the place where they originally grew, but were uprooted and transported into place before burial.[28]

Another important observation concerns *the proportion of modern-day species represented in the fossil record*. The conventional interpretation of the sedimentary rocks suggests that they were laid down over hundreds of millions of years, which means that average sedimentation rates throughout this interval must have been very low. All other things being equal, lower average rates of sedimentation will preserve fewer fossils, so if the conventional view is right, the 250,000 fossil species documented so far ought to represent a very low percentage of all the species that have ever existed.

On the other hand, if a significant proportion of the sedimentary rocks and their enclosed fossils were deposited rapidly, as in the Flood theory of geology, a much larger percentage of species should have been 'captured' in the fossil record. Observations suggesting that a very large percentage of modern species have a fossil record[29] are consistent with the creationist claim that the sedimentary layers were deposited much more rapidly than the conventional interpretation allows.

In the next chapter we continue our geological investigation with a look at some of the events that took place *after* the global flood— in particular the growth of the ice sheets that were responsible for many of the features of our present landscape.

15

The coming of the ice

The most recent geological event of extremely wide occurrence was the 'ice age' which took place after the global flood. During this time, the climate over the Earth's northern hemisphere deteriorated and ice sheets extended over much of North America and Europe, including Britain. Today there are only two large ice sheets on the continents—in Greenland and in Antarctica. However, we know that the glaciers were much more extensive during the ice age because the ice has left its mark on the landscape around us.

Many landforms produced by ice erosion can be observed in the mountainous regions of the north. Semicircular basins called corries were carved out around the highest peaks where mountain glaciers were born. Distinctive U-shaped landforms were produced as these glaciers moved down slopes, widening and deepening the sides of the valleys confining them. Ground-up debris carried by the ice scraped against the underlying rock, polishing it smooth and scouring out grooves marking the direction in which the ice was moving.

The lowland regions near the southerly margins of the ice sheets were, by contrast, blanketed with glacial sediments. Much of this material was in the form of till, an unsorted mixture of pebbles and boulders set within sand or clay, deposited directly by the ice

A classic U-shaped glaciated valley in the eastern Teton Mountains of Wyoming, USA.
Photograph © Michael J. Oard. Used with permission.

or by streams of melt water issuing from the glaciers. Hummocky mounds or ridges of till mark the place where the sides, or snout, of a glacier used to be. And scattered boulders of rock—called erratics—are sometimes found sitting directly on exposed bedrock where they were dumped by the melting ice sheets.

The requirements for an ice age

There seems little doubt that much of the present landscape of the northerly continents owes its origin to the former existence of these ice sheets. However, trying to explain how an ice age might have been started is not at all easy. The requirements for an ice age are a combination of much colder summers and higher snowfall.[1] Cooling is needed because an ice sheet will only develop where one

A ridge of glacial till in Clark Canyon, south-east of the Beartooth Mountains in the western Bighorn Basin of north central Wyoming, USA.

Photograph © Michael J. Oard. Used with permission.

winter's snowfall is not completely melted away during the following summer. However, cooling alone cannot generate an ice age because cold air holds less moisture—and that means less snow. We must also account for an abundant supply of moisture to maintain the snowfall. Furthermore, this unusual set of circumstances must persist for some time so that the snow can accumulate year after year and become compacted into an ice sheet.

The magnitude of this ice-age problem is often not appreciated. One attempt to simulate the conditions necessary to glaciate north-east Canada concluded that at least 10–12°C summer cooling and twice the present snowfall would be required.[2] Under uniformitarian conditions, in which the present is thought to be representative of the past, it is extremely difficult to see how an ice age could have been initiated. In fact, the problem is multiplied for conventional reconstructions of Earth history, according to which there was, not one, but a succession of perhaps fifty ice ages during the last 2.6 million years.[3]

So how did the ice age start? In this chapter we shall discover that the Flood of Noah provides the key that unlocks the mystery.

A wet post-Flood world

In chapter 13 we described the catastrophic rearrangement of the Earth's plates that took place at the time of Noah's Flood. During this event an enormous amount of heat must have been generated by the production of the new ocean floor. It is probable that some of this heat was lost to space as the fountains of the great deep erupted high into the atmosphere.[4] However, much of the heat would inevitably have been transferred to the ocean waters, with

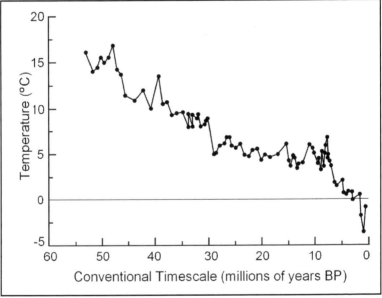

The cooling of the oceans over the conventional time interval from sixty million years ago to the present day ('BP' stands for 'before present'). In the creationist model this represents the period following Noah's Flood.[5]

the result that they would have been warm by the end of the Flood—perhaps as warm as 30°C.[6] Furthermore, the tremendous sea-floor upheavals would have thoroughly mixed the ocean waters so that they were uniformly warm from pole to pole and from top to bottom. Chemical studies of the shells of minute sea creatures buried in sea-floor sediments confirm that the oceans were once much warmer and have cooled down over time to the present average of 4°C.[7]

The warmth of the oceans after the Flood would have led to the evaporation of a great deal of sea-water into the atmosphere. All other things being equal, sea-water evaporates three times faster at 30°C than at 10°C and seven times faster than at 0°C.[8] As a result, the air over the oceans would have been full of moisture. As the moist air circulated over the continents, it would have cooled and condensed as heavy and prolonged rain.[9] This helps to explain why many of today's arid regions were once much wetter. Beneath the sands of the Sahara Desert, for example, there are ancient river channels, some as large as the Nile River Valley.[10] Fossil animals found there include aquatic and semi-aquatic creatures such as crocodiles and hippos.[11] Large lakes, some of which no longer exist today, developed in many areas. The famous Fossil Lake of the Green River Basin in Wyoming is one such example.[12] Another is Lake Manly, a 180-metre-deep (590-feet-deep) lake that once occupied California's Death Valley.[13] Many modern lakes are also known to have been more extensive in the past. The Great Salt Lake of Utah was seventeen times larger at its maximum extent than it is today[14] and Lake Chad in north Africa was nearly 1,000 kilometres (620 miles) long, requiring a water intake sixteen times greater than at present.[15] Indeed, it may have been the overfilling and catastrophic draining of two large lakes in the western USA that led to the rapid down-cutting of the Grand Canyon.[16]

The heavy rainfall after the Flood must have resulted in erosion and sedimentation on a massive scale and helps to account for many otherwise enigmatic features of the Earth's

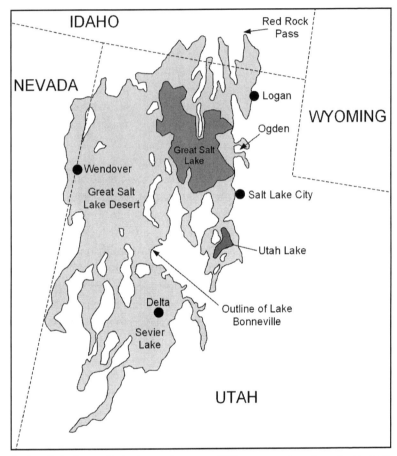

Ancient Lake Bonneville in the south-western USA was seventeen times larger at its maximum extent than its modern remnant, the Great Salt Lake of Utah.

surface. Consider pediments, for example, which are broad, flat wedges of sediment found at the base of many mountains. Pediments are apparently not forming today; rather, they are being gradually destroyed by modern-day stream erosion.[17] It seems that extensive sheet-flooding is necessary to produce them. Other features probably associated with the heavy run-off of rainwater at this time include widespread erosion surfaces called peneplains, thick wedges of river-deposited material called alluvial fans, and the extensive delta deposits found near the mouths of many modern rivers.

The beginning of the ice age

These unusual climatic conditions set the scene for the onset of glaciation. As the oceans cooled by evaporation, the moisture in the atmosphere eventually fell in the mid and high latitudes as snow. Where the snow was able to accumulate, ice sheets began to develop.

Several factors contributed to the accumulation of the snow. Perhaps the most important of these was volcanic activity, which was declining over time since its peak during the Flood but was still very energetic.[18] Before and during the ice age there were gigantic eruptions dwarfing any that occur today. More than sixty-eight falls of volcanic ash, coinciding with the ice age, have been identified in the western USA alone.[19] One exceptionally large ice-age eruption in New Zealand deposited a layer of ash over at least ten million square kilometres (almost four million square miles) of the South Pacific Ocean.[20] These eruptions injected huge amounts of volcanic dust into the atmosphere, which had a profound cooling effect by reflecting more of the Sun's radiation back to space. This resulted in much cooler summers than today. It has been acknowledged that a series of closely spaced massive eruptions could trigger a glacial episode by allowing snow to survive throughout the summer.[21] However, most scientists reject this idea because they think that the volcanic eruptions were spread out over too long a period. The biblical timescale, on the other hand, is sufficiently short for the mechanism to work.

Once a permanent snow cover had become established, the initial cooling would have been strongly reinforced.[22] Fresh snow reflects far more sunlight back to space than bare ground. Old or wet snow is less effective in this regard, but snowfall was high at

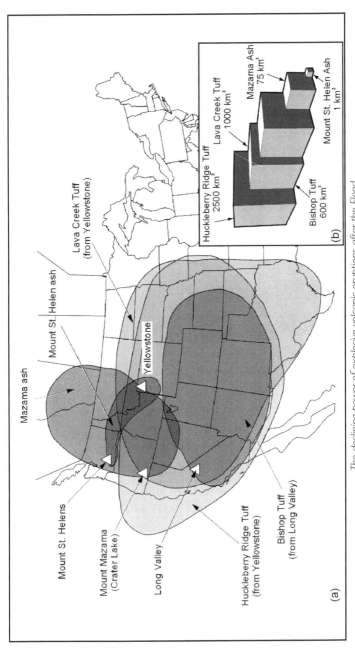

The declining power of explosive volcanic eruptions after the Flood
(a) The declining area of ash-fall beds with time in western North America
(b) The declining volume of the explosion products with time.[23]

this time, so the surface layer probably stayed fairly fresh. Another factor promoting cooling would have been an increase in cloudiness. The high rates of evaporation from the warm oceans would have led to much more cloudy skies and it is known that regional cloudiness results in cooler surface temperatures.[24] These factors—and others—combined to cause temperatures across the mid and high-latitude continents to drop significantly.

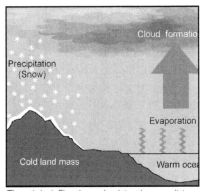

The global Flood resulted in the conditions needed to start an ice age—higher snowfall combined with cooler summers.[25]

In this way, the Flood of Noah provided the conditions necessary for the onset of the ice age—higher snowfall combined with cooler summers.

The peak of the ice age

Meteorologist Michael Oard has done much work to develop this model of a rapid, post-Flood ice age. He has shown that the temperature contrast between the cold continents and the warm oceans would have caused storm after storm to develop along the eastern coastlines of Asia and North America. The result would have been a 'snowblitz'—with ice sheets building up rapidly and simultaneously across very large areas.[26] This is in contrast to the conventional ice-age theory in which the glaciers first developed in the far north and then moved slowly southwards. Favourable areas for the early development of ice sheets were Canada, the north-eastern United States and East Antarctica. The mountains of Scandinavia, Greenland, West Antarctica and western North

America would also have been glaciated from the start. However, many areas close to, or surrounded by, the warm oceans, such as Britain and the lowlands of continental Europe, would have been too warm for the ice to build up at the beginning. In these regions, glaciation was delayed until the oceans had cooled sufficiently, although eventually ice sheets would have developed even in these areas.

One of the most surprising conclusions from Michael Oard's work is how rapidly the ice age would have developed under these conditions. Assuming an initial ocean temperature after the Flood of 30°C, he calculated that it would have taken between 174 and 1,765 years to reach the peak of glaciation—a very short time compared with conventional estimates. Oard's 'best guess' falls between these two extremes and is about 500 years.[27] If the initial temperature of the oceans was lower—say, 25°C or 20°C—the time to maximum glaciation would have been even shorter.

The thickness of the ice sheets after 500 years of glaciation would have depended on the amount of available moisture and how much of it was dropped on the ice sheets. There were two sources of moisture—the warm mid to high-latitude oceans and the water vapour transported in the atmosphere from lower latitudes. On the basis of estimates of the available moisture, Michael Oard has proposed that, on average, the ice would have been about 700 metres, or 2,300 feet, thick in the northern hemisphere and about 1,200 metres, or 4,000 feet, thick in the southern hemisphere.[28] This is considerably less than in the conventional ice-age theory, which assumes that the past ice sheets would have been comparable in thickness to the present-day Antarctic ice sheet (averaging about 2,100 metres, or 6,900 feet in depth). However, this assumption is based on the conventional idea that the ancient ice sheets built up over a long period. There is, in fact, a great deal of evidence suggesting that the ice sheet in North America was comparatively thin.[29] This helps to explain how some areas apparently stayed free from ice even though they were surrounded by glaciers.

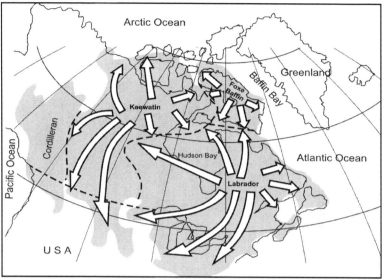

The ice-dome over Keewatin was one of two main centres of the ice sheet that covered North America. The other was over Labrador. The arrows show the proposed flow paths out from these ice-domes.[30]

It is significant that the post-Flood ice-age model is the *only* one that has been able successfully to explain the development of ice sheets where we know they once existed.[31] Consider, for example, the thick dome of ice that is known to have covered Keewatin, north-west of Hudson Bay in Canada, during the ice age. The only obvious source of moisture to develop a thick ice sheet in this region is the Arctic Ocean to the north. However, in the conventional ice-age model the Arctic Ocean was just as cold and covered with sea ice as today.[32] Consequently, Keewatin would have been too dry to develop an ice sheet. The post-Flood ice-age model resolves this problem because it proposes that the Arctic Ocean was initially warm and ice-free—thus providing a ready source of moisture for the growth of the Keewatin ice-dome.

An ice-free Arctic Ocean also explains why the lowlands of Siberia and Alaska escaped glaciation altogether. The mildness

The lowlands of Siberia and Alaska appear to have been relatively mild during the ice age and were home to many woolly mammoths and other large mammals.

of the ice-age climate in these areas has been problematic for the conventional model. However, in the post-Flood model, the warmth of the Arctic Ocean would have made these areas significantly warmer and wetter than they are today.[33] The North Atlantic and North Pacific Oceans would also have contributed to the warmth in these regions. As a result, the woolly mammoth and other ice-age mammals would have been able to live in these regions quite comfortably, with adequate supplies of food.

The end of the ice age

The post-Flood model also explains why the ice age came to an end. As the surface water of the ocean was cooled by evaporation, it became more dense and sank, to be replaced by warmer water from deeper in the ocean. This circulation would have ensured a steady supply of moisture for some time. However, the ice age would have started to wane when the temperature of the ocean reached a level at which it could no longer sustain the global build-up of ice. The amount of evaporation from the ocean surface would have declined, and the ice sheets would have stopped growing and started to melt. With less evaporation, fewer clouds would have formed and more sunlight would have penetrated to the land surface. How long would it have taken for the ice sheets to disappear? Oard's estimated melting rate is about ten metres (thirty feet) per year—comparable to the rates measured today in the melting zones of glaciers in Alaska, Iceland and Norway. At this rate, it would have taken about 100 years to melt the ice sheets near their margins and no more than 200 years in their interiors.[34] Thus, the total time for the post-Flood ice age, from the initial advance to the final disappearance of the ice sheets, was probably less than 700 years.

The rapid melting of the ice sheets appears often to have been associated with catastrophic flooding. One of the best-known examples concerns the broad network of deep channels etched into the hard bedrock of eastern Washington in the USA. These canyons were carved out, probably in a matter of hours, when glacial melt water from the former Lake Missoula burst through a dam of ice and catastrophically drained into the Pacific Ocean.[35] Recent sonar surveys of the floor of the English Channel— the narrow seaway between England and France—have revealed a similar network of large valleys which are thought to have been eroded by the catastrophic drainage of a large glacial lake. It has been proposed that large-scale discharges of glacial melt water may have been responsible for the permanent separation of Britain from mainland Europe.[37] Evidence

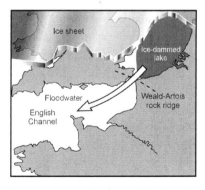

Deep scars on the floor of the English Channel were apparently cut by a sudden, massive discharge of glacial melt water. This catastrophic flood was probably responsible for separating Britain from mainland Europe.[36]

of similar glacial flooding has been found in many other locations around the world.

Another consequence of the disappearance of the ice sheets was a gradual drying of the atmosphere. Large dust storms appear to have developed south of the receding ice sheets, leaving behind the extensive layers of wind-blown dust and sand that are now found in the USA, across much of central Europe and in Siberia, Alaska and China. The changing climate was also a source of environmental stress for many of the large ice-age animals because several of them became extinct at the end of the ice age—perhaps, in some cases, helped along by man's hunting activities.

Not all the ice sheets would have melted at the end of the ice age. The ice sheets in Greenland and Antarctica continued to grow, protected from melting by their location in the polar latitudes and by the high altitude of the ice deposited there. It is sometimes claimed that cores drilled into these ice sheets since the 1960s have shown them to be many tens of thousands of years old. However, to identify annual layers in the ice cores correctly, some assumptions must be made about the amount of compression that has taken place since the ice was formed—and that depends on how old the ice is believed to be. In this case, our conclusions about time are governed by our prior assumptions about time. If the ice sheet is younger than conventional scientists believe, there has been less time for compression of the ice and each annual layer will be represented by a greater thickness of ice. What conventional scientists are counting as annual layers may, in fact, be individual storm layers or other weather cycles.[38]

Only one ice age

In some places near the margins of the former ice sheets, there are stacks of glacial sediments with non-glacial deposits in between. In the conventional model, these are interpreted as evidence of

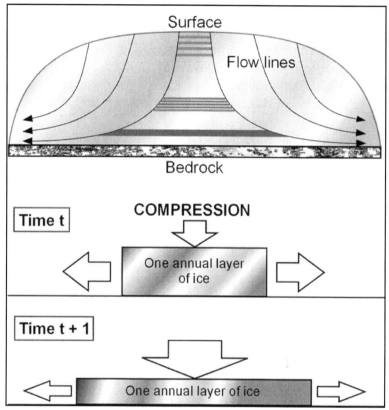

Annual layers of ice are compressed vertically and squeezed out horizon-tally because of pressure from the accumulating snow and ice above.[39]

multiple ice ages separated by warmer 'interglacial' periods. Unlike the conventional ice-age theory, however, the post-Flood model suggests that there was only one major episode of glaciation— perhaps better referred to as an 'ice advance' rather than an 'ice age'.[40] In this model, an alternative explanation for the stacked glacial sediments is that they were formed as the dynamic post-Flood ice sheets advanced and retreated, keeping track with variations in climate and the amount of volcanic dust in the atmosphere. Rapid oscillations of the ice-sheet margins would have produced layers of glacial sediment sandwiched between non-glacial material.

In fact, there are several lines of evidence which support the creationist theory of only one ice age.

1. One ice age seems inherently more probable than many

It is difficult enough to explain how the climatic requirements for an ice age might have been fulfilled once, let alone multiple times.

2. Most of the ice-age sediment has not been transported far

In the conventional ice-age theory, ice sheets developed many times over, with each successive advance transporting sedimentary material farther south. However, virtually all glacial sediments are of local origin, consistent with one ice sheet that grew in place and did not travel far before melting.

3. Most of the glacial sediment is from the 'last' ice age

The amount of material attributed to the supposed 'earlier' glaciations is very small. The conventional explanation for this is that each successive ice sheet erased the glacial deposits laid down previously. However, if this were true, we might expect a thick layer of 'reworked' sediment to mark the margins of the 'last' ice sheet—but there is little evidence of this.

4. The glacial sediment in the interior regions is much thinner than expected

In these regions, where many thick ice sheets are thought to have built up successively, we might expect to find a considerable amount of glacial sediment. However, even in these areas the sediment is fairly thin and often not all that extensive. For example, in Canada the glacial till is only two to ten metres (seven to thirty feet) thick and is found mainly filling depressions.[41] Compare this with the rate at which till accumulates today. In Glacier Bay, Alaska, it was estimated that till layers between one and five metres (three to fifteen feet) thick built up in about 200 years.[42]

5. Some areas within the glaciated regions are completely free of glacial sediments

The best-known of these areas are found covering south-west Wisconsin, small parts of south-east Minnesota and north-east Iowa in the USA. Other similar areas are the plains of north-east Montana and the extreme part of south central Saskatchewan. It is possible that one thin ice sheet might leave these areas unglaciated, but it seems exceedingly unlikely that many thick ice sheets would all miss these areas.

6. Nearly all the extinctions of large mammals occurred after the 'last' ice age

Very few are thought to have been associated with 'earlier' glacial episodes. Why did these animals survive up to fifty earlier ice ages, only to become extinct after the last? The pattern of extinctions seems more consistent with a single ice age.

In our final chapter, we turn our attention to the history of mankind—with a look at what happened to Noah's descendants after the Flood.

16

Confusion, cavemen and culture

Genesis 2:7 tells us that the creation of the first man, Adam, was a supernatural act on the part of the Maker of the universe. We are told that 'The LORD God formed man of the dust of the ground, and breathed into his nostrils the breath of life; and man became a living soul.' This verse of Scripture alone is sufficient for us to reject the idea that man came about by an evolutionary process. Man's body was specially created—it did not evolve.[1]

After creating Adam, God brought to him the animals and birds he had made to see what he would name them, but there was no suitable companion for Adam among them (Genesis 2:18-20). So the Lord God caused Adam to fall into a deep sleep, took part of his side and from it made a woman (Genesis 2:21-22).

Uniquely, these first two people were made in the image of God (Genesis 1:27). They were spiritual beings and could enjoy fellowship with their Creator. They had an understanding of right and wrong—and the capacity to obey or rebel. They were intelligent beings and could speak and exercise reason. Their offspring shared these characteristics. Adam would later call his wife Eve—'the mother of all living' (Genesis 3:20)—because from her the entire human family would be descended.

The Bible goes on to tell us that those living before the Flood were just as resourceful and creative as modern people. Among the children of Adam and Eve we find arable and livestock farmers (Genesis 4:2). Cain, their eldest son, built a city (Genesis 4:17). Other descendants were musicians and metal-workers (Genesis 4:19–22). According to the Bible, the characteristics of an advanced society were present from the earliest stages of human history.

Tragically, however, man's great sinfulness following the fall of Adam was also increasingly evident. In Genesis 6:5 the Lord indicted man with these sober words: 'Every imagination of the thoughts of his heart was only evil continually.' When the Flood came as a judgement upon mankind's increasing wickedness, the human population was reduced to just eight people—righteous Noah, his wife, his three sons and their wives (Genesis 7:7; 2 Peter 2:5).

The Tower of Babel

Upon leaving the ark, Noah and his family were commanded by God to be fruitful and increase in number and fill the Earth (Genesis 9:1). However, the former world had been destroyed and the descendants of Noah faced much that was unfamiliar (2 Peter 3:6). The landscape had been utterly transformed—lakes, rivers, mountains, and even the continents and oceans, were different. Furthermore, the upheaval of the Flood had brought about ongoing geological and climatic instability. This was now a world of explosive volcanoes, devastating earthquakes and whirling hurricanes.

This may help to explain the refusal of Noah's descendants to obey God's command to disperse. Perhaps they doubted God's covenant promise that he would never again send 'a flood to destroy the earth' (Genesis 9:11). Whatever the reason, while the animals were repopulating the new world, the people decided to settle

An artistic impression of the Tower of Babel, the location of the confusion of the languages.

on the plain of Shinar and set about building a city and a tower (Genesis 11:1–4).

This grand building project became a rallying point for the people's defiance of God. They wanted it to be a tower that reached to the heavens (Genesis 11:4). Perhaps it would have become a centre of idolatrous worship—a temple dedicated to the heavens instead of the one true God. By uniting in this purpose, they believed that they would make a name for themselves (Genesis 11:4). They would remain together and not allow themselves to be divided and scattered.

Since they were all descended from Noah's family, they had 'one language' and 'one speech' (Genesis 11:1). This enabled them to collaborate in a way that would not have been possible otherwise. The Lord saw that, while the people were united, there was nothing that would have been impossible for them and so, in his mercy, he determined to frustrate their plans by confusing their language (Genesis 11:6–7). In this way, God confounded them and caused them to be dispersed from Babel over all the Earth (Genesis 11:8–9)—just as he had always intended.

The origin of languages, cultures and races

The Babel incident had many far-reaching effects, including the origin of new languages, cultures and races.

1. *Languages*

Several different families of languages can be recognized today.[2] Since each of these groups appears to be distinct and well developed upon its first appearance, they may represent the language groups that were created at Babel. Since the dispersion, many changes have taken place within the language families, but the natural tendency is for languages to become simpler over time rather than more complex. Where languages have grown or increased in complexity, this is invariably the result of conscious and intelligent human input.[3]

2. *Cultures*

Similarly, archaeology confirms the rather sudden emergence of different cultures. Technological skills were brought into use with no apparent antecedents.[4] The oldest civilization is that of Mesopotamia, where the first cities were built, followed closely by Egypt, then India, China and South America.[5] These civilizations get successively younger the further they are from the probable location of Babel—which perhaps reflects human dispersion away from that region.

3. Races

With the confusion of languages, it is likely that different family groups would have moved away from one another, establishing new communities defined by language, culture and territory. Any physical differences that existed in the original population were divided up, with each family group being slightly different from the others. These groups, small and isolated, would have been subject to the random effects of gene assortment—what scientists know as genetic drift. This causes one characteristic to become dominant in a population even if it is no more advantageous than any other. In this way, different combinations of characteristics would have become 'fixed' in different people groups. Possession of certain characteristics may even have influenced where people chose to migrate. Light-skinned people may have avoided very hot regions where they would have been susceptible to sunburn and skin cancer; those with darker skins may have avoided places with little sunshine where they might have suffered from bone disorders such as rickets.[6]

This scenario, although admittedly speculative, seems to be consistent with the biblical account and the scientific evidence. It is important to note that the physical differences between the races are actually not that great. Each of us has the same skin pigment—melanin—and we differ only in the amount that our skin produces. There is no reason why such differences could not have arisen rapidly after Babel. Even today a range of skin colours, from light to dark, can be found in a single family provided that the parents have the right combination of genes.[7]

Cave people and the biblical record

Migration from the plain of Shinar after the Babel incident provides the context for understanding the fossil and archaeological record of humans. No doubt Noah and his family preserved a great deal of technological knowledge from before the Flood. We can assume that they would have passed this on to their descendants, so that the people at Shinar would have possessed a wide range of skills. But when the tribes began to migrate from Shinar, each took with them only a part of that knowledge.

Try to imagine what life must have been like for these families. It is likely that they would have been forced to adopt a 'primitive' lifestyle. Before they were able to find bodies of ore and extract metals from them, they probably turned to stone tools. Before they were able to settle down and build cities they probably sought shelter in caves and tents. Before they were able to manipulate their environment and become farmers they probably survived by hunting and gathering. In other words, these pioneers would have lived as we know the 'Old Stone Age' people did. But, over time, there would have been a general transition to more 'advanced' cultures— explaining the progression in the archaeological record from 'Old Stone Age' cultures to 'New Stone Age' cultures and beyond.

This transition may have taken place quite quickly—perhaps within a few hundred years at most. Conventional dating schemes suggest that these stages lasted thousands of years, but there are reasons to think that the timescale was much shorter. Consider, for example, *the low frequency of human fossils.* Human fossil remains from the 'Old Stone Age' are sparse. Even allowing for the vagaries of preservation and discovery, the low population numbers we can infer from the fossil record fit a short timescale better than a long one.[8] In Britain, for instance, there are only a handful of dwelling sites and virtually no human fossils for what, in the conventional view, represents the first 100,000 years of human occupation—a period twenty times the length of recorded history. We find a similar picture throughout Europe. This suggests that the conventional timescale is inflated and the actual period represented by these fossils was much shorter.

Another point to consider is *the persistence of stone-tool technologies.* In the archaeological record, stone-tool technologies tend to appear in a fully developed form, persist without much change for what is thought to be hundreds of thousands of years, and are then replaced by a succeeding or overlapping technology.[9] However, when we consider the capabilities of the people making these tools, it seems remarkable that their technologies would stagnate in this way. The apparent uniformity of these tools through time may cause us to question the conventional dates attributed to them.

What about the 'apemen'?

The evolutionary account of human history is very different from the biblical account. According to evolution, humans are descended from apelike ancestors who evolved upright walking as an efficient way of moving around the grassy plains of Africa several million years ago. Evolutionists point to a series of fossils which they believe document this transition.

The most completely known contender for the earliest member of the human lineage is *Sahelanthropus*—represented by a fossil skull discovered in Chad in 2001.[10] This skull, said to be about six to seven million years old, is quite small, but its discoverers say that it has a mixture of primitive and advanced characteristics. Others, however, have questioned the status of *Sahelanthropus* and regard it as an ancestral gorilla.[11] The other candidates are even more fragmentary.[12] *Orrorin* is the name given to fossils found in the Tugen Hills of northern Kenya estimated to be around six million years old. *Ardipithecus* is represented by two sets of fossils, mostly teeth and jawbones, from Ethiopia. In overall appearance, both *Orrorin* and *Ardipithecus* were probably very chimpanzee-like and there is little that distinguishes them as human ancestors.

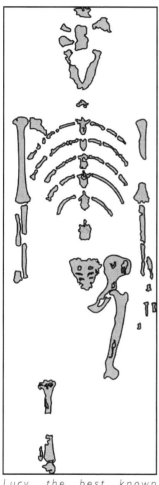

Lucy, the best known australopithecine specimen. Excluding the missing hand and foot bones, her skeleton is about 40% complete.

Next are the *australopithecines*—or 'southern apes'—which are said to have lived from about 4.5 million to two million years ago. The best known australopithecine is Lucy, a 40% complete skeleton unearthed at Hadar, Ethiopia, in 1974.[13] Lucy would have been only three and a half to four feet (105–120 centimetres) tall and very slender, although there were other southern apes that were more robustly built. They had small brains—between 300–400 cubic centimetres (eighteen to twenty-four cubic inches) for the slender forms and 400–500 cubic centimetres (twenty-four to thirty cubic inches) for the robust forms. This is comparable with chimpanzees and gorillas today. In many ways, the australopithecines were apelike. Nevertheless, an important ability is said to mark out Lucy's kind as different from other apes. These creatures had pelvis, leg and foot bones that suggest they may have walked bipedally (i.e. upright on two legs).[14] However, their style of upright walking would have been different from that of modern man, and it is likely that they were also able to climb trees acrobatically and move around on all fours.[15] A partial skull found in Kenya in 2001 and nicknamed the 'flat-faced man'—*Kenyanthropus platyops*—may be another variety of australopithecine.[16]

The australopithecines are thought by evolutionists to have given rise to the earliest members of the human genus, Homo. In 1960, Louis Leakey discovered fossil remains at Olduvai Gorge in Tanzania that were later named Homo habilis.[17] The name—which means 'handy, or skilful, man'—was given to these fossils because they were associated with stone tools. Other fossils, found at Lake Rudolf (now Lake Turkana) in Kenya by Richard Leakey in 1969, were also thought to represent early humans. There is much controversy about these fossils, partly because most of the remains are so fragmentary. Some authorities think that there are two separate species here—Homo habilis and Homo rudolfensis—while others consider the differences to be so slight that they classify both as Homo habilis. In terms of overall size and body proportions, locomotion, jaws and teeth, dental development and brain size, most of the fossils attributed to these creatures are similar to those of the australopithecines and unlike those of modern humans.[18] However, some of the fossils assigned to rudolfensis appear to be more human-like. An interesting example is skull KNM ER 1470. This specimen has an estimated brain size that approaches that of modern man (750–800 cubic centimetres, or forty-six to forty-nine cubic inches). Some also think that the inside of this skull reveals features associated in modern humans with language—an enlarged Broca's area (a part of the brain that controls speech) and a larger left side of the brain compared with the right side.[19] However, these interpretations are somewhat debatable and expert opinion remains divided.

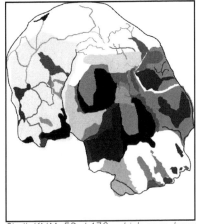

Skull KNM ER 1470, which may have belonged to a true human

Evolutionists believe that by 1.8 million years ago one of the early human populations had evolved into, perhaps, two new species—*Homo ergaster* ('action man') and *Homo erectus* ('upright man'). The *ergaster* fossils are mostly from East Africa, while the *erectus* fossils have been found in Africa, Asia and Europe. The two forms are quite similar, differing mainly in details of the skull. They had large brains, *ergaster* averaging about 900 cubic centimetres (30.55 cubic inches) and *erectus* about 1,100 cubic centimetres (sixty-seven cubic inches).[20] In 1984, Alan Walker and Kamoya Kimeu discovered the almost complete skeleton of a twelve-year-old *ergaster* in Kenya—nicknamed the 'Lake Turkana Boy'.[21] The boy would have stood five feet four inches (1.62 metres) tall and, had he reached adulthood, it is estimated that he would have been over six feet (2.08 metres) tall. His slender physique is reminiscent of the tribes living on the African grasslands today, such as the Masai. From the neck down he is essentially modern, although certain features of the skull are said to be 'primitive'. These include a sloping forehead, prominent brow ridges and a poorly developed chin.

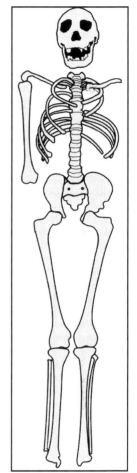

The Lake Turkana Boy, the most complete known specimen of Homo ergaster

One of the most astonishing discoveries of recent times was the 'hobbit'—*Homo floresiensis*—a diminutive fossil skeleton found in a cave system on the Indonesian island of Flores in 2003.[22] Known as LB1, the skeleton belonged to an adult, probably female, but was only one metre (three feet three inches) tall and had an extremely small brain size of 417 cubic centimetres (twenty-five cubic inches). The fossil, which was associated with evidence of stone-tool use, was conventionally dated to 18,000 years ago. Although some have dismissed the skeleton as belonging to an individual suffering from microencephaly (a disease causing an abnormally small body and brain), it seems more likely to be a dwarf form of *Homo erectus* or other human.[23]

Finally, *the Neanderthal people* are regarded as an extinct side-branch of the human family tree. They were a stocky and powerfully muscular people surviving in the harsh 'ice-age' conditions that once gripped northern Europe (which we examined in the last chapter). Their discovery dates back to 1856, when a partial skeleton was found in a limestone cave in the Neander River valley, near Dusseldorf.[24] Over the next few decades similar remains were found in many other cave sites across Europe, the Middle East and Asia. They had relatively short limbs and large, broad noses, perhaps related to the bitterly cold conditions in which they lived.[25] They also had low-domed skulls, somewhat like *Homo erectus*, but with an average brain size slightly larger than that of modern man.[26]

These fossils are usually interpreted from an evolutionary perspective, but the biblical framework provides an alternative way to understand them. In chapter 9 the concept of baramins, or basic types, was introduced. There is evidence that the species that make up each baramin are related; they are variations on a theme, expressions of latent genetic information built into each type. However, evidence for links between the baramins is lacking because each was separately created. We can apply this concept to the study of fossils thought to be of early humans.

It seems likely that *Homo erectus, Homo ergaster, Homo floresiensis,* Neanderthal man and certain of the *Homo habilis* fossils are members of the human baramin. They are united by skeletal structure, brain organization and culture. Even *erectus/ergaster* is associated with cultural remains suggestive of true humanity, such as tool manufacture, the controlled use of fire, the building of huts as dwellings and navigation of the sea in constructed vessels. Furthermore, in the fossil record there is no clear dividing line between *Homo erectus* and modern man; they appear to 'grade' into one another.[27] Thus we might conclude that these are all descendants of Adam, through Noah.

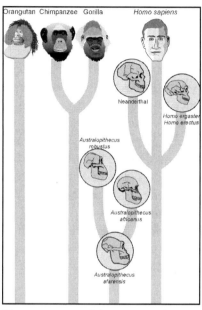

The ancestry of humans and apes interpreted from a creationist perspective. The australopithecines probably represent a unique group of primates unrelated to modern apes and human beings.

However, the australopithecines and the smaller-brained *Homo habilis* specimens appear to belong to a different baramin. They seem to have been peculiarly specialized primates, now extinct. They are best interpreted as unrelated to the human baramin, and perhaps distinctly different from modern apes too.[28] *Sahelanthropus, Orrorin* and *Ardipithecus* may belong to the same baramin as modern chimpanzees and gorillas.

In 1994, additional support for these conclusions came from computerized X-ray (CAT) scans of several fossil skulls. These scans revealed the structure of the semi-circular canals in the inner ear. The semi-circular canals are an organ of balance, and their shape and size in different creatures at least partly reflect modes of movement. Fred Spoor and colleagues were able to show that the australopithecines and certain *Homo habilis* fossils had apelike semi-circular canals (reflecting a predominantly tree-dwelling lifestyle), while *Homo erectus* had human-like semi-circular canals (reflecting upright walking).[29]

The biblical account also helps us to understand the order in which these groups appear in the fossil record. While the people banded together after the Flood, the animals were spreading across the face of the Earth in accordance with God's will. By the time the people began to disperse from Shinar, the animals would already have been widely distributed. Thus, animal fossils—including those of apes—would be expected to appear earlier in the record than human fossils.[30] Evolutionists interpret this as evidence that humans evolved from the apes, but it is also the fossil order that we would expect based on the Bible's account of history.

We can see that what the Bible tells us about the origin and subsequent history of mankind helps us to make sense of the evidence being revealed by science and archaeology.

Epilogue

We have now concluded our brief overview of the biblical and scientific data concerning origins. In the preceding chapters, I have sought to demonstrate that the insights provided by the book of Genesis are indispensable if we are to understand correctly how the universe, the Earth, living things and man himself came into being.

We have seen, firstly, that the book of Genesis provides us with *the facts of history*. The first eleven chapters of Genesis, written in the same style as the other historical books of the Bible, are full of genealogical, geographical and cultural detail—elements associated with narrative rather than poetry or parable. Furthermore, the historicity of Genesis is affirmed time and again by the rest of Scripture. There are two hundred quotations from, or references to, Genesis in the New Testament.[1] More than half of these references are from Genesis 1–11, and sixty-three are from the first three chapters. Twenty-five are from the lips of the Lord Jesus himself. The characters of Genesis 1–11—including Adam, Eve, Cain, Abel, Enoch, Noah and Shem—are referred to in the New Testament as real people; the events of Genesis 1–11—including creation, the Fall and the Flood—are referred to as real events. This surely has implications for our understanding of the origins and development of the world in which we live. If we do not take these statements of Scripture seriously, and seek to build upon the insights they give us, we will surely fail to glorify God in our thinking. We need to be those who seek to cultivate the mind of Christ in every area of life and study—including in the realm of origins.

Secondly, we have also seen that the book of Genesis provides us with *the framework for good science*. In order to study the world by the scientific method, we must presuppose three things: first, that the universe really exists and is not an illusion; second, that the universe can be understood because it operates by regular laws and principles; and, third, that the human mind is able to come to an understanding of the way in which the universe operates. None of these things can be proved to be true, but in order to 'do' science we must accept them by faith anyway. What is significant is that the Bible's account of origins uniquely provides us with the basis for accepting these presuppositions of science:

- The universe is real because God created it in the beginning (Genesis 1:1).
- It can be understood because God is a God of order and desires to be known through the things he has made (1 Corinthians 14:33; Romans 1:20).
- Man can understand the world because he alone was made in God's image and given dominion over the works of God's hands (Genesis 1:27–28).

Only the Bible—and the world view that it presents to us—provides this holistic framework for scientific study.

Furthermore, as we have seen throughout this book, the biblical record of the early history of the world helps us to make sense of the scientific evidence. Successful theories in cosmology, geology and biology can be constructed on the basis of what Scripture reveals to us. Of course, most of these creationist theories are in their infancy, and much work remains to be done to test and develop them. Nevertheless, when we take into account the fact that creationists have generally lacked the resources and manpower that evolutionary scientists have available when developing their theories, the scientific fruitfulness of these ideas has proved to be very encouraging.

Thirdly, there is one other thing that the book of Genesis provides for us. We have only touched upon it obliquely in this book so far, although it is really the most important thing of all. It is the fact that Genesis provides us with *the foundation to the Christian gospel*. This is ultimately why the question of origins is so important—because it has enormous implications for understanding who we really are, our relationship to God, the nature and consequences of our sin, and God's plan of salvation. In the first book of the Bible we are confronted with the sobering fact that the rebellion of the first man, Adam, brought God's curse upon mankind. As descendants of that first man, we have inherited his sinful nature and are likewise subject to God's righteous judgement. What is more, the Bible tells us that if we persist in our rebellion, we will one day be separated from God for ever. This is what the apostle Paul means when he speaks about the 'everlasting destruction' that will come upon those who do not know God (2 Thessalonians 1:8–9). The worst news of all is that, because we are spiritually dead in our transgressions and sins, there is nothing we ourselves can do to turn this situation around. We face the fearsome prospect that, left to our own devices, we are hopelessly lost and will spend an eternity shut out from God's presence and from all that is good.

But the Bible also brings us the supremely good news that God has taken the initiative to rescue sinful people by sending his only Son, Jesus Christ, into the world. Unlike us, the Lord Jesus Christ did not rebel against God. Instead, he lived a perfect and sinless life, fulfilling God's law in every way. And although he was without sin, he allowed himself to be executed on a cruel wooden cross, taking the fury of God's wrath in the place of sinful people. He paid the debt that was owed to God by those who had rebelled against him, so that they might experience God's forgiveness and pardon. What is more, the resurrection of Jesus Christ from the dead was God's seal of approval upon the sacrificial death of his Son. What an act of mercy on the part of God towards those who were his enemies! It opens the way for sinners like us to enter into a new life of fellowship with our Creator. We can now know the joy of having our sins forgiven and receive the hope of heaven to come.

This is the heart of the gospel message, but it is a message which only makes sense in the light of the foundational historical truths of Genesis 1–11. As the apostle Paul says in 1 Corinthians 15:21–22, 'For since by man came death, by man came also the resurrection of the dead. For as in Adam all die, even so in Christ shall all be made alive.' The death and resurrection of the real man, Jesus Christ, were necessary for salvation because of the actions in the beginning of another real man, Adam. One is logically founded upon the other. The issue of origins is so important because it has eternal implications for every one of us.

At the conclusion of this book, I want to urge you to consider the implications of what you have just read. If you, as a member of Adam's fallen race, have not yet personally come to Christ and trusted in him for the forgiveness of your sins, would you do so right now? It will be the most important thing you ever do. And if you have already trusted in Christ for salvation, I pray that your love for him as your Creator, Sustainer, Redeemer and King will have been deepened by what you have learned in this book and that you will continue to live, study and work for him, and for his glory alone.

Glossary

Abiogenesis. The concept that living organisms developed from non-living matter by purely natural processes.

Alpha decay. A type of radioactive decay which occurs by the emission of an alpha particle (two protons and two neutrons).

Altruistic genetic elements (AGEs). Mobile pieces of DNA that were originally created by God to co-operate with the genes of living organisms to produce rapid biological change.

Amino acids. The building blocks of proteins. Only about twenty amino acids are used to build the thousands of proteins needed by living cells.

Anthropic principle. The observation that the universe has all the necessary and narrowly defined characteristics to make man and his sustained existence possible; the view that the universe is conspicuously 'fine-tuned' for human existence.

Arthropods. A group of animals with hard external skeletons made of chitin, segmented bodies and jointed limbs. Insects, spiders, crabs, lobsters and trilobites are types of arthropod.

Astronomy. The scientific study of the planets, stars, galaxies and the universe.

Atom. The basic component of all matter. The atom is the smallest particle of an element possessing all the chemical properties of that element. Atoms consist of a nucleus of protons and neutrons surrounded by electrons.

Australopithecines. Extinct, small-brained and possibly bipedal (upright-walking) primates of the genus *Australopithecus.*

Bacteria. Single-celled micro-organisms which can exist independently or as parasites.

Baramin. A word meaning 'created kind'; a basic type of organism created separately from other kinds.

Baraminology. An explicitly creationist method of classifying and categorizing organisms proposed by Kurt Wise in 1990.

Bases. The chemical units (adenine, thymine, guanine and cytosine) in a DNA molecule that constitute the genetic code.

Basic-type biology. A method of classifying and categorizing organisms which uses hybridization to determine membership in basic types.

Beta decay. A type of radioactive decay which occurs when a neutron decays into a proton and an electron, with the emission of the electron as the beta particle.

Big Bang. The most widely accepted theory of the origin of the universe, which says that it began in a hot, infinitely dense state almost fourteen billion years ago and has been expanding and cooling ever since.

Biology. The scientific study of living organisms.

Black hole. A region in space where gravity is so strong that not even light can escape from it.

Breccia. A coarse-grained sedimentary rock composed of angular, broken fragments of pre-existing rocks, held together by a fine-grained matrix of sediment or mineral cement.

Catastrophic Plate Tectonics. A creationist theory similar to plate tectonics, except that most of the continental movement occurred rapidly during the Flood.

Catastrophism. The theory that a significant portion of the geological record of the Earth was formed during catastrophes of short duration.

Cenozoic Era. In conventional geology, the time between sixty-five million years ago and the present day.

Chimeromorph. Any organism which displays a mosaic distribution of character traits.

Chronology. The determination of dates and the sequence of events; the arrangement of events in time.

Cladistics. A biological classification system based on the order of evolutionary branching.

Class. A taxonomic group containing one or more orders.

COBE. A satellite (COsmic Background Explorer) developed by NASA to study the cosmic microwave background radiation.

Comet. A small solar-system object, composed mainly of ice, dust and rocky material, in orbit around the Sun.

Concordance. The situation when multiple dates for a rock or mineral sample agree with each other.

Conglomerate. A coarse-grained sedimentary rock composed of rounded fragments of pre-existing rocks, held together by a fine-grained matrix of sediment or mineral cement.

Convergence. The process by which a characteristic evolves independently in two or more groups of organisms.

Core. The central part of the Earth, thought to consist mostly of iron and nickel.

Cosmic microwave background radiation. Diffuse microwave radiation with an average temperature of 2.7 Kelvin, which pervades the whole universe. In conventional cosmology it is interpreted as the red-shifted remnant of the hot Big Bang that formed the universe.

Cosmology. The scientific study of the origin, evolution, structure and composition of the universe as a whole.

Creation. The model of origins that assumes that God created the universe.

Cross-bedding. A series of sedimentary layers inclined at an angle to the more nearly horizontal bedding planes of the larger rock unit.

Crust. The thin outer layer of the Earth, averaging about ten kilometres (six miles) thick in the oceans and up to fifty kilometres (thirty miles) thick on the continents.

Discordance. The situation when multiple dates for a rock or mineral sample disagree with each other.

Diversification. A rapid process by which a baramin gives rise to new species and varieties.

DNA. Deoxyribonucleic acid; the molecule that carries the genetic information in most living cells.

Eclipse. The darkening of the Sun when the Moon comes between the Sun and the Earth (solar eclipse), or the darkening of the Moon when the Moon is in the Earth's shadow (lunar eclipse).

Ecological zonation theory. A creationist theory which explains the succession of fossil organisms as a result of the ecological distribution of organisms before the global flood, rather than evolution over long ages.

Electron. A sub-atomic particle carrying a negative charge.

Element. A substance that cannot be broken down by normal chemical means into simpler substances. All atoms of an element have the same number of protons in the nucleus.

Erosion. The wearing away of the Earth's crust by the action of water, wind or glacial ice.

Evolution. The model of origins that assumes that all organisms on Earth descended from a common ancestor by natural processes of variation and selection.

Family. A taxonomic group containing one or more genera.

Floating forest. A unique ecosystem of aquatic and semi-aquatic plants thought to have extended around the margins of the pre-Flood supercontinent. In creationist theory, it was broken up and buried during the Flood, producing many of the world's coal layers.

Flood geology. A creationist sub-discipline which seeks to explain many features of the Earth's geological record by reference to the global flood.

Fossils. The remains or traces of animals, plants or other organisms that have been preserved in the Earth's crust.

Galaxy. A large assemblage of stars, gas and dust, typically containing millions to hundreds of billions of member stars. A galaxy is held together by the gravitational attraction of all its members on one another.

Gas giant. A planet much larger than the Earth and composed primarily of gas.

Genealogy. A list or family tree of ancestors or descendants.

Genetic drift. Random changes in gene frequencies in a population.

Genome. The total DNA for a given organism.

Genus (pl. Genera). A taxonomic group containing one or more species.

Geology. The scientific study of the origin, history and structure of the Earth.

Glacial. A cold period during which ice sheets build up; also referred to as an ice age.

Horizontal gene transfer. The process by which one or more genes are copied or transferred between organisms, other than by sexual reproduction.

Hybridization. The result of mating between two parents of different species or varieties. The offspring of hybridization are called hybrids.

Ice age. The period of time which saw the build-up of ice sheets on the mid to high-latitude continents. In conventional theory, there were numerous, successive ice ages during the last two million years. In creationist theory, there was one rapid ice advance shortly after the global flood.

Interglacial. A warm period between glacial episodes.

Isochron dating. A common method of radiometric dating which requires no assumptions about the initial amounts of daughter isotopes. This method can be applied to different minerals obtained from a single rock, or to several whole rock samples without any separation of individual mineral constituents.

Isotope. Forms of an element having the same number of protons but a different number of neutrons.

Junk DNA. Stretches of DNA that do not apparently code for genes.

Kelvin. A unit of temperature equal in size to the Celsius degree, but with the zero set by the absolute zero of temperature, $-273.15°C$.

Kingdom. The highest category in the taxonomical hierarchy (kingdom, phylum, class, order, family, genus, species).

Kuiper Belt. A large ring of icy objects beyond the orbit of Neptune. Some astronomers believe Pluto and Charon to be Kuiper Belt objects.

Light elements. Hydrogen, deuterium, helium, beryllium and lithium. In conventional cosmology, these are the chemical elements said to have been forged in the Big Bang.

Light year. The distance that light travels in one year—about ten trillion kilometres (six trillion miles).

Magnetic reversal. The process by which the Earth's magnetic north pole and its magnetic south pole reverse their positions.

Magnetic stripes. The alternating stripes of normally and reversely magnetized ocean floor arranged symmetrically either side of the mid-ocean ridges.

Mantle. The part of the Earth that lies directly below the crust and above the core. The Earth's mantle extends from a depth of about ten to fifty kilometres (six to thirty miles) to 2,900 kilometres (1,800 miles).

Mesozoic Era. In conventional geology, the time between 251 and sixty-five million years ago.

Mid-ocean ridge. A long mountain chain formed at the divergent boundary between two oceanic plates.

Mutation. A permanent structural alteration in DNA that can be transmitted from one generation to the next.

Natural selection. The process by which the individuals in a population that are best able to survive and reproduce in their environment pass on more of their genes to succeeding generations than other individuals.

Neanderthal man. An extinct, robust human of Europe and Western Asia.

Nested hierarchy. A hierarchical classification scheme involving levels which consist of, and contain, lower levels.

Neutron. A sub-atomic particle carrying no electrical charge.

Neutron star. The collapsed core of a star remaining after a supernova explosion.

Order. A taxonomic group containing one or more families.

Palaeozoic Era. In conventional geology, the time between 542 and 251 million years ago.

Parallelism. A literary device, common in the Psalms, in which grammatical or semantic elements repeat.

Parasite. An organism of one species that lives at the expense of an organism of another species.

Pathogen. A disease-causing organism.

Phylum (pl. Phyla). A taxonomic group consisting of one or more classes of organisms.

Planet. A spherical ball of rock or gas that orbits a star.

Planetary nebula. A shell of gas thrown out by a star near the end of its lifecycle.

Plate tectonics. The theory that the Earth's crust and upper mantle are divided into a number of rigid plates that move in relation to one another. The movements of these plates are involved in the generation of earthquakes, volcanoes and mountain ranges.

Precambrian Eon (or Supereon). In conventional geology, the time between

4,500 and 542 million years ago. Precambrian sediments are regarded as the oldest known, dating back as far as 3,800 million years.

Preformism. The outmoded belief that the embryo exists in the sperm or ovum as a diminutive adult and simply unfolds during gestation.

Primordial soup. The hypothetical ocean in which organic molecules were accumulating and where abiogenesis is said to have occurred.

Proton. A sub-atomic particle carrying a positive charge.

Radiohalo. A microscopic, spherical shell of discoloration in a mineral caused by the emission of alpha particles from decaying radioactive nuclei.

Radiometric dating. A set of methods for estimating the age of rocks and minerals using the relative abundances of radioactive and stable isotopes of certain elements.

Recapitulation. The idea that organisms retrace their evolutionary ancestry as they develop from a single cell to an adult.

Red giant. A large star with a relatively cool surface temperature that gives it a red appearance. According to the theory of stellar evolution, it is thought to represent one of the last stages in a star's lifecycle.

Red-shift. The displacement of electromagnetic radiation to longer wavelengths because the source of the radiation is moving away from the observer; the larger the red-shift, the faster the object is moving.

Red supergiant. A cool, red star that is at least eight times more massive than the Sun.

Reef. A mound-like structure built by marine organisms, especially corals, and consisting largely of their remains.

Retrograde rotation. Rotational motion which is backwards relative to the orbital motion possessed by an object.

Rhythmite. A repeating sequence of two or more sedimentary rock units—for example, alternating layers of siltstone and sandstone.

Runaway subduction. The process by which the ocean crust sank into the Earth's interior at rates of metres per second, initiating the catastrophic break-up of the continents during the global flood.

Sedimentary rock. A rock that was formed by the erosion of earlier rocks. The eroded sediment is transported into a basin and deposited in layers.

Solar nebula theory. The theory that the solar system evolved from a hot gaseous nebula.

Solar system. The Sun and the objects surrounding it, including planets, asteroids and comets.

Species. A population of interbreeding organisms that is reproductively isolated from other such populations.

Star. A large sphere of gas that produces its own light and heat.

Stratum (pl. *strata*). A sedimentary rock layer.

Stromatolite. A layered, dome-shaped structure usually thought to have been built by colonies of microscopic algae.

Subduction. The process by which one tectonic plate descends beneath another and is consumed in the Earth's mantle.

Supernova. The explosive destruction of a star triggered by the collapse of the star when its nuclear fuel is exhausted.

Taxonomy. The science of naming and classifying organisms.

Till. A sediment made up of pebbles and boulders set within sand or clay, deposited by a melting glacier.

Time dilation. An effect caused by gravity, or by acceleration, in which the rate at which time passes in one location will be measured differently by a clock located there and another clock somewhere else.

Toxin. A poison.

Transform fault. A fracture in the Earth's crust where two tectonic plates are sliding past one another.

Transitional forms. In evolutionary theory, transitional forms are the organisms that arose during the transformation of one group into another.

Turbidite. A distinctive sedimentary deposit produced by a turbidity current, a rapid flow of water and sediment down a very gentle slope under water.

Uniformitarianism. The concept that geological processes occur by the action of natural laws that are always the same, and by processes that can be observed today. Charles Lyell included the now-rejected concept that these processes are always slow and gradual.

Varves. Series of alternately fine and coarse sediment layers believed to comprise an annual cycle of deposition in a body of still water.

Vestigial organ. A remnant or vestige of a body part which was fully developed or functioning in an ancestral organism.

Virus. A disease-producing particle consisting of a coat of protein molecules surrounding a DNA or RNA genome. Viruses can only reproduce inside other cells which they parasitize.

White dwarf. A small, white star which, in stellar-evolution theory, forms when an average-sized star uses up its fuel supply and collapses.

White hole. A region of space from which matter and light emerge—in other words, the reverse of a black hole.

WMAP. A satellite (Wilkinson Microwave Anisotropy Probe) developed by NASA which has given us the first detailed full-sky map of the cosmic microwave background radiation.

Zircon. Mineral of zirconium, silicon and oxygen (zirconium silicate). Most commonly formed in igneous rocks.

Notes

Introduction

1. Henry M. Morris, *Men of Science, Men of God: Great Scientists Who Believed the Bible*, Master Books, El Cajon, California, revised edition, 1988.

Chapter 1—In the beginning

1. Various methods are used to estimate astronomical distances. All involve uncertainties, and actual distances in space may be considerably shorter or longer than current estimates. It seems conclusive, nevertheless, that the universe is immense.

2. Cited by Des MacHale, *Wisdom*, Prion Books, London, 2002.

3. Many examples are listed in Kurt P. Wise and Matthew S. Cooper, 'A compelling creation: a suggestion for a new apologetic', Robert E. Walsh (ed.), *Proceedings of the Fourth International Conference on Creationism*, Creation Science Fellowship, Pittsburgh, Pennsylvania, 1998, pp.633–44.

4. John D. Barrow and Frank J. Tipler, *The Anthropic Cosmological Principle*, Oxford University Press, Oxford, 1986.

5. Kurt P. Wise, *Faith, Form, and Time: What the Bible Teaches and Science Confirms about Creation and the Age of the Universe*, Broadman and Holman, Nashville, Tennessee, 2002, p.80.

6. Martin J. Rees, *Just Six Numbers: The Deep Forces that Shape the Universe*, Basic Books, New York, 2001.

7. James S. Trefil, *The Moment of Creation: Big Bang Physics from Before the First Millisecond to the Present Universe*, Collier Books, New York, 1983.

8. In fact, the galaxies are not thought to be moving away from one another *through* space; rather, the space between the galaxies is itself thought to be stretching.

9. Danny R. Faulkner, 'The current state of creation astronomy', Walsh (ed.), *Proceedings*

of the Fourth International Conference on Creationism, p.204. www.icr.org/research/ index/researchp_df_r01/

10. Karl Glazebrook, Roberto G. Abraham, Patrick J. Mccarthy, Sandra Savaglio, Hsiao-Wen Chen, David Crampton, Rick Murowinski, Inger Jørgensen, Kathy Roth, Isobel Hook, Ronald O. Marzke and R. G. Carlberg, 'A high abundance of massive galaxies 3–6 billion years after the Big Bang', *Nature*, vol. 430, 2004, pp.181–4. A. Cimatti, E. Daddi, A. Renzini, P. Cassata, E. Vanzella, L. Pozzetti, S. Cristiani, A. Fontana, G. Rodighiero, M. Mignoli and G. Zamorani, 'Old galaxies in the young universe', *Nature*, vol. 430, 2004, pp.184–7.

11. John Hartnett, 'Francis Filament: a large scale structure that is big, big, big bang trouble. Is it really so large?', *TJ*, vol. 18, no. 1, 2004, pp.16–17.

12. Jonathan Henry, 'The elements of the universe point to creation: introduction to a critique of nucleosynthesis theory', *Journal of Creation*, vol. 20, no. 2, 2006, pp.53–60.

13. John Byl, *God and Cosmos: A Christian View of Time, Space, and the Universe*, Banner of Truth, Edinburgh, 2001, pp.53–5.

14. As above, pp.42–75.

15. E. Lerner, 'Bucking the big bang', *New Scientist*, vol. 182, no. 2448, 2004, p.20.

16. www.cosmologystatement.org

17. According to the Bible, the Sun, Moon and stars were made on the fourth day *after* the creation of the Earth. However, according to the Big Bang theory, most stars formed *before* the Earth, and the Sun and Moon at about the same time as the Earth.

18. Illustration based on D. Russell Humphreys, *Starlight and Time: Solving the Puzzle of Distant Starlight in a Young Universe*, Master Books, Colorado Springs, Colorado, 1994, p.12.

19. D. Russell Humphreys, 'A biblical basis for creationist cosmology', Robert E. Walsh (ed.), *Proceedings of the Third International Conference on Creationism*, Creation Science Fellowship, Pittsburgh, Pennsylvania, 1994, pp.255–66.

20. D. Russell Humphreys, 'Progress toward a young-earth relativistic cosmology', Walsh (ed.), *Proceedings of the Third International Conference on Creationism*, pp.267–86.

21. D. Russell Humphreys, 'Our galaxy is the centre of the universe, "quantized" red shifts show', *TJ*, vol. 16, no. 2, 2002, pp.95–104. www.answersingenesis.org/tj/v16/i2/galaxy.asp www.answersingenesis.org/home/area/magazines/tj/docs/TJv16n2_CENTRE.pdf

22. John Hartnett, 'New evidence: we really are at the centre of the universe', *TJ*, vol. 18, no. 1, 2004, p.9.

23. Humphreys, *Starlight and Time* (see note 18 above for full details).

24. John Hartnett, *Starlight, Time and the New Physics*, Creation Book Publishers, Powder Springs, Georgia, 2007.

25. Danny Faulkner, *Universe by Design: An Explanation of Cosmology and Creation*, Master Books, Green Forest, Arkansas, 2004. Alex Williams and John Hartnett, *Dismantling the Big Bang: God's Universe Rediscovered*, Master Books, Green Forest, Arkansas, 2005.

Chapter 2—The Sun, Moon and stars

1. John C. Whitcomb and Donald B. DeYoung, *The Moon: Its Creation, Form and Significance*, Baker Book House, Grand Rapids, Michigan, 1978, p.132.

2. Stuart Burgess, *He Made the Stars Also: What the Bible Says about the Stars*, Day One Publications, 2001, pp.72–6.

3. Michael A. Seeds, *Astronomy: The Solar System and Beyond*, Brooks/Cole, Pacific Grove, California, second edition, 2001, p.278.

4. As above, p.232.

5. In other words, about 70,000 million million million stars (See David Derbyshire, 'More stars at night than grains of sand', *The Daily Telegraph*, 23 July 2003, p.11). A team of astronomers, led by Dr Simon Driver of the Australian National University, came up with the estimate by counting the number of galaxies in one small region and extrapolating for the entire night sky.

6. Danny R. Faulkner and Don B. DeYoung, 'Toward a creationist astronomy', *Creation Research Society Quarterly*, vol. 28, no. 3, 1991, pp.87–91. www.creationresearch.org/crsq/articles/28/28_3/starevol.html

7. Robert Newton, '"Missing" neutrinos found! No longer an "age" indicator', *TJ*, vol. 16, no. 3, 2002, pp.123–5.

8. Humphreys, 'Progress toward a young-earth relativistic cosmology', p.284.

9. Danny R. Faulkner, 'Does the collapse of a gas cloud to form a star violate the second law of thermodynamics?', *Creation Research Society Quarterly*, vol. 38, no. 1, 2001, pp.40–44.

10. J. Timothy Unruh, 'The greater light to rule the day: ladies and gentlemen—the sun!', *Institute for Creation Research Impact Article 263*, May 1995. www.icr.org/article/392/

11. As above.

12. Jonathan Henry, 'The sun is not an average star', *TJ*, vol. 17, no. 3, 2003, pp.35–42.

13. S. P. Maran, 'When all hell breaks loose on the sun, astronomers scramble to understand', *Smithsonian*, vol. 20, no. 12, 1990, p.37.

14. Charles Seife, 'Thank our lucky star', *New Scientist*, vol. 161, no. 2168, 1999, p.15.

15. Whitcomb and DeYoung, *The Moon*, pp.130–32.

16. Seeds, *Astronomy*, pp.24–5.

17. Danny R. Faulkner, 'The angular size of the Moon and other planetary satellites. An argument for design', *Creation Research Society Quarterly*, vol. 35, no. 1, 1998, pp.23–6. www.creationresearch.org/crsq/articles/35/astrodesign.html

18. Whitcomb and DeYoung, *The Moon*, pp.138–40.

19. Nigel Henbest, *The Planets*, Viking, London, 1992, p.58.

20. R. Jayawardhana, 'Deconstructing the moon', *Astronomy*, vol. 26, no. 9, 1998, pp.40–45.

21. S. Ida, R. M. Canup and G. R. Stewart, 'Lunar accretion from an impact-generated disk', *Nature*, vol. 389, 1997, pp.353–7.

22. J. J. Lissauer, 'It's not easy to make the moon', *Nature*, vol. 389, 1997, pp.327–8.

23. Charles M. Duke, in a letter dated 28 November 1979 to John C. Whitcomb and Donald B. DeYoung, authors of *The Moon*.

24. James B. Irwin, in an address to the Evangelical Christian Baptist Church in Moscow, June 1979. An abridged version of his address can be found in Eric C. Barrett and David Fisher (eds.), *Scientists Who Believe*, Scripture Press Foundation, Amersham, Buckinghamshire, 1986, pp.102–8.

Chapter 3—There's no place like home

1. There is a popular idea which says that Genesis 1:2 records the re-creation of the world following the destruction of a former creation. However, this theory seems to be based upon a mistaken understanding of the Hebrew text. See Weston W. Fields, *Unformed and Unfilled—A Critique of the Gap Theory*, Burgener Enterprises, Collinsville, Illinois, 1976.

2. Jeff Foust, 'Keck offers sharpest view of Uranus', *Astronomy Now*, vol. 19, no. 1, 2005, p.14.

3. David Stevenson of Caltech, quoted by Richard A. Kerr, 'The solar system's new diversity', *Science*, vol. 265, 1994, p.1360.

4. A geologist with the U. S. Geological Survey, quoted by Kerr, 'The solar system's new diversity'.

5. J. F. Kerridge and James F. Vedder, 'Accretionary processes in the early solar system: an experimental approach', *Science*, vol. 177, 1972, p.161.

6. T. Montmerle, J.-C. Augereau, M. Chaussidon, M. Gounelle, B. Marty and

A. Morbidelli, 'Solar system formation and early evolution: the first 100 million years', *Earth, Moon and Planets*, vol. 98, nos. 1–4, 2006, pp.39–95.

7.   Paul M. Steidl, *The Earth, the Stars, and the Bible*, Presbyterian and Reformed Publishing Company, Phillipsburg, New Jersey, 1979, pp.112–14.

8.   Paul M. Steidl, 'Planets, comets, and asteroids', George Mulfinger (ed.), *Design and Origins in Astronomy*, Creation Research Society Books, Terre Haute, Indiana, 1983, pp.73–106.

9.   As above, p.99.

10. Danny Faulkner, 'A biblically-based cratering theory', *TJ*, vol. 13, no. 1, 1999, pp.100–104. www.answersingenesis.org/tj/v13/i1/crater.asp

11. Venus is 12,104 kilometres (7,521 miles) in diameter and has a mean distance from the Sun of 108.2 million kilometres (67.2 million miles). The Earth is 12,756 kilometres (7,926.2 miles) in diameter and has a mean distance from the Sun of 149.6 million kilometres (ninety-three million miles). See: Danny R. Faulkner, 'The Goldilocks planet—the Earth compared with Mars and Venus', *Origins* (Biblical Creation Society), no. 37/38, 2004, pp.20–21.

12. Naomi Lubick, 'Goldilocks and the three planets', *Astronomy*, vol. 31, no. 7, 2003, pp.36–41.

13. Stuart E. Nevins, 'Planet Earth: plan or accident', *Institute for Creation Research Impact Article 14*, May 1974. www.icr.org/article/61/

14. As above.

15. Don B. DeYoung, *Astronomy and Creation: An Introduction*, Creation Research Society Books, Ashland, Ohio, 1995, p.21.

16. As above, p.19.

17. Don B. DeYoung, 'The water of life', *Creation Research Society Quarterly*, vol. 22, no. 3, 1985, pp.107–14.

18. Nevins, 'Planet Earth'.

Chapter 4—A matter of days

1.   Andrew S. Kulikovsky, 'A critique of the literary framework view of the days of creation', *Creation Research Society Quarterly*, vol. 37, no. 4, 2001, pp.237–44.

2.   Henry M. Morris, *The Biblical Basis for Modern Science*, Baker Book House, Grand Rapids, Michigan, 1984, pp.119–21.

3.   Gerhard F. Hasel, 'The "days" of creation in Genesis 1: literal "days" or figurative

"periods/epochs" of time?', *Origins* (Geoscience Research Institute), vol. 21, no. 1, 1994, pp.5–38. www.grisda.org/origins/21005.htm

4.   Russell Grigg, 'Morning has broken ... but when?', *Creation*, vol. 23, no. 2, 2001, p.52.

5.   This is not to deny that Genesis includes occasional lyrical verses (e.g. Genesis 1:27) and figures of speech (e.g. Genesis 3:14), but the overall genre of the book is not poetry. The contrast is obvious when comparing Genesis 1 with an actual poetic account of creation such as that found in Psalm 104.

6.   David M. Fouts, 'The genre of Genesis One', Robert L. Ivey (ed.), *Proceedings of the Fifth International Conference on Creationism*, Creation Science Fellowship, Pittsburgh, 2003, pp.409–16.

7.   James Stambaugh, 'The days of creation: a semantic approach', *Creation Ex Nihilo Technical Journal*, vol. 5, no. 1, 1991, pp.70–78. www.answersingenesis.org/tj/v5/i1/semantic.asp

8.   As above, p.72.

9.   As above.

10.   Jonathan Sarfati, *Refuting Compromise*, Master Books, Green Forest, Arkansas, 2004, pp.326–8.

11.   Andy McIntosh, *Genesis for Today*, Day One Publications, 1997, pp.39–40.

12.   Hasel, 'The "days" of creation in Genesis 1', pp.28–30.

13.   As above, pp.11–14.

14.   Russell Grigg, 'Naming the animals: all in a day's work for Adam', *Creation*, vol. 18, no. 4, 1996, pp.46–9.

15.   Andrew S. Kulikovsky, 'God's rest in Hebrews 4:1–11', *TJ*, vol. 13, no. 2, 1999, pp.61–2. www.answersingenesis.org/tj/v13/i2/rest.asp

16.   David C. C. Watson, *The Great Brain Robbery: Creation or Evolution?*, privately published, 1975, p.93.

17.   Jonathan Sarfati, 'Biblical chronogenealogies', *TJ*, vol. 17, no. 3, 2003, pp.14–18. www.answersingenesis.org/tj/v17/i3/chronogenealogies.asp

18.   Richard Niessen, 'A biblical approach to dating the Earth: a case for the use of Genesis 5 and 11 as an exact chronology', *Creation Research Society Quarterly*, vol. 19, no. 1, 1982, pp.60–66.

19.   Henry M. Morris, *The Genesis Record: A Scientific and Devotional Commentary on the Book of Beginnings*, Baker Book House, Grand Rapids, Michigan, 1976, pp.159–60.

20.   Jonathan Sarfati, 'What about Cainan?', *TJ*, vol. 18, no. 2, 2004, pp.41–3.

21.   For example J. A. Young, 'Septugintal versus Masoretic chronology in Genesis 5 and

11', Ivey (ed.), *Proceedings of the Fifth International Conference on Creationism*, 2003, pp.417–30.

22. The superiority of the Hebrew Masoretic text over the Greek Septuagint and the Samaritan Pentateuch has been argued by Pete J. Williams, 'Some remarks preliminary to a biblical chronology', *Creation Ex Nihilo Technical Journal*, vol. 12, no. 1, 1998, pp.98–106. www.answersingenesis.org/tj/v12/i1/chronology.asp

23. Sarfati, *Refuting Compromise*, pp.107–39.

24. William R. Brice, 'Bishop Ussher, John Lightfoot and the age of creation', *Journal of Geological Education*, vol. 30, 1982, pp.18–24.

25. John Bimson, *(When) Did It Happen? New Contexts for Old Testament History*, Grove Books, Cambridge, 2003.

Chapter 5—Is the present the key to the past?

1. Throughout the first half of the 1800s, a group of naturalists and clergymen—who became known as the Scriptural geologists, or Mosaic geologists—opposed the new geological theories. Largely overlooked by modern historians, they defended Genesis 1–11 as a reliable historical account, including Noah's Flood as a unique global catastrophe, and opposed the concept of long geological ages. See Terry Mortenson, 'The early 19th century British "Scriptural Geologists": opponents of the emerging old-earth theories of geology', Ivey (ed.), *Proceedings of the Fifth International Conference on Creationism*, pp.539–50.

2. Much of the historical information in this chapter is drawn from a paper presented at the Sixth European Creationist Congress in Amersfoort, the Netherlands, in August 1995. See David J. Tyler, 'Religious and philosophical inputs to geochronology'. www. biblicalcreation.org.uk/scientific_issues/bcs080.html

3. M. J. S. Rudwick, *The Meaning of Fossils: Episodes in the History of Palaeontology*, Macdonald & Co. (Publishers) Limited, London, 1972, p.78.

4. As above, p.82.

5. As above, p.93.

6. Davis A. Young, *The Biblical Flood: A Case Study of the Church's Response to Extrabiblical Evidence*, William B. Eerdmans Publishing Company, Grand Rapids, Michigan, 1995, p.101.

7. James Hutton, *Theory of the Earth, with Proofs and Illustrations*, 2 vols., facsimile reprint, Weinheim and Codicote, 1959 (first published 1795).

8. Charles Lyell, *Principles of Geology, being an attempt to explain the former changes of the earth's surface, by reference to causes now in operation*, 3 vols., facsimile reprint, New York, 1970 (first published 1830–1833).

9.   K. M. Lyell (ed.), *Life, Letters and Journals of Sir Charles Lyell, Bart.*, vol. 1, John Murray, London, 1881, p.268.

10. Ariel A. Roth, 'Turbidites', *Origins* (Geoscience Research Institute), vol. 2, no. 2, 1975, pp.106–7. www.grisda.org/origins/02106.htm

11. Arthur V. Chadwick, 'Megabreccias: evidence for catastrophism', *Origins* (Geoscience Research Institute), vol. 5, no. 1, 1978, pp.39–46. www.grisda.org/origins/05039.htm

12. Steven A. Austin (ed.), *Grand Canyon: Monument to Catastrophe*, Institute for Creation Research, Santee, California, 1994, pp.33–5.

13. Derek V. Ager, *The Nature of the Stratigraphical Record*, second edition, Macmillan, 1981, pp.1–2.

14. Arthur V. Chadwick, 'Megatrends in North American paleocurrents', *Symposium on Paleogeography and Paleoclimatology*, Society of Sedimentary Geologists, SEPM Abstracts with Program, vol. 8, 1993, p.5815. See also: http://origins.swau.edu/papers/global/paleocurrents/default.html http://geology.swau.edu/paleocurrents_1.html

15. Illustration based on Michael Garton, 'Rocks and Scripture: the millions of years time-scale and some geological common sense', *Origins* (Biblical Creation Society), vol. 6, no. 15, 1993, p.20.

16. Ariel A. Roth, 'Those gaps in the sedimentary layers', *Origins* (Geoscience Research Institute), vol. 15, no. 2, 1988, pp.75–92. www.grisda.org/origins/15075.htm

17. Garton, 'Rocks and Scripture', pp.17–23.

18. M. O. Hayes, 'Hurricanes as geological agents: case studies of Hurricanes Carla, 1961, and Cindy, 1963', *University of Texas, Bureau of Economic Geology, Report of Investigation Number 61*, 1967.

19. Robert H. Dott, '1982 SEPM Presidential Address: Episodic sedimentation—how normal is average? How rare is rare? Does it matter?', *Journal of Sedimentary Petrology*, vol. 53, no. 1, 1983, p.12.

20. Steven A. Austin, 'Mount St Helens and catastrophism', *Proceedings of the First International Conference on Creationism*, vol. I, 'Basic and Educational Sessions', Creation Science Fellowship, Pittsburgh, 1986, pp.3–9.

21. A. Lambert and K. Hsü, 'Non-annual cycles of varve-like sedimentation in Walensee, Switzerland', *Sedimentology*, vol. 26, 1979, pp.453–61.

22. Ariel A. Roth, 'Fossil reefs and time', *Origins* (Geoscience Research Institute), vol. 22, no. 2, 1995, pp.86–104. www.grisda.org/origins/22086.htm

Chapter 6—The clock that ran fast

1.   Andrew A. Snelling, 'Geochemical processes in the mantle and crust', Larry Vardiman, Andrew A. Snelling and Eugene F. Chaffin (eds.), *Radioisotopes and the Age of the Earth: A Young-Earth*

Creationist Research Initiative, Institute for Creation Research, El Cajon, California and Creation Research Society, St Joseph, Missouri, 2000, pp.123–304.

2. As above.

3. Illustration based on Kenneth R. Miller, 'Scientific creationism versus evolution: the mislabeled debate', Ashley Montagu (ed.), *Science and Creationism*, Oxford University Press, Oxford, 1984, p.29.

4. D. Russell Humphreys, 'Accelerated nuclear decay: a viable hypothesis?', Vardiman, Snelling and Chaffin (eds.), *Radioisotopes and the Age of the Earth*, 2000, pp.333–79.

5. For instance, a study of Miocene age volcanic glass revealed thousands of times more fission tracks than could be accounted for in thousands of years at today's rates. See Joseph W. Bielecki, 'Search for accelerated nuclear decay with spontaneous fission of ^{238}U', Walsh (ed.), *Proceedings of the Fourth International Conference on Creationism*, pp.79–88.

6. G. Brent Dalrymple, *The Age of the Earth*, Stanford University Press, Stanford, California, 1991, pp.376–87.

7. The 676-page volume that 'set the stage' for the RATE project was Vardiman, Snelling and Chaffin (eds.), *Radioisotopes and the Age of the Earth* (see note 1 above for full details).

8. Larry Vardiman, Andrew A. Snelling and Eugene F. Chaffin (eds.), *Radioisotopes and the Age of the Earth: Results of a Young-Earth Creationist Research Initiative*, Institute for Creation Research, El Cajon, California and Creation Research Society, Chino Valley, Arizona, 2005.

9. Don DeYoung, *Thousands … Not Billions: Challenging an Icon of Evolution, Questioning the Age of the Earth*, Master Books, Green Forest, Arkansas, 2005.

10. Steven A. Austin, 'Do radioisotope clocks need repair? Testing the assumptions of isochron dating using K-Ar, Rb-Sr, Sm-Nd, and Pb-Pb isotopes', Vardiman, Snelling and Chaffin (eds.), *Radioisotopes and the Age of the Earth: Results …* , pp.325–92.

11. As above.

12. Andrew A. Snelling, 'Isochron discordances and the role of inheritance and mixing of radioisotopes in the mantle and crust', Vardiman, Snelling and Chaffin (eds.), *Radioisotopes and the Age of the Earth: Results …*, pp.393–524.

13. Larry Vardiman, Steven A. Austin, John R. Baumgardner, Steven W. Boyd, Eugene F. Chaffin, Donald B. DeYoung, D. Russell Humphreys and Andrew A. Snelling, 'Summary of evidence for a young Earth from the RATE project', Vardiman, Snelling and Chaffin (eds.), *Radioisotopes and the Age of the Earth: Results…*, pp.735–72.

14. Andrew A. Snelling, *Radioactive Dating: Research Confirming the Biblical Record*, The Genesis Agendum Occasional Paper 8, 2003, pp.13–14.

15. Illustration based on D. Russell Humphreys, 'Young helium diffusion age of zircons supports accelerated nuclear decay', Vardiman, Snelling and Chaffin (eds.), *Radioisotopes and the Age of the Earth: Results...*, p.27.

16. Illustration based on D. Russell Humphreys, 'Accelerated nuclear decay: a viable hypothesis?', Vardiman, Snelling and Chaffin (eds.) *Radioisotopes and the Age of the Earth*, p.345.

17. R. V. Gentry, G. L. Glish and E. H. McBay, 'Differential helium retention in zircons: implications for nuclear waste containment', *Geophysical Research Letters*, vol. 9, 1982, pp.1129–30.

18. The actual reported helium diffusion age is 5,681 ± 1,999 years. See D. Russell Humphreys, Steven A. Austin, John R. Baumgardner and Andrew A. Snelling, 'Helium diffusion age of 6,000 years supports accelerated nuclear decay', *Creation Research Society Quarterly*, vol. 41, no. 1, 2004, pp.1–16. www.creationresearch.org/crsq/articles/41/41_1/Helium.htm

19. Illustration based on DeYoung, *Thousands ... Not Billions*, p.74

20. Andrew A. Snelling, 'Radiohalos in granites: evidence for accelerated nuclear decay', Vardiman, Snelling and Chaffin (eds.), *Radioisotopes and the Age of the Earth: Results...*, pp.101–207.

21. Andrew A. Snelling, 'Radiohalos: startling evidence of catastrophic geologic processes on a young Earth', *Creation*, vol. 28, no. 2, 2006, pp.46–50.

22. Vardiman, Austin, Baumgardner, Boyd, Chaffin, DeYoung, Humphreys and Snelling, 'Summary of evidence ... from the RATE project', pp.761–4.

23. Eugene F. Chaffin, 'Accelerated decay: theoretical considerations', Vardiman, Snelling and Chaffin (eds.), *Radioisotopes and the Age of the Earth: Results...*, pp.525–85.

24. Vardiman, Austin, Baumgardner, Boyd, Chaffin, DeYoung, Humphreys and Snelling, 'Summary of evidence ... from the RATE project', pp.764–5.

Chapter 7—A youthful creation

1. D. W. Hughes, 'The variation of short-period comet size and decay rate with perihelion distance', *Monthly Notices of the Royal Astronomical Society*, vol. 346, 2003, pp.584–92.

2. The latest observations are recorded in *The Kuiper Belt Electronic Newsletter* at www.boulder.swri.edu/ekonews/

3. G. M. Bernstein, D. E. Trilling, R. L. Allen, M. E. Brown, M. Holman and R.

Malhotra, 'The size distribution of trans-neptunian bodies', *Astronomical Journal*, vol. 128, no. 3, 2004, pp.1364–90.

4. Bill Worraker, 'Missing: a source of short-period comets', *TJ*, vol. 18, no. 2, 2004, pp.121–7.

5. Harold S. Slusher and Stephen J. Robertson, *The Age of the Solar System: A Study of the Poynting-Robertson Effect and Extinction of Interplanetary Dust*, Institute for Creation Research, El Cajon, California, revised edition, 1982.

6. Ron Samec, 'The age of the jovian planets', *TJ*, vol. 14, no. 1, 2000, pp.3–4. www.answersingenesis.org/tj/v14/i1/jovian.asp

7. Jonathan Henry, 'The energy balance of Uranus: implications for special creation', *TJ*, vol. 15, no. 3, 2001, pp.85–91. www.answersingenesis.org/tj/v15/i3/uranus_energy.asp

8. W. J. Nellis, M. Ross and N. C. Holmes, 'Temperature measurements of shock-compressed liquid hydrogen: implications for the interior of Jupiter', *Science*, vol. 269, no. 5228, 1995, pp.1249–52.

9. R. Ouyed, W. R. Fundamenski, G. R. Cripps and P. G. Sutherland, 'D–D fusion in the interior of Jupiter?', *Astrophysical Journal*, vol. 501, 1998, pp.367–74.

10. Wayne R. Spencer, 'Tidal dissipation and the age of Io', Ivey (ed.), *Proceedings of the Fifth International Conference on Creationism*, pp.585–95.

11. As above, p.589.

12. Z. Kopal, 'Gravitational heating of Jovian satellites by tidal friction', *Tidal Friction and the Earth's Rotation II*, Springer-Verlag, Berlin, 1983, pp.117–21.

13. Jonathan Henry, 'The age and fate of Saturn's rings', *Journal of Creation*, vol. 20, no. 1, 2006, pp.123–7.

14. D. B. DeYoung, 'The Earth-Moon system', Robert Walsh and Christopher L. Brooks (eds.), *Proceedings of the Second International Conference on Creationism*, vol. II, 'Technical Symposium Sessions and Additional Topics', Creation Science Fellowship, Pittsburgh, 1990, pp.79–84.

15. Karin S. Hansen, 'Secular effects of oceanic tidal dissipation on the Moon's orbit and the Earth's rotation', *Reviews of Geophysics and Space Physics*, vol. 20, 1982, pp.457–80.

16. Jonathan Henry, 'The Moon's recession and age', *Journal of Creation*, vol. 20, no. 2, 2006, pp.65–70.

17. K. A. Eriksson and E. L. Simpson, 'Quantifying the oldest tidal record: the 3.2 Ga Moodies Group, Barberton Greenstone Belt, South Africa', *Geology*, vol. 28, 2000, pp.831–4.

18. Steven A. Austin and D. Russell Humphreys, 'The sea's missing salt: a dilemma

for evolutionists', Walsh and Brooks (eds.), *Proceedings of the Second International Conference on Creationism,* vol. II, pp.17–33.

19. D. Russell Humphreys, 'Reiterating: ok to use sea sodium as evidence for a young world'. http://www.answersingenesis.org/home/area/feedback/2006/0331.asp

20. J. D. Milliman and J. P. M. Syvitski, 'Geomorphic/tectonic control of sediment discharge to the ocean: the importance of small mountainous rivers', *Journal of Geology,* vol. 100, 1992, pp.525–44.

21. Ariel A. Roth, 'Some questions about geochronology', *Origins* (Geoscience Research Institute), vol. 13, no. 2, 1986, pp.64–85. www.grisda.org/origins/13064.htm

22. W. W. Hay, J. L. Sloan and C. N. Wold, 'Mass/age distribution and composition of sediments on the ocean floor and the global rate of sediment subduction', *Journal of Geophysical Research,* vol. 93, no. B12, 1988, pp.14933–40.

23. S. R. Taylor and S. M. McLennan, *The Continental Crust: Its Composition and Evolution,* Blackwell Scientific Publications, Oxford, 1985, p.234.

24. Hay, Sloan and Wold, 'Mass/age distribution and composition of sediments'.

25. S. Judson and D. F. Ritter, 'Rates of regional denudation in the United States', *Journal of Geophysical Research,* vol. 69, 1964, pp.3395–401.

26. H. W. Menard, 'Some rates of regional erosion', *Journal of Geology,* vol. 69, 1961, pp.154–61.

27. S. Judson, 'Erosion of the land—or what's happening to our continent?', *American Scientist,* vol. 56, 1968, pp.356–74.

28. Paul Giem, 'Carbon-14 content of fossil carbon', *Origins* (Geoscience Research Institute), no. 51, 2001, pp.6–30. www.grisda.org/origins/51006.htm

29. John R. Baumgardner, '^{14}C evidence for a recent global Flood and a young Earth', Vardiman, Snelling and Chaffin (eds.), *Radioisotopes and the Age of the Earth: Results…,* pp.587–630.

30. Henry M. Morris, 'Evolution and the population problem', *Institute for Creation Research Impact Article 21,* November 1974. www.icr.org/article/67/

31. James O. Dritt, 'Man's earliest beginnings: discrepancies in evolutionary timetables', Robert E. Walsh and Christopher L. Brooks (eds.), *Proceedings of the Second International Conference on Creationism,* vol. I, 'General Sessions', Creation Science Fellowship, Pittsburgh, 1990, pp.73–8.

Chapter 8—The origin of life

1.   Charles Darwin, *The Origin of Species by Means of Natural Selection or the Preservation of Favoured Races in the Struggle for Life,* Penguin Books, London, 1968, pp.459–60.

2.   Charles Darwin, *Letter to Hooker*, Cambridge University Library, Darwin Archives, Manuscripts Room, 1871.

3.   Alexander I. Oparin, *Origin of Life*, second edition, trans. S. Morgulis, Dover Publications, New York, 1938.

4.   Stanley L. Miller, 'A production of amino acids under possible primitive earth conditions', *Science*, vol. 117, 1953, pp.528–9.

5.   Stephen C. Meyer, 'The explanatory power of design: DNA and the origin of information', William A. Dembski (ed.), *Mere Creation: Science, Faith & Intelligent Design*, InterVarsity Press, Downers Grove, Illinois, 1998, pp.113–47.

6.   Viruses are simpler, but they are not capable of an independent existence. They can replicate only by invading host organisms. This means that life could not have evolved through a virus-like stage because there would have been nothing for them to parasitize.

7.   G. Brent Dalrymple, *The Age of the Earth*, Stanford University Press, Stanford, California, 1991, p.191.

8.   Stephen J. Mojzsis and T. Mark Harrison, 'Vestiges of a beginning: clues to the emergent biosphere recorded in the oldest sedimentary rocks', *GSA Today*, vol. 10, no. 4, 2000, pp.1–6.

9.   J. C. G. Walker, *Evolution of the Atmosphere*, Macmillan, New York, 1977, pp.210, 246.

10. E. Dimroth and M. M. Kimberley, 'Precambrian atmospheric oxygen: evidence in the sedimentary distributions of carbon, sulfur, uranium and iron', *Canadian Journal of Earth Science*, vol. 13, 1976, pp.1161–85. H. Clemmey and N. Badham, 'Oxygen in the Precambrian atmosphere: an evaluation of the geologic evidence', *Geology*, vol. 10, 1982, pp.141–6.

11. Charles B. Thaxton, Walter L. Bradley and Roger L. Olsen, *The Mystery of Life's Origin: Reassessing Current Theories*, Lewis and Stanley, Dallas, Texas, 1984, pp.42–68.

12. Jonathan Sarfati, 'Origin of life: the chirality problem', *Creation Ex Nihilo Technical Journal*, vol. 12, no. 3, 1998, pp.263–6. www.answersingenesis.org/tj/v12/i3/chirality.asp

13. Meyer, 'The explanatory power of design', p.130.

14. As above, p.125.

15. Francis H. C. Crick and Leslie E. Orgel, 'Directed panspermia', *Icarus*, vol. 19, 1973, pp.341–6.

16. Fred Hoyle and Chandra Wickramasinghe, *Lifecloud*, Dent & Son, London, 1978.

17. William Martin and Michael J. Russell, 'On the origins of cells: a hypothesis for the evolutionary transitions from abiotic geochemistry to chemoautotrophic prokaryotes,

and from prokaryotes to nucleated cells', *Philosophical Transactions of the Royal Society Series B*, vol. 358, no. 1429, 2003, pp.59–85.

18. A. Graham Cairns-Smith, *Seven Clues to the Origin of Life: A Scientific Detective Story*, Cambridge University Press, Cambridge, 1986.

19. Andrew Scott, *The Creation of Life: Past, Future, Alien*, Basil Blackwell Ltd, Oxford, 1986, p.83.

20. BBC TV, *Horizon: Life Is Impossible*, 28 June 1993.

21. Scott, *The Creation of Life*, pp.111–12.

22. Carl R. Woese and Gunter Wächtershäuser, 'Origin of life', in Derek E. G. Briggs and Peter R. Crowther (eds.), *Palaeobiology: A Synthesis*, Blackwell Scientific Publications, Oxford, 1990, p.9.

Chapter 9—Diversity by design

1. Illustrations based on Kurt P. Wise, 'Baraminology: a young-earth creation biosystematic method', Walsh and Brooks (eds.), *Proceedings of the Second International Conference on Creationism,* vol. II, p.358.

2. Frank L. Marsh, *Fundamental Biology*, self-published, Lincoln, Nebraska, 1941, p.100.

3. This conclusion is also supported by an analysis of the Mosaic food lists in Leviticus and Deuteronomy. See Arthur J. Jones, 'Boundaries of the min: an analysis of the Mosaic lists of clean and unclean animals', *Creation Research Society Quarterly*, vol. 9, no. 2, 1972, pp.114–23.

4. Frank L. Marsh, *Variation and Fixity in Nature*, Pacific Press Publishing Association, Mountain View, California, 1976, p.30.

5. Siegfried Scherer (ed.), *Typen des Lebens*, Pascal-Verlag, Berlin, 1993.

6. Siegfried Scherer, 'On the limits of variability: evidence and speculation from morphology, genetics and molecular biology', Edgar H. Andrews, Werner Gitt and Willem J. Ouweneel (eds.), *Concepts in Creationism*, Evangelical Press, Welwyn, 1986, pp.219–40.

7. Siegfried Scherer, 'Der grundtyp der Entenartigen (Anseriformes, Anatidae): Biologische und paläontologische Streiflichter', Scherer (ed.), *Typen des Lebens*, pp.131–58.

8. M. Adler, 'Merkmalsausbildung und Hybridisierung bei Funariaceen (Bryophyta, Musci)', Scherer (ed.), *Typen des Lebens*, pp.67–70.

9. Reinhard Junker, 'Der Grundtyp der Weizenartigen (Poaceae, tribus Triticeae)', Scherer (ed.), *Typen des Lebens*, pp.75–93.

10. Reinhard Junker, 'Die Gattungen *Geum* (Nelkenwurz), *Coluria* und *Waldsteinia* (Rosaceae, Tribus Geeae)', Scherer (ed.), *Typen des Lebens*, pp.95–111. H. Kutzelnigg,

'Verwandtschaftliche Beziehungen zwischen den Gattungen und Arten der Kernobstgewächse (Rosaceae, Unterfamilie Maloideae)' , Scherer (ed.), *Typen des Lebens*, pp.113–27.

11. H. Kutzelnigg, 'Die Streifenfarngewächse (Filicatae, Aspleniaceae) im Grundtypmodell', Scherer (ed.), *Typen des Lebens*, pp.71–4.

12. R. Klemm, 'Die Hühnervögel (Galliformes): Taxonomische Aspekte unter besonderer Berücksichtigung artübergreifender Kreuzungen', Scherer (ed.), *Typen des Lebens*, pp.159–84.

13. F. Zimbelmann, 'Grundtypen bei Greifvögeln (Falconiformes)', Scherer (ed.), *Typen des Lebens*, pp.185–95.

14. J. Fehrer, 'Interspecies-Kreuzungen bei cardueliden Finken und Prachtfinken', Scherer (ed.), *Typen des Lebens*, pp.197–215.

15. Nigel E. A. Crompton, 'A review of selected features of the family Canidae with reference to its fundamental taxonomic status', Scherer (ed.), *Typen des Lebens*, pp.217–24.

16. H. Stein-Cadenbach, 'Hybriden, Chromosomenstrukturen und Artbildung bei Pferden (Equidae)', Scherer (ed.), *Typen des Lebens*, pp.225–44.

17. Sigrid Hartwig-Scherer, 'Hybridisierung und Artbildung bei den Meerkatzenartigen (Primates, Cercopithecoidea)', Scherer (ed.), *Typen des Lebens*, pp.245–57.

18. Todd C. Wood and Megan J. Murray, *Understanding the Pattern of Life: Origins and Organization of the Species*, Broadman and Holman Publishers, Nashville, Tennessee, 2003, pp.101–2.

19. Wise, 'Baraminology: a young-earth creation biosystematic method', pp.345–58. Kurt P. Wise, 'Practical baraminology', *Creation Ex Nihilo Technical Journal*, vol. 6, no. 2, 1992, pp.122–37.

20. See the home page of the Creation Biology Study Group (formerly the Baraminology Study Group) at www.creationbiology.org/

21. Todd C. Wood, 'A baraminology tutorial with examples from the grasses', *TJ*, vol. 16, no. 1, 2002, pp.15–25.

22. Todd C. Wood and David P. Cavanaugh, 'A baraminological analysis of subtribe Flaveriinae (Asteraceae: Helenieae) and the origin of biological complexity', *Origins* (Geoscience Research Institute), no. 52, 2001, pp.7–27. www.grisda.org/origins/52007.htm
     David P. Cavanaugh and Todd C. Wood, 'A baraminological analysis of the tribe Heliantheae *sensu lato* (Asteraceae) using Analysis of Pattern (ANOPA)', *Occasional Papers of the Baraminology Study Group*, no. 1, 2002, pp.1–11. www.creationbiology.org/content.aspx?page_id=22&club_id=201240&module_id=36813

23. David P. Cavanaugh and Richard V. Sternberg, 'Analysis of morphological groupings using

ANOPA, a pattern recognition and multivariate statistical method: a case study involving centrarchid fishes', *Journal of Biological Systems*, vol. 12, no. 2, pp.137–67.

24.   D. Ashley Robinson, 'A mitochondrial DNA analysis of the Testudine apobaramin', *Creation Research Society Quarterly*, vol. 33, no. 4, 1997, pp.262–72.

25.   Tom Hennigan, 'An initial investigation into the baraminology of snakes: Order—Squamata, Suborder Serpentes', *Creation Research Society Quarterly*, vol. 42, no. 3, 2005, pp.153–60.

26.   Timothy R. Brophy and Peter A. Kramer, 'Preliminary results from a baraminological analysis of the mole salamanders (Caudata: Ambystomatidae)', *Occasional Papers of the Baraminology Study Group*, no. 10, 2007, p.10. www.creationbiology.org/content.aspx?page_id=22&club_id=201240&module_id=36813

27.   D. Ashley Robinson and David P. Cavanaugh, 'Evidence for a holobaraminic origin of the cats', *Creation Research Society Quarterly*, vol. 35, no. 1, 1998, pp.2–14.

28.   David P. Cavanaugh, Todd C. Wood and Kurt P. Wise, 'Fossil Equidae: a monobaraminic, stratomorphic series', Ivey (ed.), *Proceedings of the Fifth International Conference on Creationism*, pp.143–53.

29.   Jean K. Lightner, 'The baraminic status of the family Cervidae as determined using interspecific hybrid data', *Occasional Papers of the Baraminology Study Group*, no. 8, 2006, pp.12–13.
      www.creationbiology.org/content.aspx?page_id=22&club_id=201240&module_id=36813

30.   Todd C. Wood, Pete J. Williams, Kurt P. Wise and D. Ashley Robinson, 'Baraminology of the Camelidae', in *Baraminology '99*, 1999, pp.9–18. www.creationbiology.org/content.aspx?page_id=22&club_id=201240&module_id=36812

31.   D. Ashley Robinson and David P. Cavanaugh, 'A quantitative approach to baraminology with examples from the catarrhine primates', *Creation Research Society Quarterly*, vol. 34, no. 4, 1998, pp.196–208.

32.   Stephanie R. Mace and Todd C. Wood, 'Statistical evidence for five whale holobaramins (Mammalia: Cetacea)', *Occasional Papers of the Baraminology Study Group*, no. 5, 2005, p.15.

      Todd C. Wood, 'Exploration of biological character space surrounding living and fossil whales (Mammalia: Cetacea)', *Occasional Papers of the Baraminology Study Group*, no. 8, 2006, pp.10–11.

      Todd C. Wood, 'Evidence that some toothed mysticetes are archaeocetes (Mammalia: Cetacea)', *Occasional Papers of the Baraminology Study Group*, no. 10, 2007, pp.23–4.
www.creationbiology.org/content.aspx?page_id=22&club_id=201240&module_id=36813

33. Todd C. Wood, 'A creationist review and preliminary analysis of the history, geology, climate, and biology of the Galápagos Islands', *CORE Issues in Creation*, no. 1, 2005.

34. Wood and Murray, *Understanding the Pattern of Life*, pp.169–86.

35. Robinson and Cavanaugh, 'Evidence for a holobaraminic origin of the cats', p.7.

36. Wood, Williams, Wise and Robinson, 'Baraminology of the Camelidae'.

37. Cavanaugh, Wood and Wise, 'Fossil Equidae'.

38. Todd C. Wood, 'Mediated design', *Institute for Creation Research Impact Article 363*, September 2003. www.icr.org/article/118/

39. Todd C. Wood, 'The AGEing process: rapid post-flood intrabaraminic diversification caused by Altruistic Genetic Elements (AGEs)', *Origins* (Geoscience Research Institute), no. 54, 2002, pp.5–34. www.grisda.org/origins/54005.pdf 40. A recent example reported in the conventional literature is Wim Broothaerts, Heidi J. Mitchell, Brian Weir, Sarah Kaines, Leon M. A. Smith, Wei Yang, Jorge E. Mayer, Carolina Roa-Rodríguez and Richard A. Jefferson, 'Gene transfer to plants by diverse species of bacteria', *Nature*, vol. 433, 2005, pp.629–33.

Chapter 10 — *Similarities and relationships*

1. Wood and Murray, *Understanding the Pattern of Life*, pp.5–10.

2. As above, p.8.

3. Douglas J. Futuyma, *Science on Trial: The Case for Evolution*, Sinauer Associates, Sunderland, Massachusetts, 1995, p.53.

4. Kurt P. Wise, 'The origin of life's major groups', J. P. Moreland (ed.), *The Creation Hypothesis: Scientific Evidence for an Intelligent Designer*, InterVarsity Press, Downers Grove, Illinois, 1994, pp.211–34.

5. As above, p.220.

6. Arthur M. Shapiro, 'Book review', *Creation/Evolution*, no. 35, 1994, pp.34–7.

7. Kurt P. Wise, 'Is life singularly nested or not?', Walsh (ed.), *Proceedings of the Fourth International Conference on Creationism*, pp.619–31.

8. J. D. Pettigrew, 'Flying primates? Megabats have the advanced pathway from eye to midbrain', *Science*, vol. 231, 1986, pp.1304–6.

9. G. J. P. Naylor and D. C. Adams, 'Are the fossil data really at odds with the molecular data? Morphological evidence for cetartiodactyla phylogeny reexamined', *Systematic Biology*, vol. 50, no. 3, 2001, pp.444–53.

10. J. G. M. Thewissen, E. M. Williams, L. J. Roe and S. T. Hussain, 'Skeletons of terrestrial cetaceans and the relationship of whales to artiodactyls', *Nature*, vol. 413, 2001, pp.277–81.

11. M. Zhu, X. Yu and P. Janvier, 'A primitive fossil fish sheds light on the origin of bony fishes', *Nature*, vol. 397, 1999, pp.607–10.

12. K. P. Wise, 'Towards a creationist understanding of transitional forms', *Creation Ex Nihilo Technical Journal*, vol. 9, no. 2, 1995, pp.216–22.

13. Wise, 'The origin of life's major groups', p.227.

14. W. Ford Doolittle, 'Lateral genomics', *Trends in Cell Biology*, vol. 9, 1999, pp.M5-M8.

15. W. Ford Doolittle, 'Phylogenetic classification and the universal tree', *Science*, vol. 284, 1999, pp.2124–8.

16. W. Ford Doolittle, 'Uprooting the tree of life', *Scientific American*, February 2000, pp.72–7.

17. Maria C. Rivera and James A. Lake, 'The ring of life provides evidence for a genome fusion origin of eukaryotes', *Nature*, vol. 431, 2004, pp.152–5.

18. V. Kunin, L. Goldovsky, N. Darzentas and C. A. Ouzounis, 'The net of life: reconstructing the microbial phylogenetic network', *Genome Research*, vol. 15, 2005, pp.954–9.

19. Kurt P. Wise, 'Creation polycladism: a young-earth creation theory of biogenesis', *Proceedings of the 1992 Twin-Cities Creation Conference*, Twin-Cities Creation Science Association, Brooklyn Park, Minnesota, 1992, pp.204–10.

20. Colin Brown, 'The pentadactyl plan', *Creation Research Society Quarterly*, vol. 20, no. 1, 1983, pp.3–7.

21. Walter J. ReMine, *The Biotic Message: Evolution Versus Message Theory*, St Paul Science, Saint Paul, Minnesota, 1993, pp.22–3.

22. The 'universal' genetic code is not quite universal. There are fifteen variants from a variety of organisms including mycoplasma bacteria, some species of the yeast *Candida*, and some sea squirts. See Wood and Murray, *Understanding the Pattern of Life*, p.29.

Chapter 11—Defects and degeneration

1. The expression 'eat dust' in Genesis 3:14 implies 'to be humbled' or 'to suffer defeat'. Compare it with the similar expression, 'lick the dust', in Psalm 72:9; Isaiah 49:23; Micah 7:17. See H. C. Leupold, *Exposition of Genesis:* vol. I, Baker Book House, Grand Rapids, Michigan, 1942, p.162.

2. Wood and Murray, *Understanding the Pattern of Life*, pp.40, 156.

3. Todd C. Wood, 'The terror of anthrax in a degrading creation', *Institute for Creation Research Impact Article 345*, March 2002. www.icr.org/article/312/

4. Joseph W. Francis, 'The organosubstrate of life: a creationist perspective of microbes

and viruses', Ivey (ed.), *Proceedings of the Fifth International Conference on Creationism*, pp.433–44.

5. Loren Eiseley, 'Charles Darwin, Edward Blyth and the theory of natural selection', *Proceedings of the American Philosophical Society*, vol. 103, 1959, pp.94–158.

6. McIntosh, *Genesis for Today*, pp.102–3.

7. James Stambaugh, '"Life" according to the Bible, and the scientific evidence', *Creation Ex Nihilo Technical Journal*, vol. 6, no. 2, 1992, pp.98–121. www.answersingenesis.org/tj/v6/i2/life.asp

8. Gerald T. Keusch, 'Ecology of the intestinal tract', *Natural History*, vol. 83, no. 9, 1974, pp.70–77.

9. Jerry Bergman, 'Understanding poisons from a creationist perspective', *Creation Ex Nihilo Technical Journal*, vol. 11, no. 3, 1997, pp.353–60. www.answersingenesis.org/tj/v11/i3/poison.asp

10. Wood and Murray, *Understanding the Pattern of Life*, p.162.

11. Gordon Wilson, 'The origins of natural evil', Occasional Papers of the Baraminology Study Group, no. 4, 2004, p.8. www.creationbiology.org/content.aspx?page_id=22&club_id=201240&module_id=36813

12. A pit viper can detect a mouse thirty centimetres away using body heat alone. See Richard Matthews, *Nightmares of Nature*, Harper Collins, London, 1995, p.131.

13. This is called the solenoglyphous arrangement. See F. Harvey Pough, John B. Heiser and William N. McFarland, *Vertebrate Life*, Macmillan Publishing Company, New York, third edition, 1989, p.542.

14. X. Wu, H. Sues and A. Sun, 'A plant-eating crocodyliform reptile from the Cretaceous of China', *Nature*, vol. 376, 1995, pp.678–80.

15. L. R. McCloskey, L. Muscatine and F. P. Wilkerson, 'Daily photosynthesis, respiration, and carbon budgets in a tropical marine jellyfish (*Mastigias* sp.)', *Marine Biology*, vol. 19, 1994, pp.13–22.

16. David Catchpoole, 'The "bird of prey" that's not', *Creation*, vol. 23, no. 1, 2000–2001, pp.24–5.

17. David Catchpoole, 'Piranha', *Creation*, vol. 22, no. 4, 2000, pp.20–23.

Chapter 12—Embryos and vestiges

1. From a Wikipedia article entitled 'Abortion'. http://en.wikipedia.org/wiki/Abortion.

2. These statistics are taken from a leaflet, *Abortion: What You Need To Know*, published by the Society for the Protection of Unborn Children. www.spuc.org.uk/documents/leaflets/Abortion.pdf

3. Peter Singer, *Writings on an Ethical Life*, Fourth Estate, 2002, pp.44–5.

4. As above, p.320.

5. Robert J. Richards, *The Meaning of Evolution: The Morphological Construction and Ideological Reconstruction of Darwin's Theory*, University of Chicago Press, Chicago, 1992.

6. As above, p.xiii.

7. As above, p.15.

8. As above, p.56.

9. Darwin, *The Origin of Species*, p.427.

10. John N. Moore and Harold S. Slusher (eds.), *Biology: A Search for Order in Complexity*, Zondervan Publishing House, Grand Rapids, Michigan, revised edition, 1974, p.434.

11. Tim M. Berra, *Evolution and the Myth of Creationism: A Basic Guide to the Facts in the Evolution Debate*, Stanford University Press, Stanford, California, 1990, p.22.

12. G. Richard Culp, 'Embryology—overlooked facts you should know', *Creation Research Society Quarterly*, vol. 25, no. 2, 1988, p.101.

13. Jerry Coyne, 'A paleontologist makes the case for evolution and against creationism', *Chicago Tribune*, Sunday Books, 30 July 2000, p.4.

14. Carl Wieland, 'Blind fish, island immigrants and hairy babies', *Creation*, vol. 23, no. 1, 2000–2001, pp.46–9.

15. S. J. Gould, 'Fascinating tails', *Discover*, vol. 3, no. 9, 1982, pp.40–41.

16. F. D. Ledley, 'Evolution of the human tail', *New England Journal of Medicine*, vol. 306, 1982, pp.1212–15.

17. Wise, *Faith, Form, and Time*, pp.125–8.

18. A. Hampé, 'La compétition entre les elements ossent du zengopode de Poulet', *Journal of Embryology and Experimental Morphology*, vol. 8, 1960, pp.241–5.

19. Illustration based on Douglas J. Futuyma, *Science on Trial: The Case for Evolution*, Sinauer Associates, Sunderland, Massachusetts, 1995, p.49.

20. Leonard Brand, *Faith, Reason, and Earth History: A Paradigm of Earth and Biological Origins by Intelligent Design*, Andrews University Press, Berrien Springs, Michigan, 1997, p.151.

21. E. J. Kollar and C. Fisher, 'Tooth induction in chick epithelium: expression of quiescent genes for enamel synthesis', *Science*, vol. 207, 1980, pp.993–5.

22. M. B. V. Roberts, *Biology: A Functional Approach*, Thomas Nelson, London, 1971, p.136.

23. J. W. Glover, 'The human vermiform appendix—a general surgeon's reflections', *Ex Nihilo Technical Journal*, vol. 3, 1988, pp.31–8. www.answersingenesis.org/tj/v3/i1/appendix.asp

24. T. E. Dowling, D. P. Martasian and W. R. Jeffery, 'Evidence for multiple genetic forms with

similar eyeless phenotypes in the blind cavefish, *Astyanax mexicanus*', *Molecular Biology and Evolution*, vol. 19, 2002, pp.446–55.

25. David P. Cavanaugh, Todd C. Wood and Kurt P. Wise, 'Fossil Equidae: a monobaraminic, stratomorphic series', Ivey (ed.), *Proceedings of the Fifth International Conference on Creationism*, pp.143–53.

26. Ernest C. Conrad, 'True vestigial structures in whales and dolphins', *Creation/Evolution*, vol. 3, no. 4, 1982, pp.8–13.

27. David J. Tyler, 'New fossil find shows a whale with hind limbs: evidence for evolutionary transformation?', *Origins* (Biblical Creation Society), vol. 4, no. 12, 1992, pp.6–7.

28. T. Sakai, 'Human evolution and wisdom teeth', *Dental Outlook*, vol. 58, no. 4, 1981, pp.615–23.

29. Jerry Bergman, 'Are wisdom teeth (third molars) vestiges of human evolution?', *Creation Ex Nihilo Technical Journal*, vol. 12, no. 3, 1998, pp.297–304. www.answersingenesis.org/tj/v12/i3/wisdomteeth.asp
    Robert Doolan, 'Oh! My aching wisdom teeth!', *Creation*, vol. 18, no. 3, 1996, p.17.

30. Wise, 'The origin of life's major groups', p.223.

31. Robert Wiedersheim, *The Structure of Man*, Macmillan and Company, London, 1895.

32. S. R. Scadding, 'Do "vestigial organs" provide evidence for evolution?', *Evolutionary Theory*, vol. 5, 1981, pp.173–6.

Chapter 13—Global catastrophe

1. David M. Fouts and Kurt P. Wise, 'Blotting out and breaking up: miscellaneous Hebrew studies in geocatastrophism', Walsh (ed.), *Proceedings of the Fourth International Conference on Creationism*, pp.217–28.

2. Gerhard F. Hasel, 'Some issues regarding the nature and universality of the Genesis Flood narrative', *Origins* (Geoscience Research Institute), vol. 5, no. 2, 1978, pp.83–98. www.grisda.org/origins/05083.htm

3. Steven A. Austin, 'Did Noah's Flood cover the entire world? Yes', Ronald F. Youngblood (ed.), *The Genesis Debate: Persistent Questions About Creation and the Flood*, Baker Book House, Grand Rapids, Michigan, 1990, pp.210–29.

4. See www.worldwideflood.com/

5. In Deuteronomy 2:25 the same phrase is used in a limited sense, but in this case it is qualified by the phrase 'who shall hear report of thee'.

6. Byron C. Nelson, *The Deluge Story in Stone: A History of the Flood Theory of Geology*, Bethany Fellowship Inc., Minneapolis, Minnesota, second edition, 1968, pp.169–90.

7. John C. Whitcomb and Henry M. Morris, *The Genesis Flood: The Biblical Record*

and its Scientific Implications, Presbyterian and Reformed Publishing Company, Phillipsburg, New Jersey, 1961.

8.   David J. Tyler, 'Flood models and trends in creationist thinking', *Creation Matters*, vol. 2, no. 3, 1997, pp.1–3. www.creationresearch.org/creation_matters/97/cm9705.html

9.   Steven A. Austin, John R. Baumgardner, D. Russell Humphreys, Andrew A. Snelling, Larry Vardiman and Kurt P. Wise, 'Catastrophic plate tectonics: a global Flood model of earth history', Walsh (ed.), *Proceedings of the Third International Conference on Creationism*, pp.609–21. www.icr.org/research/index/researchp_25_platetectonics|/

10. Antonio Snider-Pellegrini, *La Création et ses Mystères Dévoilés*, A. Franck et E. Dentu, Paris, 1859 (early release, 1858).

11. Mark F. Horstemeyer and John R. Baumgardner, 'What initiated the Flood cataclysm?', Ivey (ed.), *Proceedings of the Fifth International Conference on Creationism*, , pp.155–63.

12. John R. Baumgardner, 'Numerical simulation of the large-scale tectonic changes accompanying the Flood', Robert E. Walsh, Christopher L. Brooks and Richard S. Crowell (eds.), *Proceedings of the First International Conference on Creationism*, vol. II, 'Technical Symposium Sessions and Additional Topics', Creation Science Fellowship, Pittsburgh, 1986, pp.17–30.

     John R. Baumgardner, '3-D finite element simulation of the global tectonic changes accompanying Noah's Flood', Walsh and Brooks (eds.), *Proceedings of the Second International Conference on Creationism*, vol. II, pp.35–45.

     John R. Baumgardner, 'Computer modeling of the large-scale tectonics associated with the Genesis Flood', Walsh (ed.), *Proceedings of the Third International Conference on Creationism*, pp.49–62. www.icr.org/research/index/researchp_jb_largescaletectonics/

     John R. Baumgardner, 'Runaway subduction as the driving mechanism for the Genesis Flood', Walsh (ed.), *Proceedings of the Third International Conference on Creationism* , pp.63–75. www.icr.org/research/index/researchp_jb_runawaysubduction/

13. In fact, it appears that during the Flood the original supercontinent Rodinia broke apart, briefly came back together as another supercontinent called Pangaea, before disrupting completely to produce the familiar present-day continents. However, the earlier phase of plate motions may have been the result of an initial decoupling of the Earth's crust from the underlying mantle, rather than an episode of true plate tectonics.

14. See, for instance, J. E. Vidale, 'A snapshot of whole mantle flow', *Nature*, vol. 370, 1994, pp.16–17.

15. D. Russell Humphreys, 'Physical mechanism for reversals of the Earth's magnetic field during the Flood', Walsh and Brooks (eds.), *Proceedings of the Second International Conference on Creationism,* vol. II, pp.129–42.

16. D. Russell Humphreys, 'Reversals of the Earth's magnetic field during the Genesis Flood', Walsh, Brooks and Crowell (eds.), *Proceedings of the First International Conference on Creationism,* vol. II, 1986, pp.113–24.

17. R. S. Coe and M. Prevot, 'Evidence suggesting extremely rapid field variation during a geomagnetic reversal', *Earth and Planetary Science Letters*, vol. 92, 1989, pp.292–8.

18. R. S. Coe, M. Prevot and P. Camps, 'New evidence for extraordinarily rapid change of the geomagnetic field during a reversal', *Nature*, vol. 374, 1995, pp.687–92.

19. D. Russell Humphreys, 'Has the Earth's magnetic field ever flipped?', *Creation Research Society Quarterly*, vol. 25, no. 3, 1988, pp.130–37.

20. Tas Walker, 'Tsunami tragedy', *Creation*, vol. 28, no. 1, 2005–2006, pp.12–17.

21. John R. Baumgardner, 'Catastrophic plate tectonics: the geophysical context of the Genesis Flood', *TJ*, vol. 16, no. 1, 2002, pp.58–63. www.answersingenesis.org/tj/v16/i1/plate_tectonics.asp

22. John R. Baumgardner and Daniel W. Barnette, 'Patterns of ocean circulation over the continents during Noah's Flood', Walsh (ed.) *Proceedings of the Third International Conference on Creationism,* pp.77–86.

Chapter 14—Understanding the fossil record

1. Kenneth Oakley, 'Emergence of higher thought 3.0–0.2 Ma B.P.', *Philosophical Transactions of the Royal Society of London Series B*, vol. 292, 1981, pp.205–11.

2. Adrienne Mayor, *The First Fossil Hunters*, Princeton University Press, New Jersey, 2000.

3. Some stromatolites are considered to have had an inorganic origin. See: J. P. Grotzinger and D. H. Rothman, 'An abiotic model for stromatolite morphogenesis', *Nature*, vol. 383, 1996, pp.423–5.

4. Kurt P. Wise, 'Towards a creationist understanding of "transitional forms"', *Creation Ex Nihilo Technical Journal*, vol. 9, no. 2, 1995, pp.216–22.

5. This is called cladistics. The cladistic approach focuses on identifying natural groups, or clades, and determining the sequence in which key characteristics were acquired during evolutionary history.

6. Kurt P. Wise, *First appearance of higher taxa: a preliminary study of order in the fossil record*, unpublished manuscript.

7. Stephen C. Meyer, Marcus Ross, Paul Nelson and Paul Chien, 'The Cambrian explosion: biology's big bang', John Angus Campbell and Stephen C. Meyer (eds.), *Darwinism, Design and Public Education*, Michigan State University Press, 2003, pp.323–402. www.discovery.org/scripts/viewDB/filesDB-download.php?id=29

8. For a contrary view, see David J. Tyler, 'Recolonization and the Mabbul', John K. Reed and Michael J. Oard (eds.), *The Geologic Column: Perspectives Within Diluvial Geology*, Creation Research Society Books, Chino Valley, Arizona, 2006, pp.73–86.

9. Harold W. Clark, *The New Diluvialism*, Science Publications, Angwin, California, 1946.

10. Illustration adapted from an exhibit in the Answers in Genesis Creation Museum in Kentucky, USA (www.creationmuseum.org/)

11. Kurt P. Wise, 'The hydrothermal biome: a pre-Flood environment', Ivey (ed.), *Proceedings of the Fifth International Conference on Creationism*, pp.359–70.

12. Kurt P. Wise, 'The pre-Flood floating forest: a study in paleontological pattern recognition', Ivey (ed.), *Proceedings of the Fifth International Conference on Creationism*, pp.371–81.

13. Q. Ji, Z.-X. Luo, C.-X. Yuan and A. R. Tabrum, 'A swimming mammaliaform from the Middle Jurassic and ecomorphological diversification of early mammals', *Science*, vol. 311, 2006, pp.1123–7.

14. Kurt P. Wise, 'Swimming with the dinosaurs'. www.answersingenesis.org/docs2006/0308dinosaurs.asp

15. Wood and Murray, *Understanding the Pattern of Life*, p.190.

16. Paul Garner, 'The fossil record of "early" tetrapods: evidence of a major evolutionary transition?', *TJ*, vol. 17, no. 2, 2003, pp.111–17. www.answersingenesis.org/tj/v17/i2/tetrapod.asp

17. Illustration based on Jennifer A. Clack, 'Getting a leg up on land: recent fossil discoveries cast light on the evolution of four-limbed animals from fish', *Scientific American*, vol. 293, no. 6, 2005, pp.100–107.

18. Taphonomy, the study of the fate of organisms after they die, has revealed several factors that promote fossil preservation. They include rapid burial, possession of hard parts, burial in fine-grained sediments (which helps to preserve detail) and a low-oxygen environment. The most important of these is rapid burial.

19. N. H. Trewin, 'Mass mortalities of Devonian fish—the Achanarras Fish Bed, Caithness', *Geology Today*, March–April 1985, pp.45–9.

20. J. Vetter, 'Double tragedies frozen in lime', *Creation Ex Nihilo*, vol. 12, no. 4, 1990, pp.10–14.

21. D. M. Martill, 'The Medusa effect: instantaneous fossilization', *Geology Today*, vol. 5, 1989, pp.201–5.

22. R. Wild, 'Holzmaden', Derek E. G. Briggs and Peter R. Crowther (eds.), *Palaeobiology: A Synthesis*, Blackwell Scientific Publications, Oxford, 1990, pp.282–5. Specimens and replicas from Holzmaden can be seen in the fossil marine reptile gallery of the Natural History Museum in London.

23. L. R. Brand, R. Esperante, A. V. Chadwick, O. P. Porras and M. Alomia, 'Fossil whale preservation implies high diatom accumulation rate in the Miocene-Pliocene Pisco Formation of Peru', *Geology*, vol. 32, no. 2, 2004, pp.165–8.

24. D. M. Unwin, A. Perle and C. Trueman, '*Protoceratops* and *Velociraptor* preserved in association: evidence for predatory behavior in dromaeosaurid dinosaurs?', *Journal of Vertebrate Paleontology*, vol. 15, Supplement 3, 1995, p.57A.

25. E. N. K. Clarkson, *Invertebrate Palaeontology and Evolution*, Allen & Unwin, London, second edition, 1986, pp.315–17.

26. W. D. Liddell, 'Recent crinoid biostratinomy', *Geological Society of America Abstracts with Programs*, vol. 7, 1975, p.1169.

   D. L. Meyer, 'Post mortem disarticulation of recent crinoids and ophiuroids under natural conditions', *Geological Society of America Abstracts with Programs*, vol. 3, 1971, pp.645–6.

27. N. A. Rupke, 'Prolegomena to a study of cataclysmal sedimentation', Walter E. Lammerts (ed.), *Why Not Creation?*, Baker Book House, Grand Rapids, Michigan, 1970, pp.141–79.

28. Harold G. Coffin, 'The Yellowstone petrified "forests"', *Origins* (Geoscience Research Institute), vol. 24, no. 1, 1997, pp.2–44.

   www.grisda.org/origins/24002.htm

29. Ariel A. Roth, *Origins: Linking Science and Scripture*, Review and Herald Publishing Association, Hagerstown, Maryland, 1998, pp.188–9.

Chapter 15—The coming of the ice

1. J. O. Fletcher, 'The influence of the Arctic pack ice on climate', J. M. Mitchell (ed.), *Causes of Climatic Change*, Meteorological Monographs 8(30), American Meteorological Society, Boston, 1968, pp.93–9.

2.   L. D. Williams, 'An energy balance model of potential glacierization of northern Canada', *Arctic and Alpine Research*, vol. 11, 1979, pp.443–56.

3.   R. C. L. Wilson, S. A. Drury and J. L. Chapman, *The Great Ice Age: Climate Change and Life*, Routledge, London, 2000, p.62.

4.   Baumgardner, 'Catastrophic plate tectonics'.

5.   Illustration based on Larry Vardiman, 'Cooling of the ocean after the Flood', *Institute for Creation Research Impact Article 277*, July 1996. www.icr.org/article/406/

6.   Michael J. Oard, *An Ice Age Caused by the Genesis Flood*, Institute for Creation Research, El Cajon, California, 1990, p.97.

7.   Larry Vardiman, *Sea-Floor Sediment and the Age of the Earth*, Institute for Creation Research, El Cajon, California, 1996.

8.   Michael Oard, *Frozen in Time: The Woolly Mammoth, the Ice Age and the Bible*, Master Books, Green Forest, Arkansas, 2004, p.75.

9.   Larry Vardiman, 'A conceptual transition model of the atmospheric global circulation following the Genesis Flood', Walsh (ed.), *Proceedings of the Third International Conference on Creationism*, pp.569–79.

      Larry Vardiman, 'Numerical simulation of precipitation induced by hot mid-ocean ridges', Walsh (ed.), *Proceedings of the Fourth International Conference on Creationism*, pp.595–605. www.icr.org/research/index/researchp_lv_r04/

10.   J. F. McCauley, G. G. Schaber, C. S. Breed, M. J. Grolier, C. V. Haynes, B. Issawi, C. Elachi and R. Blom, 'Subsurface valleys and geoarcheology of the eastern Sahara revealed by shuttle radar', *Science*, vol. 218, 1982, pp.1004–20.

11.   H. J. Pachur and S. Kröpelin, 'Wadi Howar: paleoclimatic evidence from an extinct river system in the southeastern Sahara', *Science*, vol. 237, 1987, pp.298–300.

      S. Kröpelin and I. Soulié-Märsche, 'Charophyte remains from Wadi Howar as evidence for deep mid-Holocene freshwater lakes in the eastern Sahara of northwest Sudan', *Quaternary Research*, vol. 36, 1991, pp.210–23.

12.   John H. Whitmore, 'The Green River Formation: a large post-Flood lake system', *Journal of Creation*, vol. 20, no. 1, 2006, pp.55–63.

13.   R. L. Hooke, 'Lake Manly shorelines in the eastern Mojave Desert, California', *Quaternary Research*, vol. 52, 1999, pp.328–36.

14.   Oard, *An Ice Age Caused by the Genesis Flood*, p.78.

15.   A. J. Sutcliffe, *On the Track of Ice Age Mammals*, Harvard University Press, Cambridge, Massachusetts, 1985, p.22.

16. Steven A. Austin (ed.), *Grand Canyon: Monument to Catastrophe*, Institute for Creation Research, Santee, California, 1994, pp.83–110.

17. Michael J. Oard, 'Pediments formed by the Flood: evidence for the Flood / post-Flood boundary in the Late Cenozoic', *TJ*, vol. 18, no. 2, 2004, pp.15–27.

18. Steven A. Austin, 'The declining power of post-Flood volcanoes', *Institute for Creation Research Impact Article 302*, August 1998. www.icr.org/article/431/

19. G. A. Izett, 'Volcanic ash beds: recorders of Upper Cenozoic silicic pyroclastic volcanism in the western United States', *Journal of Geophysical Research*, vol. 86, no. B11, 1981, pp.10200–22.

20. P. C. Froggatt, C. S. Nelson, I. Carter, G. Griggs and K. P. Black, 'An exceptionally large late Quaternary eruption from New Zealand', *Nature*, vol. 319, 1986, pp.578–82.

21. J. R. Bray, 'Pleistocene volcanism and glacial initiation', *Science*, vol. 197, 1977, pp.251–4.

22. Oard, *An Ice Age Caused by the Genesis Flood*, pp.38–40.

23. Illustration based on Austin, 'The declining power of post-Flood volcanoes'.

24. V. Ramanathan, R. D. Cess, E. F. Harrison, P. Minnis, B. R. Barkstrom, E. Ahmad and D. Hartmann, 'Cloud-radiative forcing and climate: results from the Earth Radiation Budget Experiment', *Science*, vol. 243, 1989, pp.57–63.

25. Illustration based on Don Batten (ed.), *The Answers Book*, Answers in Genesis, Acacia Ridge, Queensland, 1999, p.192.

26. Oard, *An Ice Age Caused by the Genesis Flood*, pp.55–65.

27. As above, pp.93–8.

28. As above, pp.98–100.

29. P. U. Clark, 'Surface form of the southern Laurentide Ice Sheet and its implications to ice-sheet dynamics', *Geological Society of America Bulletin*, vol. 104, 1992, pp.595–605.

30. Illustration based on Michael J. Oard, *Frozen in Time: The Woolly Mammoth, the Ice Age, and the Bible*, Master Books, Green Forest, Arkansas, 2004, p.92.

31. Larry Vardiman, 'An analytic young-Earth flow model of ice sheet formation during the "ice age"', Walsh (ed.), *Proceedings of the Third International Conference on Creationism*, pp.561–8.

32. Oard, *An Ice Age Caused by the Genesis Flood*, pp.2–6.

33. R. L. Newson, 'Response of a general circulation model of the atmosphere to removal of the Arctic ice-cap', *Nature*, vol. 241, 1973, pp.39–40.

34. Oard, *An Ice Age Caused by the Genesis Flood*, pp.114–19.

35. Michael J. Oard, *The Missoula Flood Controversy and the Genesis Flood*, Creation Research Society Books, Chino Valley, Arizona, 2004.

36. Illustration based on Jonathan Amos, 'Megaflood "made Island Britain" ', *BBC News Online*, 18 July 2007. http://news.bbc.co.uk/1/hi/sci/tech/6904675.stm

37. S. Gupta, J. S. Collier, A. Palmer-Felgate and G. Potter, 'Catastrophic flooding origin of shelf valley systems in the English Channel', *Nature*, vol. 448, 2007, pp.342–5.

38. Michael J. Oard, *The Frozen Record: Examining the Ice Core History of the Greenland and Antarctic Ice Sheets*, Institute for Creation Research, Santee, California, 2005.

39. Illustration based on Oard, *The Frozen Record*, pp.44–5.

40. Kurt P. Wise, *Faith, Form, and Time: What the Bible Teaches and Science Confirms about Creation and the Age of the Universe*, Broadman and Holman, Nashville, Tennessee, 2002, p.216.

41. N. Eyles, W. R. Dearman and T. D. Douglas, 'The distribution of glacial landsystems in Britain and North America', N. Eyles (ed.), *Glacial Geology*, Pergamon Press, New York, 1983, pp.213–28.

42. R. P. Goldthwait, 'Rates of formation of glacial features in Glacier Bay, Alaska', D. R. Coates (ed.), *Glacial Geomorphology*, George Allen and Unwin, London, 1974, pp.163–85.

Chapter 16—Confusion, cavemen and culture

1. Some have tried to reconcile evolution with the biblical text by suggesting that the 'dust' of Genesis 2:7 symbolizes an 'apelike ancestor'. But if this is the case, we might ask, 'To which "apelike ancestor" does man return upon death?' (see Genesis 3:19).

2. John W. Oller, 'More than PIE', *Answers Magazine*, vol. 3, no. 2, 2008, pp.52–5. www.answersingenesis.org/articles/am/v3/n2/more-than-pie

3. Allan K. Steel, 'The development of languages is nothing like biological evolution', *Creation Ex Nihilo Technical Journal*, vol. 14, no. 2, 2000, pp.31–40.

4. Diana Waring, '"Pop" cultures of antiquity', *Answers Magazine*, vol. 3, no. 2, 2008, pp.34–5. www.answersingenesis.org/articles/am/v3/n2/pop-cultures

5. Steven J. Robinson, 'From the Flood to the Exodus: Egypt's earliest settlers', *Creation Ex Nihilo Technical Journal*, vol. 9, no. 1, 1995, pp.45–68.

6. There are, of course, exceptions. The Inuit (Eskimos) have brown skin, but they live in a cold climate without much sunlight. Conversely, there are some pale-skinned people who live in the equatorial regions of South America.

7. Ken Ham, 'Are there really different races?', Ken Ham (ed.), *The New Answers Book*, Master Books, Green Forest, Arkansas, 2006, pp.220–36.

8. Steven J. Robinson, *From the Flood to Pharaoh—Understanding the Old Stone Age*, The Genesis Agendum Occasional Paper 3, 1998, pp.7–8.

9. As above, pp.9–10.

10. M. Brunet, F. Guy, D. Pilbeam, H. T. Mackaye, A. Likius, D. Ahounta, A. Beauvilain, C. Blondel, H. Bocherens, J.-R. Boisserie, L. de Bonis, Y. Coppens, J. Dejax, C. Denys, P. Duringer, V. Eisenmann, G. Fanone, P. Fronty, D. Geraads, T. Lehmann, F. Lihoreau, A. Louchart, A. Mahamat, G. Merceron, G. Mouchelin, O. Otero, P. P. Campomanes, M. P. de Leon, J.-C. Rage, M. Sapanet, M. Schuster, J. Sudre, P. Tassy, X. Valentin, P. Vignaud, L. Viriot, A. Zazzo and C. Zollikofer, 'A new hominid from the Upper Miocene of Chad, Central Africa', *Nature*, vol. 418, 2002, pp.145–51.

11. M. H. Wolpoff, B. Senut, M. Pickford and J. Hawks, '*Sahelanthropus* or "*Sahelpithecus*"?', *Nature*, vol. 419, 2002, pp.581–2.

12. B. Wood, *Human Evolution: A Very Short Introduction*, Oxford University Press, Oxford, 2005, pp.65–70.

13. D. C. Johanson, T. D. White and Y. Coppens, 'A new species of the genus *Australopithecus* (Primates: Hominidae) from the Pliocene of Africa', *Kirtlandia*, vol. 28, 1978, pp.1–14.

    Lucy is about 40% complete if the 106 bones of the hands and feet are not included in the estimate, but closer to 20% if they are included. See Alan Walker and Pat Shipman, *The Wisdom of Bones: In Search of Human Origins*, Weidenfeld and Nicolson, London, 1996, p.147.

14. Matthew Murdock, 'These apes were made for walking: the pelves of *Australopithecus afarensis* and *Australopithecus africanus*', *Journal of Creation*, vol. 20, no. 2, 2006, pp.104–12.

15. Charles Oxnard, *Uniqueness and Diversity in Human Evolution: Morphometric Studies of Australopithecines*, The University of Chicago Press, Chicago, 1975, pp.65–7.

16. M. G. Leakey, F. Spoor, F. H. Brown, P. N. Gathogo, C. Klarie, L. N. Leakey and I. McDougall, 'New hominin genus from eastern Africa shows diverse middle Pliocene lineages', *Nature*, vol. 410, 2001, pp.433–40.

17. L. S. B. Leakey, P. V. Tobias and J. R. Napier, 'A new species of the genus *Homo* from Olduvai Gorge', *Nature*, vol. 202, 1964, pp.7–9.

18. S. Hartwig-Scherer and R. D. Martin, 'Was "Lucy" more human than her "child"? Observations on early hominid postcranial skeletons', *Journal of Human Evolution*, vol. 21, 1991, pp.439–49.

19. R. L. Holloway, 'Human paleontological evidence relevant to language behaviour', *Human Neurobiology*, vol. 2, 1983, pp.105–14.

20. R. E. Leakey, *The Origin of Humankind*, Basic Books, New York, 1994.

21. F. Brown, J. Harris, R. Leakey and A. Walker, 'Early *Homo erectus* skeleton from west Lake Turkana, Kenya', *Nature*, vol. 316, 1985, pp.788–92.

22. P. Brown, T. Sutikna, M. J. Morwood, R. P. Soejono, Jatmiko, E. W. Saptomo and R. Awe Due, 'A new small-bodied hominin from the Late Pleistocene of Flores, Indonesia', *Nature*, vol. 431, 2004, pp.1055–61.

23. Kurt P. Wise, 'The Flores skeleton and human baraminology', *Occasional Papers of the Baraminology Study Group*, no. 6, 2005, pp. 1–13.
     www.creationbiology.org/content.aspx?page_id=22&club_id=201240&module_id=36813

24. In fact, Neanderthal remains had already been found in Belgium (1830) and Gibraltar (1848), but their significance was not recognized at the time. See C. Stringer and C. Gamble, *In Search of the Neanderthals*, Thames and Hudson, London, 1994, p.13.

25. J. Shreeve, *The Neanderthal Enigma: Solving the Mystery of Modern Human Origins*, Viking, 1996, pp.158–9.

26. Stringer and Gamble, *In Search of the Neanderthals*, pp.81–3.

27. B. M. Fagan, *The Journey from Eden*, Thames and Hudson, 1990, p.60.

28. Kurt P. Wise, '*Australopithecus ramidus* and the fossil record', *Creation Ex Nihilo Technical Journal*, vol. 8, no. 2, 1994, pp.160–65.

29. F. Spoor, B. A. Wood and F. Zonneveld, 'Implications of early hominid labyrinthine morphology for evolution of human bipedal locomotion', *Nature*, vol. 369, 1994, pp.645–8.

30. Kurt Wise, 'Lucy was buried first', *Answers Magazine*, vol. 3, no. 2, 2008, pp.66–8. www.answersingenesis.org/articles/am/v3/n2/lucy-buried-first

Epilogue

1.   Morris, *The Genesis Record*, pp.677–82.

Bibliography

Ashton, J. F. (editor). *In Six Days: Why 50 Scientists Choose to Believe in Creation*, New Holland Publishers, Sydney, 1999. ISBN 1–86436–443–2

Austin, S. A. *Catastrophes in Earth History: A Source Book of Geologic Evidence, Speculation and Theory*, Institute for Creation Research, El Cajon, California, 1984. ISBN 0–932766–08–0

Austin, S. A. (editor). *Grand Canyon: Monument to Catastrophe*, Institute for Creation Research, Santee, California, 1994. ISBN 0–932766–33–1

Brand, L. *Faith, Reason, and Earth History: A Paradigm of Earth and Biological Origins by Intelligent Design*, Andrews University Press, Berrien Springs, Michigan, 1997. ISBN 1–883925–15–0

Brand, L. *Beginnings: Are Science and Scripture Partners in the Search for Origins?*, Pacific Press Publishing Association, 2005. ISBN 0–8163–2144–2

Coffin, H., Brown, R. H. and Gibson, L. J. *Origin by Design*, Review and Herald Publishing Association, Hagerstown, Maryland, revised edition, 2005. ISBN 0–8280–1776–X

DeYoung, D. *Thousands Not Billions: Challenging an Icon of Evolution, Questioning the Age of the Earth*, Master Books, Green Forest, Arkansas, 2005. ISBN 0–89051–441–0

Faulkner, D. *Universe by Design: An Explanation of Cosmology and Creation*, Master Books, Green Forest, Arkansas, 2004. ISBN 0–89051–415–1

Frair, W. and Davis, P. *A Case for Creation*, Moody Press, Chicago, Illinois, third edition, 1983. ISBN 0–8024–0176–7

Gillen, A. L. *The Genesis of Germs: The Origin of Diseases and the Coming Plagues*, Master Books, Green Forest, Arkansas, 2007. ISBN 0–89051–493–3

Hartnett, J. *Starlight, Time and the New Physics*, Creation Book Publishers, Powder Springs, Georgia, 2007. ISBN 978–0–949906–68–7

Ivey, R. L. Jr. (editor). *Proceedings of the Fifth International Conference on Creationism*, Creation Science Fellowship, Pittsburgh, Pennsylvania, 2003. ISBN 0–9617068–9–9

Junker, R. *Is Man Descended from Adam? Evidence from Science and the Bible*, Biblical Creation Society, 2000. ISBN 0–946362–03–3

Kelly, D. F. *Creation and Change: Genesis 1.1–2.4 in the light of changing scientific paradigms*, Mentor, 1997. ISBN 1–85792–283–2

Lester, L. P. and Bohlin, R. G. *The Natural Limits to Biological Change*, Probe Books, Dallas, Texas, second edition, 1989. ISBN 0–945241–06–2

Marsh, F. L. *Variation and Fixity in Nature*, Wipf and Stock Publishers, Eugene, Oregon, 2004. ISBN 1–59244–718–X

Moreland, J. P. (editor). *The Creation Hypothesis: Scientific Evidence for an Intelligent Designer*, InterVarsity Press, Downers Grove, Illinois, 1994. ISBN 0–8308–198–4

Morris, J. D. *The Young Earth*, Master Books, Green Forest, Arkansas, 1994. ISBN 0–89051–174–8

Oard, M. *Frozen in Time: The Woolly Mammoth, the Ice Age, and the Bible*, Master Books, Green Forest, Arkansas, 2004. ISBN 0–89051–418–6

Roth, A. A. *Origins: Linking Science and Scripture*, Review and Herald Publishing Association, Hagerstown, Maryland, 1998. ISBN 0–8280–1328–4

Terreros, M. T. *Theistic Evolution and its Theological Implications*, Marter Editions, Medellin, Colombia, 1994

Tyler, D. J. *The Guide: Creation—Chance or Design?* Evangelical Press, Darlington, 2003. ISBN 0–85234–544–5

Vardiman, L., Snelling, A. A. and Chaffin, E. F. (editors). *Radioisotopes and the Age of the Earth: A Young-Earth Creationist Research Initiative*, Institute for Creation Research, El Cajon, California and Creation Research Society, St Joseph, Missouri, 2000. ISBN 0–932766–62–5

Vardiman, L., Snelling, A. A. and Chaffin, E. F. (editors). *Radioisotopes and the Age of the Earth: Results of a Young-Earth Creationist Research Initiative*, Institute for Creation Research, El Cajon, California and Creation Research Society, Chino Valley, Arizona, 2005. ISBN 0–932766–81–1

Walsh, R. E. (editor). *Proceedings of the Third International Conference on Creationism*, Creation Science Fellowship, Pittsburgh, Pennsylvania, 1994. ISBN 0–9617068–7–2

Walsh, R. E. (editor). *Proceedings of the Fourth International Conference on Creationism*, Creation Science Fellowship, Pittsburgh, Pennsylvania, 1998. ISBN 0–9617068–8–0

Walsh, R. E. and Brooks, C. L. (editors). *Proceedings of the Second International Conference on Creationism*, Creation Science Fellowship, Pittsburgh, Pennsylvania, 1990, 2 volumes. ISBN 0–9617068–4–8 and ISBN 0–9617068–5–6.

Walsh, R. E., Brooks, C. L. and Crowell, R. S. (editors). *Proceedings of the First International Conference on Creationism*, Creation Science Fellowship, Pittsburgh, Pennsylvania, 1986, 2 volumes. ISBN 0–9617068–1–3 and ISBN 0–9617068–2–1

Williams, A. and Hartnett, J. *Dismantling the Big Bang: God's Universe Rediscovered*, Master Books, Green Forest, Arkansas, 2005. ISBN 978–0–89051–437–5

Wise, K. P. *Faith, Form, and Time: What the Bible Teaches and Science Confirms About Creation and the Age of the Universe*, Broadman & Holman Publishers, Nashville, Tennessee, 2002. ISBN 0–8054–2462–8

Wise, K. P. and Richardson, S. A. *Something From Nothing: Understanding What You Believe About Creation and Why*, Broadman and Holman Publishers, Nashville, Tennessee, 2004. ISBN 0–8054–2779–1

Wood, T. C. *A Creationist Review and Preliminary Analysis of the History, Geology, Climate, and Biology of the Galápagos Islands*, CORE Issues in Creation 1, Wipf and Stock Publishers, Eugene, Oregon, 2005. ISBN 1–59752–180–9

Wood, T. C. and Murray, M. J. *Understanding the Pattern of Life: Origins and Organization of the Species*, Broadman and Holman Publishers, Nashville, Tennessee, 2003. ISBN 0–8054–2714–7

Websites

The following websites provide further information concerning the issues addressed in this book. Please note that the author and publishers do not necessarily endorse everything on these sites. The addresses were current at the time of going to press.

Creationist sites
Biblical Creation Ministries
http://www.biblicalcreationministries.org.uk

Biblical Creation Society
http://www.biblicalcreation.org.uk/

Creation Biology Study Group
http://www.creationbiology.org/

Geoscience Research Institute
http://www.grisda.org/

Institute for Creation Research
http://www.icr.org/

Creation Research Society
http://www.creationresearch.org/

Earth History Research Center
http://origins.swau.edu/

Answers in Genesis
http://www.answersingenesis.org

Creation Research UK
http://www.amen.org.uk/cr/

Creation Resources Trust
http://www.c-r-t.co.uk/

Creation Science Movement
http://www.csm.org.uk/

Intelligent design sites
The Discovery Institute—Center for Science and Culture
http://www.discovery.org/csc/

Access Research Network
http://www.arn.org/

Education site
Truth in Science
http://www.truthinscience.org.uk/site/

Miscellaneous
Associates for Biblical Research
http://www.biblearchaeology.org/

The Genesis Agendum
http://www.genesisagendum.org.uk/

.

Index

F

W

Commendations

Quite different from many creationist books that focus on the scientific problems of evolution, this book also includes scientific ideas built on the historical account in the early parts of Genesis. Chapters are short and deal with the central issues of each topic but also include useful references for further reading.

Paul Garner has many years of experience explaining and discussing the issues of origins, often at a popular level, to both Christian and secular groups. It is his skill at unpacking the problems and developing arguments in easy stages with a minimum of technical language that makes this book such a valuable resource.

N. M. Darrall, Ph.D Botany

Paul Garner powerfully demonstrates that when starting with the foundational truths of Genesis (six-day creation, a historical fall, global flood, real Tower of Babel, etc.), creationists can build scientific models that are far superior in their explanatory power than the evolutionary ones. This book is greatly needed in helping to popularize creation model-building as it introduces the reader to the best contemporary creationist models in astronomy, geology, biology, and so on—and at a level the layperson can understand.

Ken Ham, President,
Answers in Genesis—U.S./Creation Museum

A Christian writing on Genesis and origins faces severe challenges. The task demands a rare combination of biblical and scientific skills. Few indeed have the competence to weigh theories and arguments across the wide range of relevant scientific disciplines. Paul Garner meets these demands in a remarkably readable book. If you thought you knew what creationism was, this book will probably surprise you.

Dr Arthur Jones,
Science and Education Consultant

If you are looking for a rant against evolution, and knockdown arguments for a young earth, you will be disappointed. Paul takes us on a sure-footed and wide-ranging survey of evidence informed by his involvement with the latest creationist research. Difficulties are honestly discussed, but the thrust of the book is to gently impress us with the attractiveness and power of a positive creation model. A compelling resource for pastors and church members alike to approach questions of origins with confidence.

Dr Stephen Lloyd,
Pastor of Hope Church, Gravesend, UK

Paul Garner in this book presents a cohesive scientific model for origins from a biblical perspective... His main purpose ... is to show that the science agrees with the biblical view not just in isolated instances, but so thoroughly as to give a robust structure and basis for a number of scientific disciplines, and primarily in astronomy and geology. Paul is a well-respected geologist by training and shows that the geological column can readily be understood in terms of creation basement rocks followed by Flood deposits and finally by post-Flood settling movements with a single ice age scouring much of the northern hemisphere. He ably deals with the issue of radioisotope dating, bringing in the recent remarkable findings of Flood geologists concerning the evidence of accelerated radioactive decay. Paul achieves his aim well of demonstrating that the great thrust of the scientific data fits well with the young-earth creation perspective obtained by a natural reading of the biblical text.

Professor Andy McIntosh, D.Sc, FIMA, C.Math, FEI, C.Eng, FInstP, MIGEM, FRAeS University of Leeds, UK

I have been privileged to know and work with Paul Garner in creation ministry for several years and have come to respect him for his beliefs and ability to communicate them in a helpful and non-aggressive way. This is demonstrated in this book. Paul is one of the few creationist speakers and writers who are qualified in the two key areas of science—geology and biology, and this is shown in the care he takes in his arguments.

This book covers the key subject areas that a Bible-believing Christian must consider in evaluating the different approaches to the subject of origins. He believes the Bible to be the inspired Word of God, and so utterly reliable in its teaching. Inevitably there are differences between some creationists on aspects of our interpretation of the science, but Paul is aware of this and respectful of these differences. His study of the various topics is thorough and I can detect no scientific or biblical flaw in his arguments. He tackles difficult subjects in a way that any reader will find both intelligible and helpful. I am very happy to commend this publication and trust it has a wide readership. May God bless it.

J. H. John Peet, B.Sc, M.Sc, Ph.D, C.Chem, FRSC, The Biblical Creation Society

In this small volume Paul Garner gives us an up-to-date survey of current scientific thinking that supports the biblical account of the origin of our universe. He shows how modern findings in the areas of astronomy, biology and geology are consistent with the Bible's teaching on creation and the global flood. A glossary and extensive references to other work provide the reader with resources that will assist them in further study of the scientific issues related to the current debate on evolution.

Marc Surtees, Ph.D, B.Sc Applied Biology

For those needing an up-to-date and comprehensive introduction to the science and issues surrounding biblical origins—this book stands above the rest. It is well reasoned, well referenced, biblically sound, fabulously illustrated and easy to read. Garner is a master in simplifying complex scientific issues for the lay person in the fields of astronomy, geology and biology without distorting the science behind them.

Dr John H. Whitmore,
Associate Professor of Geology,
Cedarville University, Ohio, USA

If you want a clear, concise, balanced and well-referenced overview of current young-universe creation science, *The New Creationism* is a great place to start. Paul Garner has sifted a vast amount of literature to bring you up-to-date and refreshingly biblical interpretations of the data by leading creationists in cosmology, biology and geology. Mr Garner also helps the reader understand the folly of conflating current creationist theories with the authority of the Bible. Brilliant and competent creation scientists are fallible, even when attempting to be faithful to the Scriptures and the data. Creationist theories come and go, but the Word of God stands for ever.

Dr Gordon Wilson,
Senior Fellow of Natural History,
New Saint Andrews College, Idaho, USA